Trust, Knowledge and Society

MARTIN
MIKAEL
LILIUS

TRUST AS THE
FOUNDATION
OF SOCIETAL
DEVELOPMENT

PUBLISHED BY MARTIN MIKAEL LILIUS
FIRST PRINTING, 2022

ISBN 978-952-94-6141-7 (SOFTCOVER)
ISBN 978-952-94-6142-4 (HARDCOVER)
ISBN 978-952-94-6143-1 (PDF)
ISBN 978-952-94-6144-8 (EPUB)

WWW.TRUSTKNOWLEDGESOCIETY.COM

COVER AND LAYOUT DESIGN BY DAYS AGENCY – WWW.DAYSAGENCY.FI
COPY-EDITING BY SUZANNE ARNOLD – WWW.SUZANNEARNOLD.COM
THANK YOU

Trust, Knowledge and Society

TRUST AS THE FOUNDATION OF SOCIETAL DEVELOPMENT

Contents

Introduction

TRUST, THAT LUBRICANT of life everyone instinctively recognizes as essential. Perhaps because of this immediate familiarity, trust as a phenomenon has received rather limited attention from researchers and thinkers looking at what it really consists of, and why it really matters. The concept is practically absent from everyday public discourse, especially in relation to societal development. However, possibly as a result of a long decline of trust in the west, the concept has started to attract increasing interest from scholars around the world. This book showcases the key results of recent research, and explores further into the consequences of trust. The central thesis is simple, but far-reaching – that trust affords us a deeper understanding not only of the current and foreseeable challenges in the west, but also of the development of societies in general.

Although trust has been largely missing from public and political debate, it has long been established that trust and the related concept of social capital are highly important for economic development. Likewise, no state or government can survive long without a legitimate claim to power. Turns out we can credibly argue that "legitimacy" is but another name for trust in the system and those in power. At a more fundamental level, trust is necessary to foster the cooperation that enables groups to function in the first place. This connection to cooperation links trust directly to the survival instincts of individual human beings, looking for safety within the numbers of a trusted group. A community, nation or state, and ultimately the individual within these groups, cannot survive if there is no trust enabling the cooperation that builds and maintains the larger entity. Trust is the foundation on which every successful society is built.

Worryingly, empirical evidence shows that the fundamental foundation of trust has been in a long decline in western countries. This erosion applies to both trust in our governments and trust in our fellow citizens. In light of the political instability during the past decade, which seems only to deepen with time, it is easy to believe that there is a deficit of trust. Unfortunately, what we have seen so far may represent only the early warning signs of the problems that may await us if these trends are not reversed.

Complicating the situation is the fact that trust seems to have a degree of self-reinforcing quality; growing trust plants the seeds for deeper cooperation and further flowering of trust, whereas declining trust increases suspicion and raises the bar for cooperation, risking further breaking of the ties between people. In other words, trust could be described as a kind of network effect. Social networks provide an apt analogy, where the fate of a service can be dependent on the momentum of its user base – more users make a service more valuable for old and new users alike, which then increases the attractiveness of the service and lures in new users. On the other hand, if users start abandoning the service, it soon disappears into the archives of internet history, as people see less and less value in it. Similar logic can be said to apply to trust in societies, though thankfully not quite as fast-moving.

The decline in trust is characterized by a breakdown in common narratives, most pointedly reflected in the topics of economic inequality, climate change and demographic anxieties, which have become the most vexing and inflamed issues in public discourse. This book strives to elucidate how trust is an essential component of knowledge and understanding of these issues, explaining in part the present problems in mutual comprehension across the west.

What has exacerbated these problems is the fact that political forces on the left and right often completely fail to acknowledge the issues highlighted by the other side as legitimate problems, and consequently fail to recognize the trust-eroding effects of the policies they themselves promote. The internet and social media further complicate the situation by amplifying competing messages from all ends of the spectrum in ways we are only beginning to grasp. As a result, politics has become polarized, leading to increasing problems, exemplified by Brexit, cross-party hostility in the US or the growing number of climate-related protests in Europe.

The issue is profoundly important given that high levels of trust go hand in hand with economic prosperity and political stability, and low trust may result in fractiousness and political instability, precipitating even worse outcomes and a fall further down the abyss of distrust. As such, reflecting the role of trust should be beneficial to everyone with an interest in developing our societies for the better. Trust is a phenomenon at the very base of every society – its presence, or the lack of it, manifesting in the sublime heights and brutal lows of our interactions. Understanding trust allows us to glimpse human behaviour and societal development from a new, fresh perspective.

To substantiate these claims, I invite the reader on a journey to explore the multiple dimensions of trust as they are understood in the latest research, how the policy choices and developments in the west have affected the general levels of trust in society, based on our various understandings of the concept, and what may lie ahead. Ultimately my aim is to bring forth ideas for policies that may restore the trust that has been steadily eroding during the past decades, and in the process improve the functioning of our societies and the wellbeing of our citizens.

WHY TRUST MATTERS

"Love all, trust a few, do wrong to none."

WILLIAM SHAKESPEARE, *ALL'S WELL THAT ENDS WELL*

As Shakespeare implies, love and civilized behaviour should be extended to all – but with our trust we need to be far more selective. Why is trust so valuable, then? This book is really an extended answer to that very question. To answer it, we seek to explain the many ways trust matters – to the individual, to the state, to the economy – and everything in between. But before diving deep, let us begin with a sample of findings that give us an idea of trust in action.

Do you think happiness is important? I bet you do. Then you should also be very keen on trust. Not only is trust essential for flourishing relationships in general (obviously enough, I hope), but it appears to be one of the key factors that separate the happiest countries from the rest. This is one of the key conclusions presented by the British economist and happiness researcher, Richard Layard in his book *Can We Be Happier?* On a scale of 1 to 10, one point of a nation's total happiness score can be attributed to the difference between high trust and low trust. To give some context, only freedom and the relative extent of social support from friends and family were found to have a greater impact on happiness.[1] An EU study found trust to be strongly correlated to four measures of wellbeing. Citizens in more trusting European countries had more positive emotions and reported fewer negative ones. They were also found to be more satisfied with their lives and scored better in terms of psychological functioning.[2] Altogether an impressive set of correlations, although it must be stressed that correlation is not the same as causation. But it is no stretch to think that a link exists between high trust and fewer negative emotions and, from there, better psychological functioning. In fact, it seems eminently logical, because the existence of high trust can be said to mark a state of psychological safety in a relationship.

If happiness is somehow not of interest, then perhaps a long and healthy life is. Several studies indicate that trust is directly related to mortality, specifically of the cardiovascular or heart-related type. It appears

---

1   *Can We Be Happier?* Layard, Richard. Pelican books, 2020. Pages 49–52.

2   *Quality of Life: Social Cohesion and Well-being in Europe*. Delhey, Jan; Dragolov, Georgi; Boehnke, Klaus. Eurofound, November 2018.

that trust acts as a buffer against anxiety, reducing the negative impacts of anxiety and stress on the heart and the body. A US population-based study found distrustful people have a 13% higher risk of death from cardiovascular disease than a trusting control group. To quote the authors directly: "There is a clear survival advantage for individuals who trust strangers in this US population-based study."[3]

Turns out that the presence of trust is not only conducive to happiness and health, but also a necessary condition for us to create and acquire knowledge. This is convincingly argued by the philosopher John Hardwig. We will cover his arguments thoroughly later in this book, and add our own spice to them, sourced from advances in trust studies since his original article in 1991. As a teaser, think of all the things you've learned throughout your life. Did you figure everything out by yourself, or did the information come from some other person or institution? The vast majority of our knowledge is learned from an external source – from a schoolteacher, TV news or social media, for example. It is precisely our trust in the source of information that determines whether we consider the information as real knowledge or fake news.

Travelling back from the concepts of thought and knowledge to the material world, trust is of course essential for our trading and commercial activities, the daily business of making the world go round. So much so, that the wealthiest countries seem also to be the most trusting. The research shows that trust does indeed support economic growth, which in turn can foster trust by increasing living standards and economic opportunities. In other words, there is a two-way street between trust and prosperity. These findings help explain the relationship between trust and gross domestic product, our material wellbeing by another name.

For the reform-minded, we find that trust makes market liberalizing reforms more likely to pass, while deliberalizing initiatives are less likely to pass the political hurdle. Thus, trust seems to have a two-pronged impact supporting liberalizing economic policies, so helping an evolving economy to find its shape in the changing landscape of technology.[4] Trust is key for almost all things economic, starting from being a necessary condition for much of the cooperation that underpins the operations of any organization.

3   Trust, Happiness and Mortality: Findings from a Prospective US Population-based Survey. Miething, Alexander; Mewes, Jan; Giordano, Giuseppe. *Social Science & Medicine*, 252, January 2020.

4   The Market-Promoting and Market-Preserving Role of Social Trust in Reforms of Policies and Institutions. Berggren, Niclas; Bjørnskov, Christian. *Southern Economic Journal*, Volume 84, Issue 1, 2017

But when talking about organizations, the ultimate units are of course the state itself and the society sponsoring one. By now it can't come as a surprise that trust is essential also for the state and the politics of a society. Indeed, the evidence is copious. Hans Pitlik and Martin Rode for example find, with the force of an enquiry covering 190,000 individuals in 68 countries, that social trust seems to be negatively correlated with extreme positions on various political topics. This implies that the presence of trust is associated with centrist political leanings, and with less polarization and political divergence.[5] In other words, where there is trust, there tends to be political stability too.

Whether for individual happiness, creation of knowledge, economic wellbeing or political stability, trust matters. And as we can infer from the nature of these topics, it matters a lot. These are after all the weightiest of imaginable topics – those governing the development, success and failure of individuals and societies alike.

These little appetizers on various topics correspond to the structure and contents of this book. But rather than just reviewing the many established results, this book will also delve deeper into the core mechanisms of trust and develop a more comprehensive view of how they play out in every society.

First, we will review the very basics of what trust is, how it is formed and the various ways we can approach the subject. Then we will consider trust's role in an individual's life. From there, the connections between trust and knowledge are put under our magnifying glass. Knowledge is of course the oil in the wheels of our information economy, and so we will continue to the economic dimensions of trust. Wealth for its part is a source of inequality and power fuelling political rivalry, and so the political dimensions of trust are the final part forming the essential foundation of this book. We will then build on the established foundations to paint a fuller picture of trust's very central role in social development, both in perpetuity and with present circumstances in mind.

That trust is related to so many matters of importance is by itself a reason to write about it. Trust really is an eternally relevant factor for the development of any society, as this book hopes to demonstrate. But what really motivated this book in the first place was the realization that trust seems to be seriously deteriorating in our present western societies. This started off as a hunch but, as we shall see next, it is amply substantiated by empirical data.

---

5   Radical Distrust: Are Economic Policy Attitudes Tempered by Social Trust? Pitlik, Hans; Rode, Martin. *WIFO Working Papers*, No. 594, December 2019.

WHY WE NEED TO PAY ATTENTION RIGHT NOW – KEY STATISTICS ON TRUST

At first glance the global picture of relative levels of trust among nations, as presented below, corresponds to what may be expected based on most other measures of development and wellbeing, with the usual suspects, developed western countries, coming out especially strong. Yet a few interesting things stand out. China is among the most trusting nations in the world, as is Saudi Arabia. But what about the development of trust over time in the west?

TRUST IN OTHERS AROUND THE WORLD, 2014

Share of people agreeing with the statement "most people can be trusted", 2014
Self-reported trust in others is constructed as the number of people responding to the question "Generally speaking, would you say that most people can be trusted or that you need to be very careful in dealing with people?" Possible answers include "Most people can be trusted", "Don't know" and "Can't be too careful".

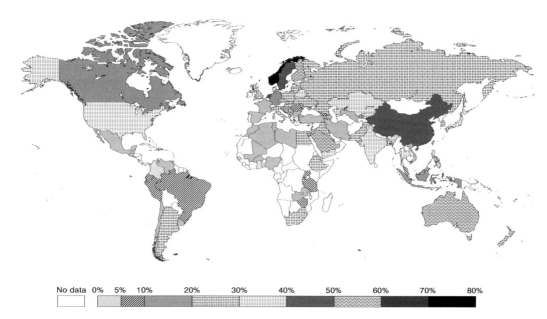

No data 0%   5%   10%   20%   30%   40%   50%   60%   70%   80%

SOURCE: World Values Survey (2014)
OurWorldInData.org/trust

For starters, some shock and horror. Americans' trust in their government has plunged from almost 80% in the late 1950s to below 20% in 2019.
And this is not merely a Trump-related phenomenon. Somewhat absurdly,
it appears that the Clinton years were good for public trust, but the direction of development has been down most of the time, and dramatically so
over the whole period. In light of the figures, it is not really a wonder that
(presumably) leftists established their own autonomous zones of control
during the summer riots of 2020, while the (presumably) right-wingers
responded with a storming of the Capitol in January 2021 after their elec-
tion loss. Trust in the government in the US is more or less at rock bottom.

TRUST IN THE GOVERNMENT IN THE US, 1958–2019

% of Americans saying they trust the government to do the right thing "just about
always" or "most of the time"

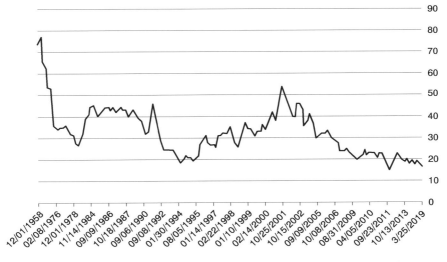

SOURCE: Pew Research Center. www.pewresearch.org/politics/2019/04/11/public-trust-in-
government-1958-2019

What about Europe? Thanks to the multitude of nations and the relative
youth of the European Union as an institution we have to content ourselves
with a more limited set of information describing European developments.
But based on the Eurobarometer data for 2004–2017, it seems that the direction of travel has been down, as in the US, when it comes to Europeans' trust
in the EU and its core institutions. Despite the downward trend, trust in the

much-disparaged EU was still at around 42% in 2017, much higher than the trust enjoyed by US governments for the past 15 years or so.

Overall trust in national governments among European countries seems to have been relatively steady in recent decades. Some nations show considerable declines, while some stay steady, and a few have even improved their trust scores during the 21st century. Combining the developments for the EU and the developments on a national level, it seems that the trajectory of trust in institutions is slightly down in the EU as well, but not quite so dramatically as in the US.

TRUST IN EUROPEAN INSTITUTIONS

For the following institutions, % of Europeans answering "Tend to trust" or the alternative "Tend NOT to trust"
% - EU - TEND TO TRUST

—— The European Union
······ The (Nationality) Government
--- The (Nationality) Parliament

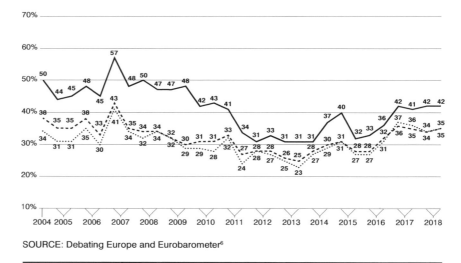

SOURCE: Debating Europe and Eurobarometer[6]

But it might be argued that distrust of the government is healthy and a natural attitude for citizens of a free and democratic country. After all, isn't it the citizen's job to keep the politicians honest and accountable, which in

---

6   www.debatingeurope.eu/2019/09/06/what-should-eu-institutions-do-to-boost-your-trust-in-them/#.YooSWKhByUk

turn requires more than a bit of scepticism and questioning? So, the loss of trust in government might be construed as a natural occurrence as citizens accustom themselves to democratic circumstances. Some have claimed this as an explanation for the declines in trust. Yet our democracies are already long-established, so the learned scepticism might have happened long ago, rather than in the past 50 years. Likewise, if the declines were only a reflection of democratic politics and its institutions, trust in other people might be expected to remain high. Yet as we see from our next set of US data, the share of respondents reporting most people "Can be trusted" has fallen from 46% in 1972 to 31% in 2018. Americans' distrust is not limited to the government but extends more and more to other Americans as well. Probably reflecting this state of affairs, the distrust between Democrats and Republicans was by now approaching legendary proportions. As an example of the cross-party polarization, in 2020 only 6% of marriages in the US were between couples supporting opposing political parties.[7]

TRUST IN OTHERS IN THE US

Generally speaking, would you say that most people can be trusted or that you can't be too careful in dealing with people?
% answering "Can trust"

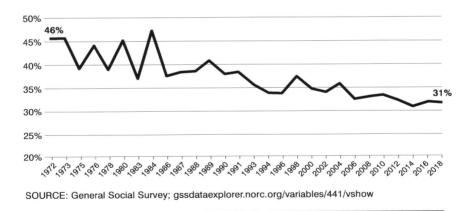

SOURCE: General Social Survey; gssdataexplorer.norc.org/variables/441/vshow

Unfortunately, we do not have similar long-term statistics on trust in others for European countries.

---

7   'Til Death Do Us Part(isanship): Voting and Polarization in Opposite-Party Marriages. Insights from the democracy fund voter study group, Fisk, Colin A.; Fraga, Bernard L., August 2020.

The data speaks clearly about the decline in trust of government institutions and fellow citizens alike. The same sorry trend continues in our attitudes towards media. In the US, trust in mass media was at around 70% in the 1970s.[8] By 2021 the figure was 36%, having recovered slightly from an all-time low of 32% in 2016. The partisan divide that is polarizing the US is reflected in the media, which has separated itself likewise to provide news and worldviews from either Democrat or Republican perspectives. Old-fashioned non-partisan, neutral reporting covering alternative and competing perspectives, aspiring to objectivity and actual understanding, has long since become an endangered species.

AMERICAN'S TRUST IN MASS MEDIA LOWEST SINCE 2016

In general, how much trust and confidence do you have in the mass media -- such as newspapers, TV and radio -- when it comes to reporting the news fully, accurately and fairly -- a great deal, a fair amount, not very much or none at all?

—— % Great deal/Fair amount

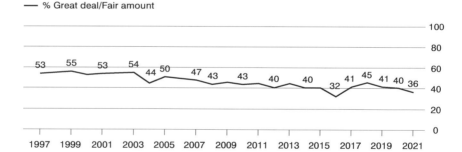

Data from 1972, 1974 and 1976 not shown
GALLUP

Source: news.gallup.com/poll/355526/americans-trust-media-dips-second-lowest-record.aspx

The same trend of increasing distrust of the media is present in Europe. From the following data we can also make out the dramatic differences in trust of different types of media. Old-fashioned media such as radio, TV and newspapers enjoy clearly greater – even net positive – trust among Europeans. The internet and social media on the other hand are seen as essentially untrustworthy sources. This is no surprise, given the vast amounts of scams, hacks and outright fabricated information floating

8   news.gallup.com/poll/321116/americans-remain-distrustful-mass-media.aspx

out there. Fake and manufactured news and reporting are nothing new, and such methods were employed extensively as tools of information warfare by the Soviet Union as well as the western countries during the Cold War, for example. But the internet has made the creation and dissemination of such material far faster, easier and more widespread. It is sadly no wonder that, in addition to the impacts of the decline in trust in general and the resulting polarization, trust in media is also in clear decline.

EVOLUTION OF EU NET TRUST INDEX (2015–2021)

Net trust index = '% of people who tend to trust' - '% of people who tend not to trust'

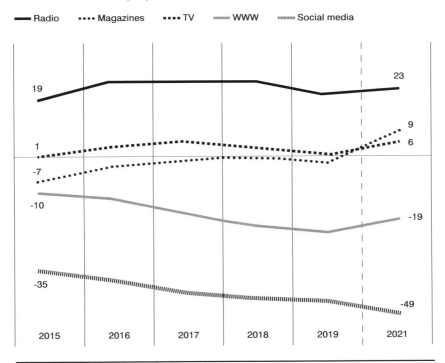

All in all, the same message keeps popping up: trust is declining, across the board. Whether it is about the core political institutions of the west, about our trust in our fellow citizens, about the meaning-making media we are all consuming one way or another, the threads holding us together seem to be coming loose. Unfortunately, the trend that is on full display in statistics is corroborated by lived experience in our increasingly divided western societies.

But what does all this mean? Should we be worried? I believe so. After all, the things we found associated with trust – such as happiness, health, material wellbeing and political stability – tend to be eminently and universally desirable regardless of one's origins or political outlook. But fuller answers to these questions will become apparent as we look in greater depth at the many essential ways trust sustains our individual wellbeing, common meaning-making and the stable development and flourishing of our societies. But first, let us get acquainted with the very basics of what trust is all about.

The definitions of trust used throughout this book

THE CONSISTENCY WITH which a partner responds to a lover's messages. The civil and fair treatment one receives when dealing with public institutions. The right-sized pint in exchange for your money. Everyday experiences such as these give us a good starting point for understanding what trust may be about. Trust is always a relationship, but the context of the relationship can be anything from warm intimacy to the cold transaction of economic interaction. The relationships of trust have a dimension of uncertain expectation, whether of an answer, of fair treatment or of just the right product. On the other side of the future-oriented expectation is the counterparty on whom our trust has been placed, and on whom we depend for something. Therefore, trust always includes a vulnerability in our relationship with the counterparty, who we hope will act in accordance with our interests. With trust we have psychological safety that things will work out for us; without, we worry about what might happen. But we can never know for sure, meaning that trust can also be seen as a gamble or an investment, with an inherent possibility of an undesirable outcome. Trust would not be trust if it could not be broken.

The everyday understanding of trust has been enriched by scholars who since the 1980s have mined the deeper qualities of the phenomenon, and have brought to the surface a treasure of knowledge that may purchase us significant insights for understanding and guiding the development of our societies.

The academic consensus on how trust comes to exist among different actors has over time coalesced around three core dimensions that determine the trustor's (the party taking the risk of trusting) assessment of the trustworthiness of the trustee (the counterparty), namely: *ability, benevolence and integrity*. In short, trust is born or broken as the individual monitors the counterparty's behaviour and adjusts their expectations according to observations of ability, benevolence and integrity in the other. These three factors (trust antecedents) are also influenced by an individual's propensity towards trust and the overall context of the situation.[9] That's it, very bluntly. But let us unpack all of this a bit, to understand what is going on.

Ability relates to our view of the other's skills, competences and essential characteristics in the domain of activity that our trust expectation relates to. In other words, it is our assessment of whether the

---

9   An Integrative Model of Organizational Trust. Mayer, Roger; Davis, James; Schoorman, David. *The Academy of Management Review*, Vol. 20, July 1995.

CONCEPTS UNDERLYING ABILITY, BENEVOLENCE AND INTEGRITY

Ability	Benevolence	Integrity
Skills	Believed will to do good	Adherence to principles
Competencies	Positive towards trustor	Personal integrity
Task-specific characteristics	Intentions	Consistency of past actions
Training	Altruism	Strong sense of justice
Knowledge		Value congruence
Perceived expertise		Character

SOURCE: Mayer, Davis and Schoorman

counterparty is actually capable of fulfilling the expectation we have of them. In practice this dimension of trust shows up for example when one has an aching tooth that needs mending; for the task at hand one prefers an experienced dentist over a random passer-by who just happens to have a drill. This is the essence of our trust in experts.

Benevolence refers to the trustor's perception of the trustee's attitude towards the trustor; the more we believe that the counterparty has our interest in mind and wants to do good to or for us, without any external motive, the more we tend to trust them. If we believe that the counterparty is benevolent towards us, the likelihood of betrayal of trust may be expected to be lower than with a non-benevolent counterparty, making us therefore inclined towards making the investment of trust with the benevolent party. This dimension thus helps explain why we tend to trust our friends more than strangers.

The final element of the triad of trust is *integrity*, which is about our perceptions of the counterparty's adherence to a set of values and behaviours we find acceptable. If we are running a project with a progression of tight deadlines, only to find ourselves halted by a party who is unwilling to keep to the agreed timetable, we may find our trust in them melt away like a cone of ice cream on a hot summer day. First there is a mess, then we get frustrated and finally trust disappears. Value congruence is also a key element of trust. Values relate to what one appreciates and wants to promote in the world. If, while trying to advance our values, we have to depend on a counterparty whose values are in direct contradiction to ours, cooperation may become difficult as both parties perceive a risk to their own values and the goals they seek to promote. This perception of competing goals will naturally lead to distrust between the parties. The connection between value congruence and trust has become particularly visible during recent times, with electorates on the left and right across the west drifting further apart and accepting as legitimate only the viewpoints of those they perceive to be promoting the same values, often regardless of facts or the complex nature of the issues at hand. Finally, research indicates that integrity is a more important factor for trust than ability or benevolence in the early phases of a trust relationship.

Context and our individual propensity to trust further regulate our perception of the trustworthiness of the counterparty. Propensity to trust is our general attitude towards trusting others, which naturally varies between individuals and is the product of our upbringing and previous experiences. Some people are more trusting, some are less. Context for its part deals with the variety of external circumstances affecting the relationship of trust between parties. Among the most impactful contextual factors for trust are, for example, the stakes involved, the balance of power between the parties, the alternatives available and the perception of the level of risk. Personal experience can quickly confirm that trust is easy to grant when nothing significant is at stake. On the contrary, if we are about to risk our lives the threshold to trust must be all the higher.

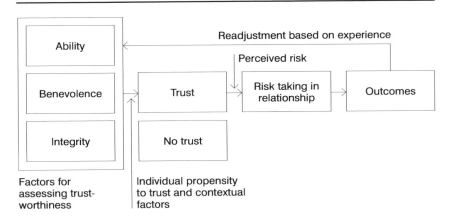

Mayer, Davis and Schoorman model of the trust process with minor adjustments by the author

This model of trust attains its completion with the feedback loop of observation and adjustment. As the relationship develops, we make new observations about the counterparty's behaviour and adjust our assessment of their trustworthiness. Should our assessment be adjusted downwards with new observations, so that our trust no longer matches the perceived level of risk in the situation, we are likely to end the relationship – in other words, we no longer trust the other party enough to continue. Alternatively, if things proceed according to our wishes or expectations, the assessment may become more approving, firming the foundation of our trust.

As with most ideas and matters of the mind, we can find antecedents for our current thinking on trust in the old world of the ancient Greeks and Romans. Whether it is about the nature of the universe (atoms as the fundamental building blocks of all matter were first proposed by the Greeks), the nature of man or the nature of society itself, our discussions in the present often tread paths first opened over 2,000 years ago on the coasts of the Mediterranean.

Although Aristotle didn't consider the concept of "trust" with the same breadth of connotations as we understand them in this book, he had an interesting definition of the credibility of an orator trying to sway a crowd of people (perhaps the citizens of a polis weighing some pressing issue): "There are three things which inspire confidence in the orator's own character – the three, namely, that induce us to believe a thing apart from any proof of it: good sense, good moral character, and goodwill."[10]

By "good sense", Aristotle meant false or correct opinions about things – essentially whether the orator actually knows what they are talking about. Elaborating on "good moral character" Aristotle mentioned a person who says what they really think – in other words, a person who is honest. He noted that a past record of good deeds and upright behaviour are hallmarks of good moral character. Finally, mutual goodwill and friendliness incline the audience to a favourable stance towards the orator. If we compare our discussion above of the three core building blocks of trust with Aristotle's thinking, we find that they are essentially identical. As if to confirm our analysis, Aristotle also commented: "It follows that anyone who is thought to have all three of these good qualities will inspire trust in his audience."

What Aristotle failed to notice in his focus on oratory and rhetoric was that trust, formed from the components he accurately perceived, is relevant to a much, much broader set of issues than just oratory, argumentation and rhetoric.

---

10   *The Art of Rhetoric*. Aristotle. Collins Classics, 2012. Page 80.

THE DUAL NATURE OF TRUST – DIMENSIONS OF TRUST ASSESSMENT AND THE DYNAMIC ADJUSTMENT PROCESS

Trust, then, is initially based on evaluations of ability, benevolence and integrity, and subsequently evolves as we experience our counterpart in action. In the course of a trusting relationship we make new observations and accumulate evidence that either supports or detracts from our earlier trust position, laying the groundwork for behavioural adjustments in response to our updated understanding. We live and learn; sometimes to trust, sometimes to distrust.

Based on this view, we have two distinct parts of trust: the three dimensions, and their dynamic adjustment process based on experience and observation. As will be elaborated throughout this book, these distinct parts of trust have deep – and very different – implications for trust in society.

When it comes to the three dimensions of ability, benevolence and integrity, we can draw some obvious conclusions about their social consequences. If ability in all its expressions is a source of trust, then it should pay off to have a highly educated populace, to create incentives and structures that allow expertise to flourish and so on. This is because the greater the abilities of the populace, and the state serving the citizens, the better things get done and the more trust there should be to go around. When it comes to benevolence, a population at peace with itself and its official institutions is undoubtedly more trusting than one racked with malevolent abuse. In terms of integrity, a nation that is united in its values and behaviours will find cooperation far easier than one split between fiercely competing habits and belief systems. All this is to say that it is easy to perceive the high-level implications of ability, benevolence and integrity at the broader societal level. This part of trust tells us why excellence and similarities are so agreeable for us; why like attracts like, why we seek harmony and unanimous agreement and have trouble with differences. The first part of the dual nature of trust (the three dimensions) thus answers the question: what qualities earn my trust?

When it comes to the second distinct aspect of trust, the dynamic adjustment process, the societal implications are more indirect and altogether quite different. This aspect of trust can be thought to answer the question: if I'm going to have to deal with you, how does trust develop over time, and under what conditions would I like to cooperate?

Here the core of the issue is first the ability to observe and, from there, to adjust one's behaviour if necessary – to deepen cooperation or withdraw from it. These aspects of trust speak for the value of information, transparency and accountability in our societies, in private and public interactions alike, as enabling trust-related observations. The more accurate our observations, the better we can react and measure actions in relation to our counterparty. This is why transparent and accountable governance is key for creating trust between the state and the people – for example, helping us assess policies effected and vote in response to them. Likewise, the ability to freely adjust our behaviour in response to our evolving assessments is highly important for the organic development of trust. This has a number of implications. It explains why we appreciate freedom in general, because it implies space for adjustment. It explains why backroom dealing, unequal laws and compulsion are not generally friends of trust, restricting us and leaving little room for manoeuvring in response to our needs, desires and perceptions of trust.

This is why we distrust secrecy and are eager to know more about the things we find important. It's why we value the ability to be who we genuinely are – because this is the best place from which to act and advance one's own interests. It also explains why democracy, tolerance and equality before the law are hallmarks of the most trusting countries. Institutions in these countries enable relatively free representation of interests and the adjustment of cooperation in response to evolving trust or distrust, and respond to citizens' needs – melting the icebergs of distrust and making way for a return to the peaceful waters of trust. Evolving laws, the changing fortunes of competing political parties and institutional evolution are concrete examples of this responsive flexibility. The great virtue of such responsive institutions is that they align with the dynamic adjustment process of trust.

The importance of these elements can be underscored by some quick thought experiments: think of the difference between working with an inept colleague and someone you know you can depend on. How do your trust and behaviour change with the situation? Taking things to a higher societal level, how much trust would you have towards a totalitarian state prohibiting free speech and representation of interests, and how would that affect your behaviour? How would your perception of the situation change if you could end the disagreeable relationship without negative repercussions? What if you could not?

Obviously, we prefer the more skilled and dependable co-workers, and a friendlier state is more agreeable and trust-inducing than a totalitarian one. Should we find ourselves in the less preferable situation of either sort, the possibility of an easy exit tends to ease our minds, whereas an unescapable situation fuels our frustration and distrust.

We might hypothesize that the dual nature of trust is linked to the fundamental instincts to survive and flourish in each of us. The dimensions of trust assessment, where excellence and commonalities reign, lead us to seek the company of those with ability, who are like and agreeable to ourselves. Such an environment is at once both easily intelligible and more supportive of our own interests – a relative safe haven for us. The dynamic side of trust shows how we update our trust assessments, and in doing so implicitly points towards the ideal conditions for the process. Thus we can understand why we prefer individual rights, information and freedom of action – in other words, personal empowerment – because these things help us adapt to changing circumstances and maximize our ability to overcome the challenges we inevitably meet.

When trust is present, we also have a sense of safety. When trust is lacking, we tend to be worried for our interests. The secure state of trust lets us focus on enjoyment and productive activity over the frustration, worrying and avoidance of cooperation that mark distrust. The aspects of trust let us approach many social phenomena and the workings of our institutions from a new angle. Indeed, this is the premise and promise of this whole book.

INTERPERSONAL TRUST AND GENERALIZED TRUST

Another way to think about trust is to divide it into two types: interpersonal trust and abstract, general-level trust. The so-called dyadic, or interpersonal, trust grows (or withers) in the context of direct interactions of individuals, such as between co-workers or a couple nurturing a new relationship. The opposite is the subtle and abstract generalized trust, representing more global attitudes towards trust, relevant in a variety of contexts.

Dyadic trust comes about through the process of interpersonal interaction as experience is gained and assessments made about the other's ability, benevolence and integrity. The level of trust towards the other is constantly refined through new observations, and the changing assessments modify subsequent attitudes and behaviours between the participants in the relationship. Thus observations made during our interactions help us form an increasingly accurate picture of the trustworthiness of the other. Getting to know another's values, their skills in relevant areas and how they respond to our expectations about proper behaviour all adjust our perceptions about our counterparts.

It's not only the quality of interactions that matters in shaping each party's view of the other. The initial level of trust each displays towards the other is also of consequence; if one has zero trust to begin with, all cooperation may be refused, the other never given a chance to prove themself, leaving the potential dyad of trust wholly unrealized.

The participants in a dyad usually reach a mutual understanding of the level of trust in the relationship, where their perceptions and expectations are in harmony, reflecting either high or low mutual trust. It is also possible, however, though less common, that the mutual learning process leads to an asymmetrical situation, where the parties of the dyad have highly divergent trust perceptions about each other. It may be guessed that in these situations the relationship is unlikely to last – misunderstandings, disappointments and conflicts appear highly probable.

Research shows many other things also affect the formation and level of interpersonal trust. Expressing initial highly trusting attitudes tends to foster further growth of trust; an unequal power distribution, such as may happen at work between a superior and a subordinate, tends to decrease trust. Finally, in an interpersonal situation trust is seen to be reciprocal, meaning that the quality of trust exhibited towards the other tends to affect the trust received in turn.[11]

Generalized trust, on the other hand, refers to the concepts and attitudes an individual, or even a whole society on average, may have about trust and trustworthiness at a general, abstract level. Generalized trust may be about anything from perceptions about the trustworthiness of a

---

11   *It Isn't Always Mutual: A Critical Review of Dyadic Trust.* Korsgaard, M. Audrey; Brower, Holly H.; Lester, Scott W. 3 September 2014.

random stranger on the street (before any contact to establish an inter-personal relationship has been made), the companies that form the clock-work of the economy or the institutions that have been built to govern the whole state. Like dyadic trust in an interpersonal relationship, generalized trust shapes action as it forms expectations about human behaviour and the wider society, and how one should conduct oneself based on these expectations. If a person has low generalized trust, they might assume others are untrustworthy, or may be highly sceptical of institutions as sources of positive contributions to society. These expectations shaped by low generalized trust may consequently manifest in various ways – for example, as a universal aversion to making acquaintance with new people or as political apathy.

Research indicates there are three factors acting as the main instruc-tors in instituting the sense of generalized trust in someone: genetics, life-time experiences and culture. Like practically every human trait, general-ized trust has been shown to have a dimension of heritability. Depending on the source, current studies indicate that some 5–57% of an individual's level of generalized trust could be explained by heritability, though the variation in results and the close connection to lifetime experiences indi-cate that there is further work to be done in elucidating the exact role genes play. It can be speculated that the genetic element has a larger effect in youth because the other key elements, lifetime experiences and cultural influences, have yet to impart their full impacts. Following this reasoning, the explanatory power of social experiences and culture as determinants of trust should increase with age, leading to a decreasing relative share of genetic impact; the culture is the same for everyone in a given society, but imbibing it fully takes time; and learnings accumulated from cumula-tive social experiences tend to mitigate either exceptionally low or high levels of generalized trust inherited from family. These effects could thus be expected to moderate the relative impact of the genetic component of trust over time.

If generalized trust has an element of heritability, it seems logi-cal that family environment might be the most significant class in the school of trust. Parents pass on to their children not only their genes, but also behavioural models and associated experiences about sociability and trust. As such, the childhood home environment and the quality of care experiences as an infant are especially important in establishing a sense of whether others can be trusted. We will look at this further in the following section on the role of trust in an individual's life. While early childhood is a key period for trust formation, the specific social

experiences we accumulate during our lifetimes all affect our evaluation of others' trustworthiness in general – that is, our level of generalized trust. However, the observations that tune our understanding of
trust are not limited to those coming from our own struggles – we learn
nearly as effectively from the people in our close social circles and their
encounters with issues of trust.

External influences that mould our views are many, and those
closest to us are just the most obvious sources. In fact, everything we
learn about human nature guides our expectations about others, and
these learnings may come from many sources besides personal experience. Universities scrutinize human behaviour from various angles
and propagate views in proportion to the latest academic trends
(which are often mere theory, rather than actual empirical knowledge)
in given fields, and these lessons tend to get repeated elsewhere as
the concepts spread to the wider society. Perhaps the most infamous
example of academic assumptions about human behaviour is found
in economics. The so-called homo economicus is a central assumption guiding economic theory, whereby the agents in an economy
(consumers, workers, also known as human beings) are considered to
be rational utility maximizers, always seeking the best outcomes for
given needs through rational weighing of alternatives. Sadly, this is of
course a highly idealistic view of human behaviour. Precisely because
of the glaring contrast with common experience, homo economicus
is a prime example of an academic assumption about human behaviour that is at odds with reality. To be fair to economics and economists (full disclosure: I studied economics and have a soft spot for the
discipline), assuming humans are rational beings is rather defensible,
because irrationality would be a challenging starting point for any analysis. Furthermore, recent decades have seen considerable efforts to
bring irrationality into economics. Nonetheless, this working assumption fails the test of reality quite dramatically, and is but one example
of academic frameworks scarcely in line with actual human behaviour.
Here we have to express our hope and sincere belief that the story of
trust recounted in these pages, based largely on academic research, is
at the more accurate and useful end of theorizing.

Academia is but one stream contributing to the wider river of ideas
affecting generalized trust in us. The news we see on TV, the things we
read on social media, the stories we tell in one form or another – all of
these impart lessons about other people and society. Collectively these
influences may be considered to compose the environment of culture we

find ourselves immersed in, the third major constituting factor of generalized trust in addition to genetics and lifetime experiences.[12]

What these two ends of the trust spectrum, dyadic and generalized, represent is trust at its most personal, particular and individually tangible, and at its most abstract and general. Each has implications for the other – the generalized influences our particular personal relationships; and specific experiences affect our interpretation of a broader range of phenomena. Generalized trust is built from and affected by the trust experiences in interpersonal relationships, just as the level of an individual's generalized trust affects how the person conducts these relationships. The view taken in this book is that the dyadic and generalized versions of trust are but different manifestations of the same phenomenon, with broadly equivalent implications in situations of low or high trust, and therefore the word "trust" throughout this book may refer to one or the other form, the particular or the general.

THE SEPARATE STATES OF TRUST – TRUST, MISTRUST AND DISTRUST

If trust is the party you are heading to, mistrust is a wrong address on your map app and distrust is never getting the invite in the first place. So far we have established that trust is a bright influence on the horizon of humanity, but let us for a moment venture to the dark side of the moon, to the company of mistrust and distrust.

Mistrust can be understood as misplaced trust, where the investment of trust does not result in the expected return, regardless of the outcome we were waiting for. This tends to mean that whether or not we granted our trust, our initial position may later turn out to be the wrong choice. Following this definition, mistrust is a relatively common state in the early phases of any relationship, before enough observations have been made to arrive at an accurate understanding of the other party. Given time and

---

12   Generalized Trust: Four Lessons From Genetics and Culture. Van Lange, Paul A.M. *Current Directions in Psychological Science*, February 2015; Exploring the Genetic Etiology of Trust in Adolescents: Combined Twin and DNA Analyses. Wootton, Robyn E., et. al. *Twin Research and Human Genetics*, December 2016.

increasing understanding the state of misplaced trust will yield to either positive trust or its opposite, distrust.

With distrust we travel to the territory of negative expectations. Distrusting something can be considered to mean, at the mellower end of the spectrum, a lack of faith in the ability of the other party to deliver what is expected of them. At its darkest end, distrust is a natural state in a situation where the opposite party is thought to have contradictory or even hostile interests and intentions towards us. What is fundamental to distrust is that there is no expectation that the other party will align with or fulfil our interests and hopes; instead, there is the expectation that we would be wrong to invest our trust in them. Taking the ability, benevolence and integrity (the basic constituents of trust formation) perspective, distrust can for example denote a situation at work where we perceive a lack of ability in the trustee to accomplish a certain task, or perhaps in a political context knowing our interlocutor to have diametrically opposite values to us, making us certain that they will act against us regarding the motion at hand.

In common parlance and academic output alike the words mistrust and distrust are often happily mixed and used to refer to the same thing, corresponding closely to a lack of trust, here defined as distrust. To console those not content with simplicity, various alternative and additional meanings can also be fished from the pond of research around the subject, such as the concept of untrust, used to refer to the uncertain or neutral middle ground between trust and distrust.[13] In this text we keep to the simple triad of trust, mistrust and distrust.

While mistrust can be seen as a step on the way to better information, distrust represents an established view on the situation. In other words it is trust or distrust that may turn out to be mistrust, and mistrust may give way to trust or distrust. In our real-life situations we tend to start from a position of trust or distrust, based on our prior knowledge and assumptions informed by generalized trust. Because trust is needed for sustained cooperation and its attendant benefits, distrust for its part can be seen as an adaptive response when cooperation and trusting behaviour could be harmful to us, such as in highly risky situations, limiting the potential damage.

---

13   Trust, Untrust, Distrust and Mistrust – An Exploration of the Dark(er) Side. Stephen Marsh, Stephen; & Mark R. Dibben, Mark R. Conference paper in *Lecture Notes in Computer Science* 3477:17–33, May 2005.

FACTORS OF TRUST AS
MOTIVATORS OF COOPERATION

As we've seen, assessments of trustworthiness are made on the basis of ability, benevolence and integrity, enhanced by contextual and individual elements that add their own spice. This typical conceptualization of trust explains how the often unconscious anticipation acts as a yes/no gate for cooperation. In other words, trust is a sort of qualifying stage that gives permission for the business of cooperation to proceed if the necessary level of trust is met. Another way to perceive trust's impact on cooperation is to see it as a description of attractors, rather than as a threshold to be passed.

Think about your friends and loved ones, favourite colleagues or the people you play sports with. What makes them special for you? Because they're interesting conversationalists, fun to be with and care for you? Or maybe you just have common interests, whether through work or leisure, that draw you together to enjoy some activity or other. The reasons we associate with those we do can quite well be understood with the antecedents of trust.

When it comes to sports, we tend to group up with people who are at roughly the same skill level as we are. It is simply most enjoyable to compete when there is enough of a challenge, but not too little or too much of it. This means those far below or far above our level tend not to make for fun teammates or opponents. Thus, matching ability can often be a relevant factor in bringing together a group for sports and other activities such as gaming, arts and crafts and the like.

It is not just that matching abilities often make for good fun. Complementary knowledge, skills and abilities also make cooperation worthwhile. Indeed, it is precisely through the symphony of complementary skills that the music of the modern economy is produced. A firm cannot flourish if it is made up only of salespeople or accountants. But working together with people of different skills, they do produce results. This applies in nearly every field of activity, but especially in productive endeavours. The expansion of know-how through education and other means over the past few centuries has certainly made cooperation more lucrative. As people gain skills and knowledge, they can provide more value to others, making cooperation more attractive for everyone involved.

Most often the people closest to us – our families, spouses and lovers – are also people who care a great deal about us, just as we care about them. Caring relationships are by definition marked by deep sympathy and profound benevolence (although, yes, sometimes it is more complex than that). It is no surprise that familial relationships are among the most lasting and trustful. With family it is not necessarily the mutual benevolence that makes members stick together, but the ties of kinship. But certainly, if there is no goodwill or mutual respect, families too can break apart. More casually, friendships perhaps best epitomize the attracting magic of mutual goodwill. Friendships are formed on the basis of common interests and the enjoyment of matching wits and humour. Finding those who greet you with kindness, a smile and a joke to brighten your day is certain to bring joy and sunshine to anyone's life. Our social nature encourages us to seek such company, the type that is benevolent towards us and our mental well-being.

We are also drawn to people who possess values and standards of behaviour that are acceptable and agreeable to us. This of course connects back to the enjoyment of benevolent company: it is more pleasant to associate with people you don't have to argue with all the time. More importantly, people with similar values are more likely to have congruent goals in many areas of life. Common objectives draw people together to achieve their goals. Having similar standards of behaviour in general will make for a more enjoyable time working together, because unpleasant surprises should be less common. And so the integrity dimension offers another perspective on why we seek out the company of others.

The same factors that we use to evaluate others' trustworthiness can also be seen as things drawing us to others, though perhaps without the element of risk inherent in typical trust relationships. The more we see something good through the prisms of ability, benevolence and integrity, the more likely we are to have an interest in engaging with someone. In many ways it is a corroboration of the old adage that "birds of a feather flock together". Common values and interests bring people together to advance causes or maybe the success of some sports team. But this is not the whole story. As we saw with skills and knowledge, it is also often precisely the different strengths and weaknesses that lead people to seek each other out, to reach a goal that would be unattainable for them alone.

Trust and the individual

"We are, all of us, molded and remolded by those who have loved us, and though that love may pass, we remain none the less their work – a work that very likely they do not recognize, and which is never exactly what they intended."

FRANÇOIS MAURIAC, *THE DESERT OF LOVE*

TRUST IS A topic nearly as diverse as the world we find ourselves in, and our journey of exploration started with getting acquainted with the symbols adorning the map – the definitions that serve to guide us rest of the way. Now, with the basics covered, we can start to discover the real meaning and importance of trust by looking at the role it plays in an individual's life.

TRUST AS THE FOUNDATION OF SOCIABILITY IN PSYCHOLOGICAL THEORIES

Trust is to social interactions what cutlery is to dining; without the former, the latter tends to turn into a mess. This becomes evident as we turn our enquiring gaze on some of the principal theories of the foundations of human sociability in psychology. Let us start out with the insights of attachment theory, which allow us to build a bridge between trust and broader psychological development.

The flower of insight known as attachment theory has at its root the idea that our earliest experiences with our caregivers continue to resonate in social interactions throughout our lives, showing up variously as the speed bumps, wrong turns or smooth rides on the roads of our lives. From our first years to early childhood, we are continuously absorbing new experiences and information, which in turn mould our concepts of the world and how we see our place in it, and in this way forge our personalities. The circumstances of our infancy and youth teach various lessons to the young mind, which tend to be adaptive in the initial family environment but may later turn out to hinder personal development in the larger world of adult society.[14]

The process of learning is ongoing throughout our lives, but the early years are especially critical, because the initial concepts formed during childhood affect our interpretation and understanding of later experiences, setting a course for our psychological development. Of course all experience tends to inform subsequent interpretation, which leads us to the

---

14   Attachment Theory: Basic Concepts and Contemporary Questions. Rholes, W.S.; Simpson, J.A. *Adult attachment: Theory, research, and clinical implications*. Guilford Publications, 2004. Pages 3–14.

insight that the earliest ones will be the most influential because there's much more to come, in contrast to a mind-bending insight at your 95th birthday. Moreover, learning has been found to be connected to the intensity of emotional experience at the time of the lesson, whatever form it may take. We may safely assume that the first experience of anything elicits a stronger response than subsequent repetitions. Childhood and youth are a wonderland of the new, but the passage of time familiarizes and accustoms us to the ways of the world, slowly eroding the emotional intensity of our experiences – dulling the sharpness of the lessons on the way.

In other words, the earliest lessons of experience have an outsized influence, painting the first strokes on the virginal canvas of the young mind, thanks to the way they affect our way of seeing everything that comes after. Attachment theory deals specifically with how these early experiences translate into behaviour in social and intimate relationships in adolescents and adults alike. Successful attachment to a primary caregiver during infancy, through maintenance of safe proximity to the caregiver, is seen to provide the infant advantages in regulating their emotions and physical security, improving the odds of survival and thus forming the evolutionary basis for attachment. The safety provided by secure attachment creates space for exploration of the unknown, easing the way to healthy psychological growth and individuation of the child.

The quality of our childhood interactions with our primary caregivers can vary widely, and this variation plays a part in forming the spectrum of approaches to intimacy and sociability we see in the world. In an ideal situation the infant receives consistent care, emotional availability and loving attention from a primary caregiver over their first years and childhood, resulting in secure attachment as the child learns to trust the caregiver. This secure attachment comes with many advantages for the child, which may continue into adult social relationships, in forms such as lower levels of personal distress, low fear of failure, comfort with closeness and intimacy, and good conflict resolution and communication skills. As a consequence of these favourable traits, the securely attached tend to hold positive views of themselves and their relationships, and of others. Relationships between two securely attached persons have been found to be more stable, more intimate and more emotionally satisfying than relationships between insecurely attached people.

If infants are deprived of consistent caregiving, or suffer from abuse, neglect or rejection, the results may be very different. Attachment theory assigns three categories for the non-secure attachment outcomes: anxious, avoidant or fearful attachment. These categories reflect negative views either of oneself (anxious) or of others (avoidant), or both (fearful). The anxiously attached have a fear of rejection and abandonment; the avoidantly attached seek to avoid dependency and closeness; and the fearful combine both elements. Regardless of the source, all of the non-secure attachment styles result in difficulties forming stable intimate and other relationships, arising from problematic experiences with the childhood caregiver that have shaped the person's mental model and expectations of social interactions. Example behavioural patterns of the insecurely attached include seeking excessive approval and intimacy, leading to dependence (anxious); avoidance of attachment and intimacy altogether (avoidant/dismissive); and being simultaneously desiring of attachment while feeling intense discomfort in intimate situations (fearful). As the opposite of secure attachment, the non-secure attachment styles are found to be highly correlated with many negative outcomes such as higher rates of depression and criminal behaviour.

At this point it is appropriate to note that childhood experiences do not alone determine one's personality or social inclinations, and so even a child from the most broken background can grow into an exemplary adult with a secure attachment style. Besides the quality of childhood care experiences, biological factors such as the individual's sensitivity to stress, with variance based on differing neurological systems, are seen to play a part in the formation of the attachment style. Even more comforting is the fact that although one may have trouble with intimacy and social relations in general, exemplified and driven by a non-secure attachment style, secure attachment and its attendant advantages may be learned later on – for example, through positive new experiences or therapy.

This brief tour of the main arguments of attachment theory underlines the importance of secure attachment for everyone's wellbeing and flourishing social relations in general. What leads to such secure attachment is a consistent, responsive and responsible caring relationship between the caregiver and the infant, which in turn forms the guiding mental model of intimate and social relations for the developing young person. This consistent caring relationship is by its nature also a relationship of trust, in that secure attachment can only be built on a firm basis of trust. Psychological safety is created for the infant from the caregiver's steady presence, responsive and dependable meeting of the needs that arise, and a warm, loving and understanding way of interacting with the child. Thus the exemplary adult shows to the child benevolent behaviour no matter what and consistency of care, which become internally modelled as hallmarks of safety and trustworthiness. Notice how a caregiver's kind behaviour and consistent care correspond with benevolence and, to a lesser degree, integrity, two of the three sources of trust. Later on children also learn values, expectations and assumptions about ability from their parents, encompassing the whole breadth of sources of trust, though these lessons are perhaps most prominent after the initial years of infancy. Despite the importance placed on youth here in general, the caregivers' influence remains strong throughout our lives.

Conversely, experiences leading to insecurity and associated dysfunctional attachment types appear likely to contain significant breaches of trust. Showing up to nurture at one moment – emotionally, physically or both – but not at another, making care inconsistent and unpredictable, is bound to instil anxiety in a child and lower their propensity to trust and rely on others. Should the caregiver(s) fail to account for and give weight to the child's needs and emotions, the person may be predisposed to grow up unable to trust themselves, having been neglected all their life. Rejections and abuse in turn may make closeness and intimacy feel outright dangerous, pushing the child further apart from everyone else in proportion to the pain. The message of experiences such as these is very obvious, telling the child not to trust themselves or others. The damage to their subsequent development can be enormous.

In summary, someone who learns to trust their childhood caregiver is more inclined to trust others as well, with all the attendant social benefits. Someone who doesn't will find trust harder to come by, and without trust the fruits of sociability will be hard to reach. In this way, trust is found at the very heart of our psychological development and successful social relations at large.[15]

In the field of psychology attachment theory provides but one prominent explanation of the role of trust in an individual's life. Closely mirroring attachment theory's view of the consequences of early childhood care, Erik Erikson's theory of psychosocial development considers individual psychological development as the outcome of a series of universal challenges confronted throughout life, and resolved with more or less success. Erikson identifies eight of these challenges, each corresponding to unique circumstances at different stages of life. For example, his final stage of psychosocial development is in old age, as one comes to reflect on the life lived in the face of its imminent end. The challenge that lies in this situation is to find meaning, pride and happiness with how one has spent their years. Attaining a positive view of the life led and choices made yields a peaceful and content old age, whereas feelings of regret and wasted life tend to make for despair-filled final years.

---

15   Attachment Theory and its Place in Contemporary Personality Theory and Research. Fraley, R. Chris; Shaver, Phillip, R. *Handbook of Personality: Theory and Research*, 2008.

At the other end of the age scale, we find teenagers struggling with questions of identity. The central challenge of this development stage is to form a stable sense of self. During teenage years young humans explore their autonomy and potential social roles, navigating through a sea of issues such as personal beliefs and values, independence and control. Successfully tackling these issues results in the formation of an identity that helps guide the individual in society and through its standards and expectations. Failure to form a stable sense of self leaves one mired in confusion and insecurity, hindering personal growth and progress.

But where does trust come to play according to Erikson? Echoing attachment theory, Erikson finds trust to be the essential element of the earliest childhood experiences. Up to the age of 18 months, the key learning in this first stage of psychosocial development is of trust and distrust. Because the infant is fully dependent on the caregiver for having its needs met, the quality of care received is directly reflected back into the mental model of the world the child builds, consequently modulating future expectations – just as with attachment theory. Perhaps this can be demonstrated best with a minor mind-game. Put yourself into the diminutive shoes of the infant and picture two versions of your childhood environment. In the first one you are cared for with consistency, lovingly nurtured in a warm environment of steady safety, with the nourishment of food, shelter and emotional support provided in proportion to need; not too little to deprive, not too much to smother. In the second one, your only consistency is that there is none. Warm care alternates with abandonment and emotional unavailability, safety is broken by shouting, with parental strife polluting the home. Whichever environment you grow up in makes up the whole of your experience of the world in this infant state of complete helplessness. How would these different environments affect the foundational assumptions of your nascent mental model of the world? Quite dramatically, comes the answer from a considerable number of empirical studies supporting the hypotheses of Erikson and attachment theory.[16]

---

16   For example: Attachment Security: A Meta-analysis of Maternal Mental Health Correlates. Atkinson, Leslie; Paglia, Angela; Coolbear, Jennifer; Niccols, Allison; Parker, Kevin; Guger, Sharon. *Clinical Psychology Review*, November 2000, Volume 20, issue 8. A Prospective Longitudinal Study of Attachment Disorganization/disorientation. Carlson, E.A. *Child Development*, August 1998. Differences in Parenting Stress, Parenting Attitudes, and Parents: Mental Health According to Parental Adult Attachment Style. Kim, Do Hoon; Kang, Na Ri; Kwack, Young Sook. *Journal of the Korean Academy of Child and Adolescent Psychiatry*, 2019, 30. Are Close Relationships in Adolescence Linked with Partner Relationships in Midlife? A Longitudinal, Prospective Study. Möller, Kristiina; Stattin, Håkan. *International Journal of Behavioral Development*, 2001, 25. When Marriage Breaks Up – Does Attachment Style Contribute to Coping and Mental Health? Birnbaum, Gurit; Orr, Idit; Mikulincer, Mario; Florian, Victor. *Journal of Social and Personal Relationships*, 1997, volume 14.

The connections between the home environment, mother's attachment style and mental health, and infants' emotional states and attachment styles have been the subject of many empirical investigations. A meta-analysis of 35 studies on the subject concluded that maternal social support, marital satisfaction, stress and depression of the parent are significantly related to attachment security in the child. Social support for the mother, in the form of wider circles of friendships, familial ties, community and professional groups and the like, were reflected as greater attachment security in the child. A similar effect was found for marital satisfaction. Stress and depression were predictably negatively correlated with attachment security outcomes. Taken together these results highlight the importance of the home environment and caregivers' mental states in the establishment of secure, and therefore trustful, attachment capacity in people.

Another study highlighted the correlations between adolescent relations with parents and friends and later adultlife romantic relationship satisfaction in a Swedish context. The longitudinal study investigated relationships with friends and parents at 13–18 years of age, and those individuals were questioned again about their romantic relationships at the age of 37. In line with expectations, good relationships with parents in adolescence were found to be positively correlated to relationship satisfaction at 37 years of age. More surprising was the fact that this connection was especially robust for father–son relations. For women, the young ladies who were more worried about cross-gender relationships in adolescence were also less satisfied with their relationships as adults. In a mirror image, boys who were less worried about girls as teenagers were also happier about their romantic situations later on.

In Korea, a study evaluated how parents' attachment styles were reflected in the stress they experienced during parenting, their parenting attitudes and mental health. Compared with the securely attached, anxious and avoidant parents were more stressed out by their parental duties, and perhaps in response also had more negative parenting attitudes. The avoidant parents reported the least affectionate parenting style. Anxious attachment, on the other hand, was significantly correlated with negative mental health markers. All in all the results imply how attachment styles become transmitted between generations, in that the anxious and avoidant mothers appear to replicate the problematic parenting styles they themselves were likely subject to.

The impacts of attachment style show up in divorce situations, as well. In general, most divorcees reported more distress than the married, regardless of attachment style. But the level of distress was clearly higher for those with avoidant or anxious attachment styles. The differences continued in situation appraisal and coping strategies between the groups. The securely attached viewed their circumstances as less threatening and appraised themselves as more able to cope. The anxious and avoidant, on the other hand, evaluated the divorce as more threatening and their ability to cope as lesser. In response, they also employed less adaptive coping tactics, such as social withdrawal, wishful thinking and self-defeating thought patterns.

On the basis of the many empirical studies about the subjects of childhood conditions and attachment, it is well established that a psychologically secure home and parenting translates into secure children, who grow up to be more secure adults – in line with the theories we have covered. This security for its part predisposes a person towards more trustful interactions with the world, aided by more realistic situational assessments and better coping strategies when facing the many challenges of life. Trust is something that grows in stable and loving homes, and is passed on from parents to children, from generation to generation.

From this we can infer an old piece of wisdom from a new angle – the wider social importance of upbringing. Stable and safe homes produce psychologically safer and sounder individuals, who as a result are also more trustful and thus on average more likely and able to cooperate with others. The home environment is of course a private setting to which the state or society has limited rights and abilities to intrude, not to mention the quality of relationship between the parents. Yet it is also obvious that things such as financial security and social support do impact the home, and are in the state's control. Another thing affecting the ways we bring up our children, and our conduct at home in general, is the values held and promoted by a given society, which also connects back to the choices made at the state level. If we keep in mind the lessons from the studies about the impacts of home on attachment, it seems apparent that values promoting an ideal environment would be desirable. In practice this would mean things such as: valuing and putting effort into the care and nurture of the children; honesty, kindness and an open and forthright manner of solving family issues, teaching productive problem-solving strategies; and fidelity among the parents, all providing security and acting as first-order examples of trust for the children.

Let us next consider these lessons from psychology in the context of our model of trust. The findings indicating that the securely attached perceive their situations as less threatening, and thus less distressing, provide a good starting point. According to our model of trust, trusting can be described as risk-taking in relation to an external party, who we hope will act in our interests but we don't have certainty that they will. If the securely attached, compared with the anxious or avoidant, have a tendency to view their situations as less threatening, then it would likely follow that they also appraise the risk of unpleasant trust outcomes as lower – and thus are on average more likely to trust. The inverse would obviously apply to the other attachment styles.

Those with avoidant or anxious attachment styles used unproductive strategies for resolving their situations more frequently, such as avoidance, wishful thinking and self-blame. It is easy to see how these tendencies arise in a family setting, perhaps from parents avoiding difficult topics or emotional expression, thereby teaching the habit of avoidance to their off-spring through constant examples. Less effective coping strategies by definition should lead to more negative experiences than productive strategies, and from a trust-theory perspective thereby explain why situations can be perceived as more threatening by the insecurely attached, raising the bar for trust.

The impacts of varying assessments of threat might be conceptualized through the benevolence element of trust representing the evaluation of positive or negative intent towards the trustor. As articulated in the psychological theories, a person will form expectations about the world in relation to the self based on childhood experiences. If one is accustomed to negligent, uncaring and dismissive attention in the childhood home, these lessons will form the baseline expectations for interactions with others in general. In assessing the trustworthiness of others, a person from such a background will therefore inevitably expect others to be less benevolent and caring than might actually be reasonable. A similar logic might apply also for the ability antecedent of trust. If a child experiences parents consistently unable to provide for their changing needs, this might lead them to assume everyone is incompetent in contexts wholly separate from the family home. The consequence is again a lower level of trust than might actually be warranted.

Thus, the Eriksonian and attachment theories and the empirical findings corroborating them find a welcoming home within our framework of trust. And through the workings described by the psychological theories, the inclination to trust is found among the many aspects of life where nurture and learning matter alongside nature. Healthy attitudes towards oneself and others are the foundation for trust and flourishing social relations in general. The foundations are built from stable and loving care by parents who not only provide consistent attention to the child, but also remember to nurture their own relationship. All this seems to place tremendous demands on parents, who have to raise the child, maintain the mutual relationship and take care of their careers and everything else on the side. No doubt knowledge of the delicacy of the child's situation is enough to stress the parents even if nothing else does. However, wisdom and peace of mind are probably achieved with the recognition that "perfect" can be the enemy of "good", and that the good is well enough.

Trust develops as people demonstrate a willingness to invest in a relationship, often forgoing some immediate interest to take the needs and concerns of their partner into account. As evidence of the partner's commitment to the relationship accumulates, so do confidence and trust that the relationship will last and grow stronger. This dynamic applies to the child just arrived in the new and strange world, just as well as to relationships between adults and to interactions in society at large.

But interacting with others is not merely dependent on our assessment of the other party's trustworthiness. An important motivating force in our behaviour is the view we hold of ourselves, and of our capacity to achieve the desired ends. If we believe we can succeed, we are more likely to try, whatever we are aiming for. The belief in self commonly carries the name self-confidence. The Merriam-Webster online dictionary offers as its definition "confidence in oneself and in one's powers and abilities", and gives "self-trust" as a synonym. In many ways, the impacts of upbringing and home environment manifest as differences in self-confidence, or self-trust.

TRUST AND THE SELF

Every young person quickly learns to appreciate the importance of self-confidence in dating. It's not just relevant for those looking for amour and excitement, however – self-confidence is a central quality called for in many situations, from giving a presentation to maintaining composure in adversity.

Given its broad areas of application and importance, self-confidence is widely acknowledged as an important factor for wellbeing. But the concept suffers from slight fuzziness about its exact nature, given interference from oft-used related terms like self-esteem and self-efficacy. Let us therefore clear up our analytical toolkit and define the meaning of self-confidence, or self-trust, as a starting point to understanding its significance.

When it comes to self-confidence, the American Psychological Association defines it as "self-assurance: trust in one's abilities, capacities, and judgment".[17]

For contrast, the APA's definition of self-esteem: "the degree to which the qualities and characteristics contained in one's self-concept are perceived to be positive."[18]

Self-efficacy was originally defined by Albert Bandura, and here is APA in his footsteps: "An individual's subjective perception of his or her capability to perform in a given setting or to attain desired results."[19]

The difference between self-confidence and self-esteem is that although self-confidence pertains to trust in one's abilities, capabilities and judgements, it does not include the component of positive or negative general self-evaluation – the broader feeling of the self. If one considers oneself to be capable, and trusts one's abilities and judgements, then it is likely that the broader internal evaluation would also be mostly positive. But there are many capable people who know they are highly skilled, yet suffer from low self-esteem. And of course the opposite exists, too.

Self-efficacy in turn refers to an evaluation of capability in some specific context, in contrast to the more global evaluation that is self-confidence. Again, the difference is small, but warranted. Given all this, it is not so surprising that the terms are often confused or used as synonyms.

Turning the definitions around and starting from our understanding of trust as an outcome of ability, benevolence and integrity, we can attain another perspective. Self-trust may be thought to result from satisfactory perceptions of our own abilities, behaviours and values (integrity) reflecting judgements about the world, and from a generally positive and supporting attitude towards the self (benevolence). The first two fall neatly under the umbrella of self-confidence, while a benevolent stance towards the self is obviously equivalent to good self-esteem. Self-trust as an inward relationship based on ability, benevolence and integrity would thus encompass both self-confidence and self-esteem, as defined by the APA.

Having clarified the definitions, let us turn to an investigation of self-trust as self-confidence, focusing thus specifically on the consequences of internal evaluations of ability and integrity (judgements) in an individual's life. Self-confidence or trust in your own abilities and judgements could be thought to develop along a similar process to trust – by observing one's

17   dictionary.apa.org/self-confidence
18   dictionary.apa.org/self-esteem
19   dictionary.apa.org/self-efficacy

own actions, thoughts and behaviour and the outcomes they generate. The more one sees one's own actions leading to the outcomes aimed for, the more one develops trust in one's own capabilities, reinforcing successful behaviour just as positive experiences strengthen trust and cooperation with others. The same applies to judgements, with confidence developing in step with the ability to read one's environment and the course of events, and act in accordance with these situations and one's own values. The more correct one's judgements turn out to be, the higher the self-trust one develops. Should the outcomes turn out to be consistently negative, the unfortunate outcome is likely to be that self-confidence and trust in one's own abilities or judgements declines or fails to develop. At some point the disappointments may lead to either a change of course towards more successful strategies or declining interest in making any effort at all, because the expected low outcome does not seem to merit the exertion.

As is typical in the rollercoaster of real life, noise is introduced into the development of self-confidence by all sorts of events, such as the varied situations one encounters, the society one grows up in, the family environment and parental examples, as well as genetics or the chance distribution of wealth and other challenges and advantages in life.

Being able to connect an action to a desired outcome teaches not only self-confidence or self-trust, but also an industrious and hard-working attitude. Should you get accustomed to the fact that your capabilities are enough to achieve positive results, and thus gain the blessing of healthy self-confidence, you become programmed by nature to expect good outcomes in the future. With the higher expected likelihood of success, the value of expended effort increases, as do thereby the incentives to get out there and get things done. The more we trust our abilities, the more we believe we can achieve and therefore are willing to try. Higher confidence in the ability to achieve may be presumed to lead to not only more frequent, but also more persistent and long-range efforts. The likes of Elon Musk are probably not lacking in self-confidence.

If severe lack of confidence can easily turn into a problem, so too can an excessive amount of confidence. Overt and unwarranted trust in one's own abilities, judgements and knowledge in the face of a reality screaming otherwise is often a recipe for disaster. Yet this happens all the time. The various consequences of overconfidence are perhaps most visible in the fields of business and economic life. Think of asset bubbles driven by wild optimism, or the CEO with sky-high self-confidence constructing castles in the sky. At first glance it would seem that the problems arising from overconfidence, such as excessive risk-taking, unrealistic expectations, biased assessments and the like, would seem inferior next to accurate evaluations and so would not be favoured by evolutionary pressures. Yet it appears that, at least to some extent, the opposite is true.

Indeed, there exist fundamental incentives for overconfidence that may be adaptive from an evolutionary perspective. As the poster boys and girls of overconfidence, CEOs help us explain the forces maintaining overconfidence in society.

Several studies indicate that when people are more confident in their abilities (whether that confidence is warranted or not), others too will assume them to possess greater competence. Other research provides another important, if not surprising, detail by confirming that people afford social status (including leadership positions) to people they perceive to be competent. Competence – a component of ability in our trust framework – is valued because it helps generate contributions in group and company settings, and trust on the side. Confidence is often seen as a proxy for competence. Therefore, confidence gets mixed with competence, and indeed research confirms higher confidence leads to higher status in both newly formed short-term groups and longer-term groups.[20] It is no surprise that the CEO types tend to have high self-confidence long before they achieve mastery in their line of business, or a position of power.

In circumstances where competence cannot be quickly or comprehensively verified, it becomes difficult if not impossible for others to identify overconfidence and differentiate it from actual confidence derived from ability. In today's often very abstract working world, there can be no doubt that contributions can be hidden, embellished or taken credit for in many ways – making it difficult to accurately establish the level of competence in others. This obviously creates incentives to present confidence regardless of actual level of capability, when social status afforded by confidence is valuable.

And so it is that many benefits derive from high social status, such as access to resources and influence in decision making, not to mention general admiration and respect. Likewise, high social status is understood to be an advantage in mating. With so many desirable associations, it is no surprise that social status is highly sought after. CEOs, especially those of large public companies, sit on top not just of the hierarchies of their organ-

20   When Overconfidence is Revealed to Others: Testing the Status-enhancement Theory of Overconfidence. Kennedy, Jessica A.; Anderson, Cameron; Moore, Don A. *Organizational Behavior and Human Decision Processes*, 2013, 122.

izations, but also of income distributions. Quite naturally, the prestige of high social status has followed these facts. As such, we may expect those reaching for the CEO position, or having achieved it, to be those with high confidence – warranted or not.

Self-trust as self-confidence means one is secure in one's abilities to cope with the challenges that arise, whatever the context of the moment. In a group situation this explains why others, should they feel less confident, defer authority and status to the confident. The (often unconscious – and unwarranted) expectation is that the confident have the answers or the ability to find them to meet the task at hand. Whether it is based on real or imagined resources and competence, the facade of confidence can often shield one from uncomfortable doubt and questions, both from others and from oneself. As such, confidence helps maintain a peaceful and content state of mind, in addition to its status-related blessings.

The French economists Roland Bénabou and Jean Tirole (who won the Riksbank Nobel memorial prize in economics 2014 for his research on market power and regulation) weighed the value of self-confidence in a delightful article *Self-Confidence and Personal Motivation*. In keeping with their training, they came up with several explanations for the value of confidence, dubbing them as either "demand" or "supply" factors. On the demand side we have drivers representing the things that make self-confidence useful and desirable, and encourage a person to support their self-confidence, even to unrealistic levels. These include the consumption, signalling and motivational value derived from self-confidence.[21]

The argument for *consumption value* approaches genius with its simple insight: it is much more enjoyable to feel good about yourself and your abilities, than not to. That is hard to argue with. Therefore, a predisposition for self-aggrandizing thoughts is a quite natural source of happiness. Bénabou and Tirole seem to use self-esteem and self-confidence interchangeably here, but the argument remains valid despite our stricter definitions of the terms – recalling that both can fit under our own definition of self-trust.

The *signalling value* of self-confidence relates to its status-bestowing impacts, as already mentioned. Regardless of actual ability, confidence is inferred by others to imply competence. Our economists, however, take the reasoning a step further. Bénabou and Tirole note here that irrespective of genuine or imagined basis, should you genuinely believe yourself to be capable in various contexts, then you should also be more effective in

---

21   Self-Confidence and Personal Motivation. Bénabou, Roland; Tirole, Jean. *Quarterly Journal of Economics*, February 2002.

convincing others of this. In other words, they assume confidence to have some degree of transparency as to its origins, and potentially elements of bluffing when it comes to the respective displays. But if you genuinely believe your own bluff, you become more convincing to others.

The third demand factor for self-confidence is the *motivational value* it provides. As noted already, self-confidence not only creates an expectation of success that by itself can motivate more action. It also helps us persist in difficult and adverse circumstances. The high morale and effort in turn are essential components of achievement in every field.

On the supply side of the fence we find the means through which the positive effects demanded may be secured.

One source of self-confidence may be *wired-in optimism*, a hypothesis according to which nature has endowed us with a systematic and unconscious cognitive bias for overweighting positive information about ourselves and underweighting the negative. This explanation seems problematic, though, for multiple reasons. First, confidence and overconfidence are not stable across all domains of activity, but vary depending on the skill or task at hand. Likewise, poor self-confidence and the defensive strategies that people employ to support their confidence show that even if a wired-in optimistic bias does exist, it is not a sufficient explanation for the phenomenon. Indeed, the various strategies for boosting self-confidence seem more fruitful sources of understanding.

Blissful ignorance is one cognitive strategy by which people seek to shield their confidence, attempting to remain oblivious of information adverse to them. In other words, the stock of self-confidence can be thought of as an asset, which can either grow or decline in response to new information and evidence about one's own abilities. In these circumstances it may sometimes be better to remain uninformed, by whatever means that can be achieved. To this end people may even engage in self-handicapping behaviours that pre-emptively provide excuses if performance is insufficient in some measure, while simultaneously increasing the likelihood of poor performance. This cognitive strategy provides an "external" reason for failure, but an opportunity to attribute a positive outcome to the self.

Often information cannot be avoided, however, and therefore another key factor impacting our self-confidence is how we orient ourselves to the inevitable. *Self-deception* is the third and last of our "supply-side" mechanisms for maintaining and developing self-confidence. Repression, denial and self-serving attributions are all well-known and common methods used by the individual in coping with the often-negative experiences and information concerning own abilities. Selective memory is a prime example of self-deception strategies, its operation perfectly captured by Nietzsche in one of his aphorisms: "'I did that', says my memory. 'I could not have done that', says my pride, and remains inexorable. Eventually – the memory yields".[22] This is what cognitive dissonance and Freudian repression are all about.

Demand for self-confidence is generated by the value of its consumption, signalling and motivational aspects, each making the thing desirable to the individual in their own ways. This demand is met by the supply-side strategies, of which Bénabou and Tirole see the cognitive (wilful) ignorance and self-deception as the foremost, being something the individual may control with conscious or unconscious effort. They model various situations involving confidence-related information processing. The results and analysis shed light on many effects of self-confidence on behaviour, of ourselves and of those travelling beside us.

In their formulation successes in new tasks lead to gains in confidence due to revealed ability in new areas. In addition, we may assume that the self-confidence gains from success will decline as the particular challenge becomes more familiar and more robustly learned. Less obviously, failure can theoretically also be a net positive for an individual, even if not from a confidence perspective: should one "suffer" from extreme overconfidence, they are likely to waste time on impossible or too difficult tasks. If failure brings confidence down to a more realistic level, the person should in theory start to focus on things more in line with their actual ability, and therefore become more productive in their lives. Here the key is of course whether the person is willing to acknowledge failure, or explain or repress it away to persist in overconfidence.

The way Bénabou and Tirole explore the utility of memory manipulation, repression and other cognitive and behavioural strategies in the maintenance of self-confidence is especially interesting. These strategies are essentially about how to engage with or avoid information that may increase or decrease one's confidence. A key factor in determining the sorts of strategies a person may employ is the level of confidence they are currently working with, because it affects how much they have to gain or lose from new information. The economists propose that those with higher initial levels of self-confidence are more interested in maintaining their self-confidence, rather than exposing themselves to new information that might change the situation.

---

22 *Beyond Good and Evil*. Fourth Chapter: Apophthegms and Interludes, 68. Nietzsche, Friedrich. Wordsworth Editions, 2008.

Given the importance of self-confidence to effort and thereby success, a person who has a vested interest in the success of another will also have an interest in supporting their confidence. Another peculiar yet intuitively understandable behaviour occurs when high self-confidence is threatened, or alternatively at a very low level; behaviour may change towards more risky, high-value projects, or gambles, that if successful would result in a "resurrection" of self-confidence.

A common way of managing self-confidence and others' perceptions, however counterintuitive it may seem, is to consciously or unconsciously create obstacles to our own performance and success. This is called "self-handicapping". Common examples include the myriad ways of withholding effort and failure to prepare, or drinking and partying the night before an important exam at university. Choking under pressure and test anxiety are the more involuntary forms of self-handicapping. But how could these things be in any way helpful to a person's self-confidence? The idea put forth by Bénabou and Tirole, in line with much psychological research, is that self-handicapping provides a convenient excuse for failure and mitigates the confidence hit from potential failure, yet retains the opportunity to attribute a potential success to the self. As such, self-handicapping skews the payoffs from the event so that the upside potential is heightened while the downside is mitigated – at the expense of decreasing the odds of actual success. If the short-term costs of self-handicapping are low enough, the strategy might appear quite enticing to anyone regardless of their initial level of confidence. Indeed, research seems to be inconclusive on whether those with higher or lower self-confidence are more likely to self-handicap; the strategy seems to be quite universal. Although it might seem that those with more robustly built high confidence would have a lesser interest in resorting to potentially counterproductive strategies, experimental research indicates the opposite is often true. Indeed, high-confidence individuals seem to be more active in employing strategies of confidence enhancement, which offers at least a partial explanation for their higher self-confidence.

The many forms of motivated cognition and self-deception help us take the self-manipulation of confidence to even greater heights, or perhaps depths in the more absurd cases. Bénabou and Tirole recount numerous psychological studies showing how people colour their self-histories to create more pleasing stories to support their self-confidence. Recalling successes more readily than failures is a common escape from bad memories, as are other self-serving biases in the way we recall past events. Other studies indicate that people attribute positive qualities and moral virtues to themselves but, when they are the cause of bad outcomes, they will readily reason and explain away the facts by depositing the responsibility elsewhere. In other words people like to see themselves as instrumental in the good, but not the bad, and will manipulate their perceptions accordingly – for example, by framing the situation anew ("they are stupid so they deserved it"). Perhaps the most classic instance of self-serving bias comes from the firm belief professed by the majority of people that they are better than average drivers, obviously contradicting statistical possibilities.

As an example of a tactic to dismantle confidence-threatening situations Bénabou and Tirole offer a taste of their own experiences as researchers. As is par for the course in research, criticism will inevitably arise, whether in response to a seminar or lecture or as a rebuttal of a published article. When this happens, the researcher will often tend to look for reasons to discount the critique, such as the commenter's poor taste, vested interests in previous theories or perhaps inadequate understanding of the issue at hand. Finding such reasons is the mind's way of lessening the threat to our confidence by discounting the value of the critique.

A similar way to avoid processing difficult feedback is used in relationships at home and elsewhere, by instigating a verbal fight in response to unpleasant feedback. By creating the distraction of the fight the mind avoids engaging the potentially more painful information and focuses on the trivialities around the fight. Thus, the first painful bit of information may become overshadowed in memory by the response and its consequences, decreasing the accuracy and odds of recollection.

Manipulations of memory and attention are also used for productive ends. Studies and lived experience alike confirm that things recently encountered or oft repeated become more easily remembered. In light of these factors the habit of last-second cramming the night before exams gains some credence. Although one may easily have completely forgotten the information a month (or a week) later, the strategy is often enough to clear the hurdle of the exam the next day, even if not enough for lifelong wisdom. This type of short-term memory manipulation is probably a nearly universal experience for school-goers of all ages and levels of education.

In other words, plain old denial of adverse information and repression of painful memories are constantly with us, whether we are aware of it or not, alongside the tendency to play up more positive or useful explanations and recollections. These observations hark back to the quote by Nietzsche about the malleable nature of memory, and indeed these tendencies are a common feature of all humanity.

The various forms of self-deception and denial are a peculiar phenomenon in that they effectively require us to be simultaneously aware of and yet not acknowledge some piece of information and its consequences. To be in denial about something requires one first to be aware of it – you cannot deny something you do not know. Self-deception was defined in a 1979 article by Ruben Gur and Harold Sackeim as a situation in which (a) a person holds two contradictory pieces of knowledge, (b) that person is not aware of holding one of the pieces and (c) this lack of awareness is motivated.[23] This definition and the lessons of this chapter are worth keeping in mind as we consider the dynamics of trust and knowledge in the next chapter.

Avoiding inconvenient information to support one's self-confidence is just one reason to manipulate our cognition. Maintaining motivation in the face of uncertainty is another. One example of motivational distortions of the mind is pessimism about our own achievements – defensive pessimism, as it is dubbed by economists. By minimizing or discounting one's prior successes, perhaps by considering them the results of pure luck or otherwise benign circumstances, we may be able to increase the motivation to work harder in the face of present or future challenges.

Situations where the benefits of some action or behaviour precede the costs of it offer a similar example of motivational information manipulation. Think of a smoker, for example. They enjoy their vice at the cost of long-term risks to their health. To combat the risks, regulators have decided to cover tobacco packages with information about the adverse effects, accompanied by gruesome images of the physical damage smoking can cause. With prominent displays of information and imagery about the long-term consequences, the attempt is to make the costs of smoking more relevant in the present, and thus skew the cost–benefit calculation towards abstinence. The climate change battle over present prosperity and future risks is an almost exact analogue, except on a global rather than individual scale.

These descriptions of memory manipulation and self-deception imply that maintaining self-deception and using various other strategies of cognitive manipulation entail effort and thus costs for the person. Proceeding from this, Bénabou and Tirole assume that the individual must also be aware to some extent that they are possibly not wholly honest with themselves – meaning they cannot be quite sure about their memories and self-image. Understanding their own motivations for favourable filtering, they may suspect themselves to have forgotten or willed away memories and information that was not the most agreeable to them. This in turn may

---

23   Self-Deception: A Concept in Search of a Phenomenon. Gur, Ruben C; Sackeim, Harold A. *Journal of Personality and Social Psychology*, February 1979.

incur self-doubt, somewhat offsetting the confidence-maintaining effects of the cognitive strategies employed.

All in all Bénabou and Tirole cover a broad swathe of psychological and behavioural findings and develop a rich analysis of the various ways cognitive manipulation can be used for self-confidence and motivation enhancement under different circumstances such as the level of confidence to begin with, high or low costs of memory management, varying time preferences and so on. Their work finds its place among the wave of behavioural economic research making room for real-life humans with their psychological peculiarities within the framework of economics, which for so long had focused mostly on the activities of the idealized utility-maximizing homo economicus.

SUMMARY – THE BROADER IMPLICATIONS OF SELF-TRUST/SELF-CONFIDENCE

For our ongoing enquiry about trust and its broader impacts on individuals and society at large, the implications of the preceding findings are quite remarkable. First, it is clear that self-confidence – as in self-trust – is a powerful motor of motivation and persistence in adversity, exerting a strong influence on how people's lives unfold. Quite simply, people who trust their own abilities and judgements are more likely to go out there and get things done, which in turn helps them achieve better outcomes. Second, incentivized by the value of self-confidence and motivation, people employ (mostly unconsciously) many cognitive and behavioural strategies to manipulate these traits. These manipulations often include selective processing of information, whether in memory or freshly encountered in the present moment. Finally, being aware of these incentives and the resulting manipulations can help us understand many strange-seeming phenomena from a new perspective.

Let us now consider how the dynamics of self-confidence might relate to a challenge to a person's established worldview. Because correctness of judgement is part of self-trust, or self-confidence, encountering information that might invalidate previously held understandings or beliefs is clearly negative for self-confidence. Thus the defences and manipulations described by Bénabou, Tirole and other psychologists are sure to come immediately online in such a situation. Outright denial or seeking faults in the source of the challenge are no doubt among the immediate reactions and, if those don't cut it, the information might be simply repressed and forgotten.

This has immense and direct implications for our understanding of broader societal developments. As values between the left and the right in the west seem to drift ever further apart, it seems that the challenge to self-confidence posed by claims and information from the other side becomes all the more severe – and therefore much more likely to be resisted and repressed. This of course means ever greater fortifications around own positions, making even the compromising middle ground that much scarier a place.

The findings around self-handicapping, where individuals may engage in self-defeating behaviours to protect their confidence, effectively indicate that in many situations a person might self-sabotage to create some excuse rather than expose themselves to admitting having been wrong about something in the first place. Combine this with the observation that those with threatened or low self-confidence may engage in highly risky gambles to resurrect it, and it becomes more understandable why some might believe in absurd conspiracy theories or pour their life savings into an insanely risky stock speculation incited by some message board. If you have nothing to lose, you are ready to gamble everything. The research on self-confidence and trust helps us understand these sorts of highly risky behaviours.

To summarize, low or threatened self-confidence, or self-trust, seems not only to provoke highly risky behaviour, but can also entrench people in their perspectives to such a degree that they start accepting even absurdities to defend that position. As our societies seem to continue to splinter in nearly every manner imaginable, it is no surprise absurd ideas and behaviours seem to be spreading in every direction. On some level this comes back to the diverging values, beliefs and ideas people hold. Of course, not all values need to be accepted, just as different ones can be defended. Regardless, new information needs to be assimilated and compromise found if a society hopes to hold together. And our built-in resistance to adjusting our perceptions often gets in the way.

The strange operations of the mind in relation to self-confidence might also be placed in the same continuum with cognitive biases, such as those explored by Amos Tversky and Daniel Kahneman,[24] among others. It would seem probable that many cognitive biases could be thought of as shortcuts and distortions of the mind serving some psychological need, of which self-confidence maintenance would be one. Of the more well-known biases, the Dunning-Kruger effect is the tendency of unskilled

---

24   Most famous for the book *Thinking, Fast and Slow* exploring the themes and impacts of cognitive biases.

people consistently to overestimate their knowledge in some area, while experts conversely underestimate theirs. This is clearly in line with the findings and mechanisms presented by Bénabou and Tirole. Overestimation of knowledge in a particular situation can be seen as a sign of high self-confidence, while underestimation of it might serve as a motivating bias for someone highly interested in the particular subject.

Perhaps shockingly, it even appears that our psychological wellbeing may actually be dependent on our biases and misrepresentations to some extent. This is strongly suggested by a number of studies indicating those with realistic and accurate assessments of their selves are also more likely to be depressed. To perceive the reality as it is, is to be depressed? Luckily, since the original hypothesis about the connection in 1979 the subsequent research and empirical studies have been mixed, indicating that measurement, reporting and methodology-related factors play a meaningful role in the results. Although the depressed seem a tad more realistic in some respects, the differences appear small, and in some cases reversed.[25]

Trust in self and others is fundamentally shaped by experiences in the childhood home, as we saw earlier. Confidence in our own judgements and capabilities is nurtured with loving support in an environment where progressive development of skills big and small is made possible. The implication here is that the stimulation provided by parents and early school experiences is key. Thus, a home that provides opportunities and encouragement for mastering new skills, whether through games, sports or even just learning to read and write, also gives the building blocks for healthy self-confidence. If you can develop skills in sports, for example, this helps develop a mental model connecting effort with development and success, thereby wiring the motivating effect of confidence. Parents are instrumental in fostering opportunities for this sort of healthy development. It is not just activities that matter here. The examples, values and attitudes of the parents are also essential. Should everything be considered bad, should effort be for the untalented, should excellence be snobbery and modesty the highest virtue, such environment would not help the development of motivated children with high self-confidence.

School is a (nearly) universal experience, but its contribution to confidence can be highly variable. Consider two contrasting youngsters as an example, one with high aptitude and the other less lucky in the

---

25   The original thesis: Judgment of Contingency in Depressed and Nondepressed Students: Sadder but Wiser? Alloy, Lauren B.; Abramson, Lyn Y. *Journal of Experimental Psychology: General*, Volume 108, 1979. See also Depressive Realism: A Meta-analytic Review. Moore, Michael T.; Fresco, David M. *Clinical Psychology Review*, Volume 32, Issue 6, August 2012.

lottery of life. The first can coast along without much effort, because everything comes easily. They might initially develop strong self-confidence as a result of this easy successes. A second, less fortunate, outcome of this may be that in the absence of any challenge they may not learn to properly connect effort with success, lowering their performance when they encounter actually difficult tasks, because they have not acquired the habit of hard work.

Now let us think of how the other, less gifted, student might fare. Should school pose relatively greater challenges to this child than to others, our student cannot help but notice this. Two outcomes seem likely. Either they become demoralized with low self-confidence and let schoolwork slide, or they double down on the challenge and conquer it with hard work, developing a healthy sense of self and an understanding of the value of effort in achievement. Of course, these are speculative hypotheses about likely or possible outcomes. In real life there will be a wide variety of students with different backgrounds giving rise to a diverse set of behaviours. Yet it is intuitively clear that these sorts of impacts seem to be among the more probable outcomes.

This example brings us back to the importance of family background. The young are especially prone to imbibing the examples set by their parents, and imitation forms a significant transmission channel for self-confidence and motivational development, as children model after their parents. The essential supports of self-confidence and industriousness are thereby transferred in some degree to the next generation through the habits of the parents. It is undeniable that propitious circumstances such as the upbringing received by the parents and their level of wealth and education, in the absence of other factors, are likely to have a positive effect on the legacy of confidence they will bestow on their own children. Several studies describe, for example, how financial security is often connected to greater future orientation and lesser anxiety about present circumstances, which eases the ground for growth and development rather than wasting time on firefighting present problems.[26]

Those at the extreme end of less fortunate circumstances are liable to develop the symptoms of learned helplessness, a state of being that is practically the opposite of self-confidence and high motivation. If someone has deeply absorbed the lesson that no matter what they do, the outcome will always be negative, they internalize their acceptance of help-

---

26   Adolescent Future Orientation: An Integrated Cultural and Ecological Perspective. Seginer, Rachel. *Online Readings in Psychology and Culture*, 6(1), 2003.

lessness. This in turn leads to a state of near-complete apathy. Nothing will be attempted because there is no belief in the capability to achieve anything. Learned helplessness is a commonly observed outcome of torture, but can surface in varying degrees after persistent exposure to circumstances where one is completely at the mercy of others and no action by the self is enough to help. Children of drug addicts may be among those at risk of developing symptoms of learned helplessness. Not surprisingly, learned helplessness is strongly correlated with depression and other mental illnesses.

Self-confidence – trust in our own abilities and judgements – develops on a diet of effort, healthy expectations and realistic standards of success. Excessively critical caregivers or other influences can be highly detrimental to the development of self-confidence, but so too can parents who praise the child excessively and demand nothing from them. The problem with both is the same: they set up unrealistic expectations in the children about what they can or cannot achieve, which will inevitably lead them into conflict with reality. This leads to wasted time, either through lack of effort due to low confidence or persistent hitting the head on a wall due to a misperceived level of ability. Given time and experience the self-correcting nature of self-confidence will become evident. Excessively low confidence will improve, and excessively high confidence tempered. But this process can take decades, is bound to be painful and can persist throughout life if it is deeply ingrained.

Thinking more broadly, the problems of confidence can be replicated in circumstances where people are for example hired on merits other than their actual fit and ability related to the job; if their skills and talents are not adequate, the person will be a low-performer relative to the others who have been hired on more relevant grounds. Thus such biased practices for workplace hiring may end up costing the hired person their self-confidence, as well as the trust the other employees have in their new co-worker and the hiring manager.

Trust in the self accompanies a productive and happy life. It enables greater engagement with life on our own terms, including with others. The more you trust yourself and your ability to cope with whatever life may bring, the less you see risk elsewhere and in engaging with others. Thus trust in the self is also connected to trust in others and our social tendencies. When one is distrustful of the self, suffering from low self-confidence, time is wasted on useless rumination, distracting procrastination and the like, leading to lower effort and achievement, regardless of actual ability.

The trust we have in our abilities and judgements affects how we conduct our lives, how we exert effort and work with the information we encounter. The mental manipulations elaborated by various psychologists and used by Bénabou and Tirole in their modelling represent different strategies for engaging the world, depending on the state of self-confidence and the needs flowing from it for the individual. The practical strategies and mechanisms, such as memory repression or defensive pessimism, show that the trust we have in ourselves and the incentives for supporting it will inevitably play a meaningful role in how we see the world, and affect our relationship with knowledge as well. Understanding the existence of these foundational individual-level influences gives us a stepping stone to our next subject: the broader interplay between trust and knowledge.

Trust and knowledge

"We do not normally notice the air we breathe. Similarly, we epistemologists have not noticed the climate of trust that is required to support much of our knowledge."

JOHN HARDWIG, PHILOSOPHER[27]

27   The Role of Trust in Knowledge. Hardwig, John. *The Journal of Philosophy*, December, 1991

THIS VOLUME PRESENTS several claims about the essential, if often unseen, roles trust plays in various contexts. Perhaps the most fundamental of these is performed on the stage where every aspect of our life plays its part, a stage on which every experience leaves its mark – the stage of knowledge itself.

It can be claimed, with some credibility, that our present prosperity flows from the revolutionary distrust of received wisdom displayed by leading scientists and thinkers since the renaissance. As Europe emerged from the deep dark of the economic and intellectual winter that covered most of the medieval period, the first rays of light revealed the remnants of ancient learning stored in monasteries and the newly born universities. In the growing light of this springtime of the intellect, new observations and ideas started to accumulate, slowly making the ancients seem outdated rather than eternal in their insights. Reporting these findings, and thereby contradicting what was considered true based on both the ancients and the revelations of Christian faith, was of course highly controversial, as Galileo among others found out. Eventually the summer heat of conflicting views produced its fruit: a paradigm shift in what was considered true knowledge, and a new understanding of how it should be achieved – with an approach today often described as the scientific method. This new paradigm of scientific thinking, resulting in continuous challenging and renewal of established views to more accurately explain new observations of reality, has ever since the 16th and 17th centuries provided the template for enquiry that has yielded massive increases in learning and, through the use and application of this burgeoning store of knowledge, the material basis of our society today.

Indeed, excessive subservience to and trust in authorities, ancient or contemporary, has probably limited the advancement of knowledge in every society through the ages. The cause for this can be discerned in the seemingly universal inborn resistance both to information contradicting that which is previously known and comfortable, and to the independent critical thinking required for generating, digesting and applying such information – a condition afflicting everyone in varying degrees and contexts. The reasons for our reluctance to know and reassess can be speculated about: the confidence manipulation tricks may account for some of it, but perhaps it is also that sticking with the known is often the easiest thing to do. Peer pressure can also make us avoid potentially awkward conclusions; likewise, anything that would be painful to us personally or those close to us is difficult to admit. Generally anything that is small, insignificant and impersonal should be easy enough to acknowledge and assimilate into one's view of the world and resulting actions, and anything that is beneficial to us tends to be acquired with haste; but anything painful or difficult is often resisted.

Anything contrary to a prevailing public opinion, even if it is insignificant in the larger scale of things, requires first some effort of thought to understand the issue profoundly enough to produce a differing view and second the courage to go against the commonly held position. These are by themselves not insignificant tasks, and become all the more challenging as the issue at hand gains in significance, perhaps because challenging publicly held views may be seen as a risk to personal credibility, acceptance by others and ultimately one's own welfare. Thus, in challenging the most sacred things one risks being considered either ridiculous or a heretic worth purging. This not only makes voicing a different opinion difficult, but also disinclines us to search for and accept alternative explanations.

Typically issues involving fundamental values are the most sensitive, questioning them easily resulting in furious or even violent rebuttals. And these countervailing forces reside not just on the outside, but also inside us. The shifting of internal tectonic plates of views, values and the emotions attached to them can easily result in eruptions of confusion and pain. Indeed, questioning our own most deeply held values is the stuff of identity crises, and resolving the resulting internal storm can be a very long and arduous process. With issues of a more technical and impersonal nature a challenge is perhaps easier to digest. But all the same, where egos are in play, disputing established notions can easily yield a fray.

Scientific thinking counters blind trust (or, to be precise, mistrust) characterized by excessive deference to established doctrines, by promoting a system of enquiry in which verifiable empirical evidence is used to prove or discard hypotheses, with the merit of an argument being independent from the personal attributes of the author of the claim. At least, this is the ideal. The weight of the argument should be fully dependent on the evidence gathered and the quality of the theory bridging explanation to observation. This is in stark contrast to the pre-renaissance situation in Europe, where the church or the ancients were considered to be the ultimate authorities, their unquestionable primacy demeriting any new contradictory knowledge and thus retarding the development of the sciences. As new ideas continued their relentless siege, the bastions of official truth started to yield one by one. Unshackled from the restrictions of faith and tradition, and armed with Gutenberg's printing press, thought broke out of its old moulds. Having attained its full freedom, the new mode of enquiry upended our concepts of science and initiated a continuous flood of new ideas in every sector of knowledge, which themselves multiplied and mutated into the forms we recognize today. This revolution in understanding brought about a deep realignment of the foundations of our societies, with everything transformed, from beliefs about the origin of life to economies and political systems.

So, does this mean trust and science are at odds, that a high level of trust is an opponent of new knowledge and therefore a negative influence on the long-term development of societies? As always in life, it is complicated.

To draw a clearer map of this land of confusion, let us venture deeper into the bushes and look at what we consider knowledge itself to be. The commonly held definition is that knowledge consists of justified true beliefs. Justified, because we have viable reasons and explanations to support the belief; true, because the belief is actually true as far as can be known and aligns with real-world observations; belief, because we truly believe a thing to be just so, but ultimate certainty about the state of affairs remains always out of reach. Critiques of this type of definition can be traced all the way back to Plato, not to mention the existence of many competing interpretations throughout the ages. Regardless, this remains the commonly held explanation of knowledge and so is a suitable reference for the purposes of our enquiry about the relationship between knowledge and trust.

If knowledge is defined as a (true) belief that is justified, we may start to suspect that trust is lurking in the background of (at least) the belief and the justification components of true knowledge, and therefore directly linked to knowledge itself. Trust formation being an iterative process of observation and expectation formation, it will most certainly have something to do with coming up with justifications and beliefs.

Reviewing the history of the scientific revolution and the attendant rise of new methods for reaching a new standard of knowledge, the immediate reaction may be that a highly trusting attitude and the effective production of knowledge through questioning established views are likely to be engaged in a wrestling match, with both trying to throw the other out of the ring. An antagonistic relationship certainly seems plausible when we consider the sceptical mindset that is required for generating new ideas, which are by definition in opposition to (or distrustful of) at least parts of the presently understood state of affairs. Whether the proposed idea is a more accurate description of a previously known phenomenon or something truly novel, the old ways would have to yield to make way for the new.

Even more fundamentally, if real knowledge must be based on verifiable empirical evidence, then how can it be a matter of trust? Trust, we remember, is always a state of uncertain expectation rather than a solid hard fact. But if we take a step closer to the practical operations of knowledge production, a more complex picture starts to emerge.

The philosopher John Hardwig illustrated in a pioneering fashion the paradoxical relationship between trust, research and the concept of knowledge itself in his aptly named 1991 article *The Role of Trust in Knowledge*. Hardwig's first and fundamental observation was that the scientific enterprise, based on data and logical arguments acquired from earlier work or new observations, is sustained by trust, without which there can be neither data nor the arguments arising from it. A convincing example comes from a review of a physics experiment about the lifespan of charm particles, which are among the quarks forming the peculiar world of subatomic particles. The experiment and resulting report had no less than 99 co-authors, who had collectively worked some 280 years to come up with the results. From this we can immediately notice two things: no single human being could have lived long enough to accomplish alone what the team did; likewise, the team of 99 persons probably included specialists from different areas, meaning the shared knowledge of the group must have far surpassed the knowledge of any individual member, no matter how clever. In other words, no individual person could have had the time or the range of skills necessary to put together the experiment.

From this example, we can safely surmise that contemporary research is increasingly a team effort, rather than a soloist's sport. This tendency became more apparent in the 1960s, when the trend away from single-author papers towards multiple authors was first documented. Teamwork naturally concentrates the efforts of the team within a timeframe on a given research project, and most importantly enables task- and skill-based specialization of individual team members, enhancing productivity by reducing the waste of time and resources that comes from switching between tasks, while also promoting superior skills and knowledge in the area of specialization that enjoys the researcher's full focus. Taken together, thanks to these characteristics, teamwork often produces superior outputs compared with what a similar number of individual researchers working alone could accomplish, and enables projects that would not be otherwise possible. This is of course exactly what Adam Smith and economists since have noticed about the effects of collaboration, specialization, trade and market sizes on economic production in general.

What does this mean from a trust perspective? Teamwork and specialized skills in practice lead to the distribution of work across the research group, with considerable autonomy for every specialist, each using their own and often highly differing methods and approaches to tackle their specific issues. From these individual efforts and results the common fabric of the final finding is woven. The drawback of specialization in skills and responsibilities, however, is that it may in turn leave members of the team unable to evaluate each other's results. Hardwig highlighted this with an example from mathematics, where a group of mathematicians produced a novel proof, with each using their own arcane techniques and domain-specific knowledge, so that each member of the group was unable to personally confirm the work of the others. This meant that final verification of the different parts of the proof had to come post-publication from the small number of top experts working in these separate branches of mathematics around the globe, who could one by one untangle each of the knots securing the solution. In producing and publishing their findings the group of mathematicians relied on trust on several levels: first to cooperate and submit their own partial findings for the common use of the team; then to accept the results of the others without the ability to independently verify them; and finally publishing the results to the wider scientific community with the trust that they would review the findings in a fair manner, thus providing the ultimate judgement of their case.

So what made the feat possible was the fact that the mathematicians trusted each other, knowing they were experts in their given areas. From here it emerges crystal clear that these results, and indeed much of what we consider to be knowledge, could not have been created without trust as the key component underpinning the common work. Trust is not only essential for teamwork itself, but especially so in situations where the scientist or the layperson cannot independently verify the information claimed as knowledge. Without the independent ability to fully understand and assess the argument, we are left to choose either to trust the experts or not. And these situations cover most of what we know. Evaluating the advantages of trust in knowledge acquisition, Hardwig notes that through it we may increase not only the amount of information we can possess by accessing the insights of the rest of humanity, but also the quality of our knowledge, because we can thereby gain from those who may have a much better understanding of a given issue than we ourselves have. Because our capacity to retain information and learning is limited, insights from others provide compressed versions of the most essential bits of data, enabling us to fill our limited storage spaces with more impactful data.

As for our concept of knowledge, this also implies that much of what we personally consider known cannot be said to consist of justified true beliefs, knowledge as traditionally defined, because we may simply lack the first-hand data to provide the necessary justification or evaluate the truthfulness – and so these are in turn compensated for with trust. This observation yields the dramatic realization that either we know much less than we thought we did or perhaps that many things cannot really be known individually, but socially through group efforts mediated by trust. Hardwig acknowledges the concepts that either we may have less knowledge than we thought or much of our knowledge may be socially constructed rather than individually owned, but deems them unacceptable and gets around them by considering that trusting another's testimony about A or B yields an individual full possession of knowledge without having clarity on every detail, thereby maintaining the standard justified true belief view of the issue.

Given that another person's testimony, a gift given on trust, turns out to be a key element in knowledge, our focus naturally turns to the conditions of this trustful interplay between the two knowers. Hardwig wrote his article in 1991, some years before the cornerstone of this book, the ability–benevolence–integrity (ABI) framework for trust formation became fastened. Consequently, Hardwig saw trust in a somewhat narrower manner and focused on knowledge-sharing between established members of academia, rather than going for a more comprehensive examination about trust's role in knowledge-sharing in different contexts.[28]

In any event, Hardwig saw trust between researchers arise from the competence, conscientious work habits and epistemic self-competence (having a correct understanding of the limits of one's own knowledge) of the person providing information to another. Competence here corresponds neatly to the ability dimension of our ABI framework, whereas the conscientiousness and epistemic self-competence fit in with our concept of integrity, denoting mutually accepted values and standards of behaviour. This also means Hardwig did not consider the benevolence aspect of trust in his investigation. Given that his concept of trust and the resulting analysis did not take into account the full spectrum of the antecedents of trust, represented by the ABI framework, there remains something to be learned by further contemplation of the issue through this newer, broader understanding. Therefore, we shall add a few notes of our own by examining knowledge transfer in light of the ABI framework.

In short, we will accept the thesis that trust is a central factor for knowledge, making it possible for people to benefit from findings discovered by others as described by Hardwig, thus enabling the spread of knowledge throughout society. Our simple addition is to substitute ability, benevolence and integrity for Hardwig's elements of trust, which, we hope to show, will make for a more robust framework for considering trust's effects on knowledge. In effect the argument put forth here is that knowledge as justified true belief relies significantly on the ABI elements of trust, both in relation to ourselves as assessors and towards the interlocutor we assess through the ABI prism. Diving into the depths of ability, benevolence and integrity under the surface of knowing, the aim is to look for the effects they have specifically on the justification and truthfulness part of knowledge.

As we have seen, whether we are creating or receiving knowledge, we often cannot fully ascertain the quality of the empirical observations or the justifications given for our beliefs. Thus, we are left with trusting those who claim to know. And our trust in others is determined by our perceptions of their ability, benevolence towards us and values. This applies whether they are a person, an organization or even a government; therefore we are more likely to grant the status of knowledge to claims from sources we deem capable and friendly to us, and with whom we are in agreement over relevant core values. If we identify a lack of these necessary qualities, or even hostile intent, we are disinclined to accept claims that could otherwise present a bright window to reality. How often do we discount the claims of our government, regardless of their actual validity, because we consider their authorities either inherently incompetent or (mis)guided by opposing political ideologies?

Perhaps, then, instead of "justified true belief", knowledge should be understood as "justified true belief, qualified by our ability to trust" (in the absence of a less cumbersome definition).

Just as a watermelon may be described as a green sphere or an edible fruit, both of which are truthful observations, so too can knowledge about a thing take multiple forms that may appear to have nothing in common but describe parts of a more complex whole. For a person inexperienced in the subject of watermelons, to acquire a fuller understanding about the plant would of course require one to acknowledge both of these two observations and add a host of others. Should the person enquiring about watermelons receive these two bits of data from two different persons, the information coming from the more trusted source would probably gain prevalence in the mind of the knowledge seeker. Watermelons are thankfully not especially controversial as a subject, and new information about them should be relatively easy to absorb and verify independently with a visit to the local supermarket. Therefore, we may expect that trust is ultimately not a decisive factor when trying to learn about watermelons, although it might be so initially. Here we find a more general distinction, between things that may be verified empirically and those that may not. The role of trust in knowledge is no doubt heightened on matters of more indefinite quality, such as when talking about optimal social arrangements or political ideologies.

Plainly, there may exist different, superficially contradictory yet equally valid, pieces of knowledge about a subject. The superficial contradictions tend to rise from narrow or limited perspectives on some larger multidimensional phenomenon that is not fully perceived. Given the limitations of our intellectual faculties, this is a common state of affairs. Ultimately fundamental knowledge must include and reconcile all of its constituent parts, as shown in the watermelon example. The tendency to ignore or accept one or another aspect of the knowledge, instead of conceding a more comprehensive view, may specifically be a product of the interactions of our trusting facility, with its perceptions about the ability, benevolence and integrity of the source of information. If we deem the informant deficient in these dimensions, we are more careful in investing trust in their claims, whereas the testimony of a close friend speaking about an area of personal expertise is more readily accepted.

Our trust-related evaluations are context-sensitive and based on the standards we ourselves have about ability and our values and assumptions about right and wrong, which form the umbrella of integrity, and the quality of our relationship with the information provider. As a demonstration of the interplay of context and trust, think about the difference between reading a political manifesto and witnessing in person a speech by a politician. When you're reading the manifesto, at your leisure in the quiet of a study, you can focus on the arguments and weigh them against your understanding and evidence, perhaps rereading some sections and checking facts on the net. The printed medium affords you an opportunity to engage and re-engage with the message, whenever you have the time, and analyse the contents and the quality of the arguments. The unfilmed speech, on the other hand, can't be revisited after the experience, and any deeper analysis is dependent on your imperfect memories of the event. Likewise, as you watch the speech among the crowd that has gathered, your experience is coloured by the reactions and behaviour of the other people present. Perhaps there is a loud group from the opposing camp heckling the speaker, constantly interrupting the speech, making you annoyed and at the same time making it more difficult to follow the argument. And, of course, the speaker uses all sorts of rhetorical devices, which would be impossible in print. Much more than with the printed argument, your impression of the speech is influenced by factors other than the content of the message itself.

So here both the medium, print or speech in the example, and the environmental factors represent different contexts for engaging with information. Contextual (or medium-related) factors in turn lead to different logics of communication and content. A thoughtfully written text yields a different argument and engagement from a social media environment with messages limited in length. Regardless of the context, our trusting facility operates through the dimensions of ability, benevolence and integrity, basing itself on our standards for evaluating these components of trust.

These standards for assessment spring from the canvas of our unique background – first shapes painted by our families, subsequent strokes added by our education, many colours appended from the wider society using techniques perhaps picked up at work or play. Where we come from influences the way we see the world – an old truth rediscovered from a trust and knowledge perspective. The knowledge gained from our prior experience informs our worldview and standards for trusting; our worldview and ability to trust direct the knowledge we acquire in the future.

Breaking down trust into its constituting elements of ability, benevolence and integrity allows us deeper insight, because we can identify the specific vectors through which opposition or acceptance of an issue, and acquisition of knowledge in general, may come about.

It may be assumed that the different elements vary in importance depending on the issue at hand; in some cases, ability as in technical know-how is everything, whereas in a political context values under the dimension of integrity may be of the highest importance; and every time there is vulnerability of some kind towards another, expected benevolence is no doubt an essential requirement for trust – and therefore for believing their claims.

In the context of trusting for knowledge, ability relates to what we can do, what we know; anything from formal education to heroics on the sporting field counts here as know-how that may form a standard of evaluation for trust. A clear example of this sort of ability-based trust is when we turn to experts in any given issue. It is precisely because of their demonstrated depth of focus on the subject that we turn to them for wisdom and advice, instead of persisting with our own ignorance. So if we want to know about the finer points of cross-country skiing technique, we are more willing to trust the Olympic winner than the comments of a neighbour who has tried the sport once on a trip to Lapland a decade ago.

When we think about the exchanges that might lead to knowledge, the content of what is being said and how it is expressed, the quality of the argument being made, is of course of paramount importance. What is ultimately being argued is one thing, and how it is said another. But both aspects are relevant when we consider the transmission of information. Let's say someone proclaims that the moon is indeed made of cheese; you would probably think they have finally lost their mind. But if they then proceed to build the argument and present credible evidence of new samples brought from NASA lunar drillings showing that the material unearthed is physically identical to the finest Parmesan, you might at least become a bit puzzled. Recognizing the legitimacy of the sources of evidence, you also start to relax the hypothesis of lunacy in your interlocutor. Later on, hearing the news that the finding was the result of a prank by the technology students who were involved in building the landing vehicle for the mission, you realize how skilful construction of evidence and argumentation can provide a believable foundation for even the sublimely ridiculous. Coming back to the ground and reality, and the topic at hand, the specific skill in constructing ingenious arguments can be thought to lie within the realm of ability in our trust framework, connecting neatly to how knowledge is communicated.

It appears that there may be a relative quality to our trust perceptions, where we can be aware of different scales of credibility when considering the ability of another in relation to a given task. As an example, let us ponder for a moment the credibility of an economic commentator. Imagine a Nobel-prize-winning economist is commenting on some country's chosen policies. For a layperson without strong views on the subject, the commentator would likely appear credible and trustworthy, and their word could be readily taken as fact and incorporated as knowledge about the economy. Another person, this time with a degree in the subject, might recognize that the Nobelist is talking about a situation outside the scope of their expertise, and therefore see that the claims made may not come from the deepest well of knowledge in this particular case. So although the commentator is otherwise a highly capable and credible source, there may be some room for doubt. Finally we might have a fresh PhD in the specific subject area in question, who might recognize outright that the old Nobelist is basing their comments on data that was relevant 10 years ago, but was recently disputed and over-turned, making the claims false in light of the latest evidence – therefore making the fresh PhD distrust and refuse the knowledge shared by the Nobelist.

From this example we can make some inferences about the nature of our trusting facility. When it comes to knowledge, it is clear that our ability to accept the claims of others as knowledge is dependent on our own ability relative to the claimant. The lay-person in the example is more ready to accept the Nobelist's claims as knowledge due to their own inability to evaluate the basis of the claims made, whereas the person at the avantgarde of the economic art can ignore the Nobelist when appropriate because they themselves possess a superior framework of understanding that is able to explain and improve on the foundation from which the Nobelist's approach springs. Therefore, ability as a factor of trust in general and as a component of knowledge is varying in its effect, with the dynamics determined by both parties in the relationship, their stores of knowledge and the subject matter itself. It can be guessed that similar effects may be found with the operations of the other antecedents of trust, namely integrity and benevolence. For example, whether you find another's values agreeable depends on the particular values you both hold, how much your values differ or overlap, how important those values are to you both and how they relate to the given situation.

Integrity for its part reflects the more abstract explicit and implicit lessons learned throughout life, about what is of high or low value, and what are the rules and boundaries within which a proper life should fit. The often-mentioned social media bubbles, composed of self-reinforcing spheres of opinion and information sharing by politically likeminded people, represent the effects of integrity on knowing in action. We are far more willing to consider as truthful the claims of those we know to appreciate things like we ourselves do. Opposing views, when they are engaged, are trashed and ridiculed in a routine fashion without much effort to weigh the merits of the information at hand. As such, values and attendant standards of behaviour – integrity, in trust parlance – have a profound effect on our ability to receive and transmit knowledge.

The importance of common values was also stressed by Francis Fukuyama in his sprawling examination of trust, published in 1995. In his words "The ability to associate depends, in turn, on the degree to which communities share norms and values and are able to subordinate individual interests to those of larger groups. Out of such shared values comes trust, and trust, as we will see, has a large and measurable economic value."[29]

A schoolbook example of the economic value of social values Fukuyama refers to comes from the Protestant belief system that was claimed by Max Weber as the principal force behind the industrial revolution in Europe. Devout Protestantism was conducive to economic activity and high trust, a view that can be supported by several arguments. First, Protestantism was seen to encourage frugality, a rational approach to problem solving and a practical focus on earning salvation in the here and now rather than waiting for an abstract eternal world of the afterlife, collectively constituting the values of the famous Protestant work ethic supporting material prosperity. Second, these new Protestant values were favourably aligned with the new scientific paradigm, and as such helped advance the application of science, thereby lending new strength to the development of knowledge. Finally, Protestantism also created, especially in its myriad smaller sects, new tightly knit communities that shared a set of values that separated them from the wider world. This instigated high generalized trust and attendant spontaneous sociability, which Fukuyama credits as an important source of American economic success.

Information coming from those with a benevolent attitude towards us is more readily believed as knowledge than that from more unkind sources. Benevolence-related trust and distrust can be speculated to be closely linked to intraspecies competition, where superior or inferior knowledge about the prevailing circumstances may directly affect the odds of survival. A competitor may therefore be expected to gain from misdirecting another competitor, and likewise non-competing sources are more likely to be perceived as benevolent than competing ones. In a more practical example, let us think of wartime behaviour between belligerents. Each tries to spy as much highly detailed information about the other's strengths and weaknesses as possible, to enable them to conduct their operations as wisely as possible. As they jostle for advantage, both are simultaneously aware of the supreme worth of accurate knowledge in this situation. Therefore, both try not only to catch the enemy's spies, to reduce the information available to the other, but also to feed as much misinformation as possible to misdirect their efforts. Just as these incen-

---

29   *Trust – The social virtues and the creation of prosperity.* Fukuyama, Francis. Simon & Schuster, 1995. Page 10.

tives apply to nations at war, they might show up among people competing for a mate or, more mundanely, between colleagues in the race for a raise on the ladder of the corporate world. The value of knowledge in a competitive situation is summed up by Sun Tzu in his *Art of War*:

"If you know the enemy and know yourself, you need not fear the result of a hundred battles. If you know yourself but not the enemy, for every victory gained you will also suffer a defeat. If you know neither the enemy nor yourself, you will succumb in every battle."

If we reflect on our experiences of cooperation, the links between benevolence, trust and knowledge once again become apparent. Our arrival as a child in the world is marked by a state of helplessness, and our survival is linked to the benevolence of those taking care of us, establishing in the process an example of trustworthy behaviour that is essential for our flourishing. Later on, as we meet new people and are engaged in situations of cooperation in school or at work, experience teaches us that it is easier to work with those we get along with and who care for our needs, than with those who tend to only their own immediate and narrow benefits at the expense of others, further reinforcing the connection between success and benevolent sociability. These positive experiences with benevolence predispose us not just to seek the company of the people possessing such a stance towards us, but also to put more weight on the information received from these parties.

Competition and cooperation in their myriad forms are eternal features of human existence, and educate us to connect our perceptions of benevolence with our tendency to trust.

KNOWLEDGE AND INTERPERSONAL AND GENERALIZED TRUST

As the last part of our discussion of Hardwig's ideas about trust's role in knowledge creation, let us recall the division of trust into its interpersonal and generalized dimensions. In his exposition Hardwig did not discuss these two ends of the spectrum and was mainly focused on talking in general terms about the necessary trust that enables scientists to work together and build on each other's findings. The cooperation during research projects described by Hardwig most clearly resembles trust of the interpersonal type, but he ended his paper with a discussion of the importance of the peer review process, including its problems, in establishing the veracity of claims made in scientific papers. With academic journals and peer review the abstract generalized dimension of trust starts coming into play, because the issue is no longer merely about practical day-to-day personal interactions but rather system-level impersonal coordination founded on commonly understood aims and principles of behaviour. Indeed, if we take the analysis of the role of generalized trust in knowledge to a higher level, we arrive at the obvious realization that scientific research as it exists today, and therefore much of knowledge creation in our societies, depends on the workings of a multitude of institutions such as those offering foundational education, others collecting and channelling funding, or the political apparatus directing state policies, collectively upholding the continued existence of society and its knowledge creation processes. Equally evident is that these complex systems and the society built on them, requiring a high level of impersonal coordination, also require a basis of generalized trust to function in the first place.

As an immediately relatable example we find generalized trust in action when acquiring knowledge from an indirect source such as a research report or perhaps a schoolbook of unknown authorship. In these cases we may not be able to evaluate the trustworthiness of the author directly ourselves, but have to trust the system or process that raised the book to be the standard around which the particular lesson or course was built. Generalized trust is the cement that holds together the institutions of our society that create the room and opportunity for the scientists' work to begin with.

Every day, as we go about whatever business we are on, we meet familiar and unfamiliar people, with whom we build our societies. Our common efforts are naturally coloured by interpersonal trust that develops as we make observations about the various characters found in our lives, depending on how often we meet and in what kind of circumstances. These events give us concrete and often high-frequency evidence about the trustworthiness of the other. In this sense interpersonal trust with its specific and easily identifiable determinants can differ greatly from generalized trust, which contends with issues at a more abstract level. To say it more plainly, you can easily tell when someone has broken your trust, and how it subsequently affects your attitude and behaviour towards the person. But because generalized trust tends to our global assessments of various topics such as the government, the media or the trustworthiness of other people in general, the issue of cause and effect is more complicated.

Reflecting our more abstract attitudes, generalized trust is less sensitive to particular pieces of evidence – if we lose our trust in another once, it does not immediately lead us to designate everyone as untrustworthy. But if the negative interpersonal experience is repeated often enough, we will acquire a more cautious stance towards others, with our generalized trust having shifted lower. Or perhaps we start out with strong generalized trust in the media, based on our consumption of a select few major outlets, which then slowly evaporates as we explore new sources offering different yet valid views, allowing us to perceive the partisan leanings among different sources and thereby challenging our previous notions of unquestioned truthfulness and trustworthiness of media. This process can also be very gradual, without any one particular event that changes everything. Hence, one may become conscious of a shift in trust only much later, as one looks back on one's own thoughts about the issue 10 years ago and contrasts them with the present situation.

Ultimately this means that the particular interpersonal trust of a colleague can be rapidly adjusted with easily identifiable experiences, but the generalized trust underpinning a great variety of perceptions tends to change more slowly, and the causes of the development may often remain obscure. Of course, that is a generalization, and slow changes in interpersonal trust and fast ones in generalized trust are also very much possible. But due to its more direct, personal and particular nature, interpersonal trust yields more readily to revision.

Coming back to knowledge, we may hypothesize that the higher generalized trust a person exhibits, the more easily they can take into account information coming from both familiar and unfamiliar sources. Having a high level of this abstract form of trust can be seen to manifest when making a positive assessment of the trustworthiness and credibility of a personally unknown source in the absence of any direct evidence. In effect high generalized trust may make for a lower bar on the ABI dimensions, and thus affects whether the source is to be taken into account at all. And at the extreme, someone with too much generalized trust might also believe everything they are told – like a fish taking the propagandist's bait, no matter how obvious to others.

Likewise, the hypothesis would imply the opposite – that those with low generalized trust may be more likely to categorically deny any information from their political opponents, thus closing the door to knowledge from that particular direction regardless of the merits of the argument being made.

So we find that trust in some sense reminds us of Aristotle's virtues, finding its most beneficial expressions around some golden mean between the extremes of outright distrust and blind acceptance of everything. But while it may be true that too much trust can lead its individual possessor astray (something that should, over time, be a self-correcting situation based on our trust process model), the problem in most, if not all, societies today seems to be too little rather than too much trust, as attested by the long-term decline in trust measurements. This raises the question: if trust is too low, then why so and is it for a good reason? These are key questions this book will attempt to understand in the following sections.

At the end of the day the interpersonal and generalized dimensions are different aspects of the same phenomenon, manifested in real-life cooperation and in the deeper thoughts and attitudes we hold. Both the actual real-life trust events and the generalizations we derive from them affect each other, marking a complex relationship between our experiences and our view of the world. As for what this has to do with knowledge, it is obvious that both dimensions of trust are essential. Not just because they affect each other, but for the fact that they shape our capacity for cooperation and our ability to work with information coming from different sources.

To summarize, the proposal here is that by adding a more comprehensive understanding of trust in its many dimensions available today, we can improve on Hardwig's insights. The simple but broad and deep ABI framework enables us to understand in finer detail the nature of knowledge as it is in reality created, shared and believed in. The interpersonal and abstract ends of the trust spectrum bring further clarity on different contexts of trust in knowledge.

KNOWLEDGE AS A PROCESS AND AN OUTCOME

Perhaps it would be fruitful to separate learning, meaning here the process of acquisition, and knowledge itself, representing a ready, distinct constellation of information that has become integrated and linked with other data and representations residing in the network of one's own mind. In other words, through the process of learning we acquire knowledge, representing a specific justified true belief qualified by our ability to trust.

The process of learning in practice can refer to acts such as reading a book, having a conversation or digging through the results of an empirical experiment. Through each of these acts we engage with new information, which requires cognitive processing and digestion of the information itself, and evaluation to ascertain whether we find it justified and truthful, and consequently believable. Once we have ticked the boxes of justification, truthfulness and belief, we end up possessing a piece of knowledge.

If we think back on what we have discovered about trust's role in knowledge, it is clear that the effect of trust is particularly pronounced during the process of accessing, evaluating and integrating new data, or learning. Once the process of engaging with the new information is complete, we have chosen (consciously or not) to integrate or discard the new data, possibly forming new knowledge. The ABI dimensions of trust affect how we relate to the source of information and the information itself, acting as a sort of gatekeeper and potentially cutting short the acquisition process itself. As an extreme example of the role of the ability dimension we can think of a person unable to comprehend a particular language. Any message in that language would be fully incomprehensible and our person would be left scratching their head in confusion, unable to acquire the potential knowledge, much less trust whatever content it may be said to have.

Knowledge, then, is the outcome, a kind of final product, of the process of learning that is affected by our trust apparatus, which in turn is built from our backgrounds and resulting tendencies in assessments of ability, benevolence and integrity. This means trust comes most strongly into play when dealing with new information, while established knowledge has already passed the trust-assessment gate. This of course mirrors the general development of trust in any circumstance, through evaluation and integration of new information to adjust expectations and the choice of trust.

In reality, the process of learning is potentially always ongoing and our personal databanks of knowledge potentially always evolving, and therefore trust is always along to steer the ride. But this is only a potential. It is evident that many have fixed their worldviews at some point, choosing to live the rest of their lives with a chosen set of assumptions and knowledge, perhaps acquired at university and untouched ever since – in a way choosing the comfort of certainty over the pain of revision and growth.

THE BIOLOGICAL ROOTS OF EMOTIONS, LEARNING, TRUST AND KNOWLEDGE

If competition and cooperation are among the elementary features of the human experience, they can be thought to be found immediately downstream from the most fundamental instincts of life: to survive and to reproduce. It is on the endless quest for survival and growth that competition and cooperation present their challenges and opportunities. These underlying evolutionary pressures have over the course of human development shaped our brains to manage our physiology and behaviour in a way that aligns more successfully with the environments we live in. One manifestation of the variety of human habits aiming for evolutionary fitness is trust.

Neurobiological research during the past few decades has achieved a set of results showing an interesting connection to trust, especially in the knowledge context. What has emerged from investigations in affective neuroscience is the centrality of emotions in guiding our thinking, decision making and actions – remarkably so in realms previously considered to be guided by "purely rational" thought.[30]

During the course of history societies have developed tools to regulate internal operations and external relations: among them the various institutions, organizations, religions, traditions and formal and informal customs. All of these try to nudge actions towards whatever is deemed the desired direction. Positive emotions such as pleasure, the proud feeling of accomplishment or joy mark success in things like mating, work and socializing, which in turn are cornerstones of individual and communal flourishing. The painful emotions of shame and guilt, fear and pain are the companions of those who transgress against the rules of the community or face a threat to personal survival.

With painful emotions marking dangerous or wrong choices and pleasurable ones augmenting our successes, we are thereby naturally incentivized to avoid certain behaviours and to seek others. This emotional guidance is constructed by the interplay of our biological bodies and our environment. As an example of evolutionary lessons inscribed in

---

30   *Emotions, learning, and the brain.* Immordino-Yang, Mary. Norton Professional Books, 2016.

us, the sense of disgust when encountering spoiled food helps us avoid potentially lethal outcomes by overriding the competing feeling of hunger. Many biologically grounded emotions arise in response to our perceptions about the words and actions of our fellow citizens, coming to the surface as our reactions. A political opponent might cause rage with a statement that to us seems preposterous. The clash producing our reaction is between our values and theirs. Values reflect our ideas about good and bad. What causes the eruption of conflict is not just that many people have different views about what is desirable and not, but also the fact that often the aims promoted are mutually exclusive or in direct opposition. Values are themselves subject to their own peculiar evolution in the pressure chambers that are human societies. New ideas, new situations, new technologies – all change tends to exert a challenge to existing values. Ultimately the soundest values, providing advantages for the survival of the community holding them, will persist and flourish over the centuries; and unsound values creating disadvantages tend to become lost in one way or another.

Although the focus here is on the important role of emotions, it must be noted that emotions are a rough guide. They can, and often do, go wrong. The consciousness can interpret and attribute the physical sensations making up emotions to explanations that may have nothing to do with the real causes. Yet if we are to understand trust, a grounding in the biological and emotional factors underlying our cognition is essential.

Whatever the source of the emotion – natural environment or social construction – the effect is to impart information and behavioural guidance, allowing us to function and succeed. It is not just that emotions help us internalize the rules of engagement. More profoundly, without emotions we are unable to motivate our behaviour, make decisions and take action. This is one of the key lessons from research by Antonio Damasio and others who since the 1990s have uncovered the centrality of emotions in rational behaviour.

The initial breakthrough came from a study on a group of people who had suffered damage to a specific brain region (ventromedial prefrontal cortex), which had compromised their emotional processing capabilities, evidenced by diminished emotional reactions in general and specifically in social contexts. The outcome of the damage was that the patients had intact knowledge bases and full intellectual functionality in the traditional sense, so that in a laboratory setting they could demonstrate normal logical capabilities, the ability for future planning and understanding of the rules of social engagement. Yet in real life, since suffering the damage that affected emotional processing only, their ability to function normally had deteriorated considerably. To quote the researchers Mary Immordino-Yang and Antonio Damasio:

"They would make disadvantageous decisions for themselves and their families. They would not perform adequately in their jobs, in spite of having the required skills; they would make poor business deals in spite of knowing the risks involved; they would lose their savings and choose the wrong partners for all sorts of relationships. Why would patients suffering from compromized social conduct also make poor decisions about apparently rational matters such as business investments?"

As the researchers were able to rule out any deficiencies in logical capabilities, memory or knowledge, they gradually realized the importance of emotional processing in areas of cognition typically considered "purely rational". Losing access to emotional understanding, being unable to perceive emotional repercussions and learn from them and lacking the ability to respond emotionally in social situations together resulted in these people becoming deficient in their abilities to reason well and function in society – capabilities they had amply demonstrated before the damage. Losing access to the internal incentive system of emotions made decision making dysfunctional.

It is worth mentioning at this point that it has recently been demonstrated that losing parts of our brain and its functioning can often be compensated for elsewhere in the grey mass through practice and training that develops new connections and networks. The common term for this flexibility is neuroplasticity.

These insights about emotions, incentives and decision making have broad applicability, especially for understanding learning. Emotions are biologically grounded, manifesting as physiological effects in our nervous system, respiration, digestion and blood chemistry, which we then consciously or subconsciously interpret according to our prior experience, knowledge and cultural context. In learning, emotions guide the process in several ways. Why does a third grader at elementary school do their homework? They might want to avoid their parent's and the teacher's disapproval, the guilt of letting them down, or perhaps they yearn for the pride that comes from eventually achieving the highest grade in the class. Or maybe they are curious about the subject or just enjoy the thrill of a challenge? In just a few examples it becomes clear that the process of learning is full of emotional factors motivating and guiding the process.

On perceiving an adequate trigger, emotions direct our mind and its various faculties towards solutions for resolving the issue at hand. The researchers tested and demonstrated the issue empirically with a card game, where participants in the study drew cards from different decks. Some decks contained high-risk cards that were detrimental to succeeding in the game. Measuring the participants' skin responses, the researchers found that over time as the participants learned the game, they started to show anticipatory responses before choosing a card from the high-risk deck, evidenced as microscopic amounts of sweat in their palms. As the game proceeded further, the participants started steering away from the high-risk decks towards the safe decks, having learned their lesson.

In real life the same lesson is learned, very promptly, when a youngster sticks their finger on a hot stove or their tongue on frozen metal. Usually, one try is enough. What really makes the collection of studies recounted here stand out from the regular common sense understanding of emotions is the fact that they demonstrate the ubiquitous presence and importance of emotions in places where they have gone unnoticed or underappreciated, stemming from the initial finding that impaired emotional processing can wreak havoc on decision making and behaviour in an unexpectedly broad fashion.

The results provide a seed for an emotion-based theory of learning, which the authors proceed to nurture and grow. Let us summarize the main findings by Immordino-Yang, Damasio and company:

Emotions are bodily experiences interpreted by the brain

Emotional processing happens between the body and the brain. More specifically, emotions depend on the so-called somatosensory system, which is responsible for sensing the internal state of the body and its organs, and then transmitting the data up for assessment. Thus bodily experiences are interpreted by the brain to provide an explanation connected to the present circumstances. Sometimes this attribution process can be faulty – for example, post-traumatic stress disorder (PTSD) can lead to situations where difficult trauma-related emotions are re-triggered by something that merely vaguely resembles the previous traumatic event. In the interplay of brain and emotions, information goes both ways, so that physical experiences can precede conscious emotions, but likewise our thoughts can provoke physical experiences that then show up as emotions.

Emotional guidance can be conscious or unconscious

In general emotions provide information about what is to be desired and strived for, and what should be avoided. Many of our emotional reactions, especially those central to learning, are unconscious; some are conscious. Most of the time we are not aware of the operations of our emotional apparatus.

Learning is steered by emotion

Learning is dependent on both conscious cognitive efforts and emotional cues that steer our behaviour; the emotional cues are affected by things such as prior experience that can modify our responses, the way we interpret what is happening to us and of course the endowment of nature coded in our genes.

Emotional learnings affect our future behaviour

Positive and negative emotions become associated with the events surrounding their experiencing (sometimes spuriously) and thus start shaping future behaviour as the emotions are recalled when encountering the same or closely similar events.

Task-relevant emotions may facilitate learning and the development of knowledge

Trying to eliminate emotions from learning environments, which has often been an objective in institutional education, can be counterproductive. Instead, understanding relevant and informative task-specific emotions may support learning and knowledge creation.

Impaired emotional processing can lead to dysfunctional learning and behaviour

Disturbing or removing the processing of emotional cues in learning situations can lead to a lack of integration between knowledge, emotional reactions and cognitive strategies, impairing learning and living in general. Information alone without emotional cues attached is unlikely to affect behaviour – leaving the lesson at hand unlearned.

We learn by mirroring other people's actions and reactions

Much of our learning is achieved by observing and imitating others. It turns out the brain has systems composed of neurons that are specialized for just these tasks. These so-called mirror neurons fire when we recall things, observe others in action or do things by ourselves. This flexible interface between perception, representation and own action enables us to model internally what we see out in the world, whether it is about physical movements or mental modes. Here mirror neurons again show the links between the body, brain and emotions: internal modelling of perceived physical movements is found hand in hand with the ability to understand others, further demonstrating the way our emotional understanding is connected to our physiques.

The systems involving these socially oriented neurons are fundamental for our abilities to understand and internalize the goals and actions of other people, including understanding their emotional states. This in turn makes it possible for us to work with others, to understand why they are doing what they are doing and learn from them and empathize with them. With these characteristics mirror neurons provide the biological basis for social learning, and for sociability in general. As with many things, the internalization of other's actions, situations and emotions is a two-way street: dependent on both the observer and the observed. The way we interpret others is affected by our own preferences, culture, knowledge and psychological make-up.

Two systems govern attention

You are reading these words – your vision is fixed on the line of text and the symbols are translated into meanings filling your consciousness, a feat of simultaneous translation feeling something like holding an internal speech. The outward focus on the text when reading exemplifies one of two groupings of systems governing our attention, the so-called outward-looking and inward-looking systems. "Systems" here means networks in the brain enabling some specific capacity.

Recent research in neuroscience indicates that the outward-looking system governs active goal-oriented tasks involving attention out towards the world, such as reading, playing football (whether American or European) or simply intently admiring the undeniably agreeable views opening across Lake Geneva from the balcony of a temporary pied-a-terre in Montreux. The purpose of this system is self-evident: to get us successfully through our lives without getting eaten by tigers, for gathering and hunting food, not to mention finding the most suitable mate – and everything else involved in interacting with our environments.

What happens when we are not focused on the external environment? Our thoughts drift, we come up with random ideas in a daydreaming state, perhaps recall an event from the weekend or start planning for the future. These internally focused activities are the hallmarks of the so-called "default mode", or the inward-looking system, coming online when we are at rest and not actively engaging with our environments. This system is thought to be responsible for free-form psychosocial processing encompassing many things from self-awareness and self-reflection to imagining the future, and various sorts of conscious emotional issues including moral judgements. Indeed, although the default mode comes online during "rest", the mind is certainly not idle. It is during this inward-oriented phase that especially abstract emotional, social and moral thinking occurs.

When you're daydreaming or thinking about the future, you are not actively oriented towards your surroundings; when you're focused on getting the ball to the net and winning the game, you are definitely not daydreaming. One of the remarkable attributes of the outward and inward attention systems is that when one is engaged, the other is disengaged. Turns out the two systems regulate each other, and the quality of neural processing supporting one system tends to improve the operation of the other as well. When it comes to the inward-looking default mode, evidence indicates that poor connections between different brain regions comprising the system are linked to various psychological and cognitive problems, while strong linkages are associated with improved ability for seeing connections and patterns, perhaps an indication of intelligence. Subsystems of the outward-looking network for their part take care of alerting and orienting us, and of executive control. All of these are important for things such as following lessons and maintaining focus on homework – and are therefore highly relevant for success at school and in life at large.

As a cheeky aside, we might hypothesize from these findings the origins of different schools of philosophy: that those more empirically minded like Aristotle or Bacon are people who are oriented towards their outward-looking system, eager to appreciate the information offered by their senses and surroundings; whereas those with a more inward focus are the Platos and Descartes, creating rationalist systems by the force of their connection constructing inward-looking default mode.

EMOTIONS AND LEARNING – A SUMMARY

As with many aspects of physiology and brain function, it seems our understanding of emotions is in a phase of vigorous expansion. We are approaching the possibility of profound revisions in our concepts of human behaviour and psychology. One building block for new ideas comes from the evidence of the ubiquity of emotions, whether consciously experienced or not; another from the discovery of their essential contribution to rational and socially successful behaviour. Although the functions of emotions stem from the depths of our evolutionary history, these functions remain just as relevant in today's postmodern society as they did in the savannah. Although we are less likely to need to escape predators or hunt for food, we certainly have to avoid scammers, face competition and exploit opportunities as they arise. These encounters work our emotions and the capacity for learning they bestow. Failures and pain lead us to take a different path next time, while success and pleasure make us eager to take another step in our chosen direction.

Emotions are necessary for learning, and therefore for knowledge. What else is knowledge but a crystallized, internalized set of learnings – justified true belief qualified by our ability to trust. In other words, there is a direct link from emotions to knowledge. One might object and claim that scientific results are achieved by rational thought and practice, with little room for emotion. We must then recall how learning at school was steeped in emotions, mostly unnoticed and often below consciousness, and recognize the same factors are at play in high-level research. It is not outlandish to think that the researcher might find rational higher reasoning and empirical experimentation enjoyable in and of themselves, and that research might be a source of pleasure. Returning to the necessities of existence, it is not only that "non-emotional abstract higher reasoning" might be a source of positive emotions, but if the aim of such higher reasoning is to acquire a more complete picture of reality there is also a link to the basic survival instincts honed by evolution. Assuming survival is about fitting one's actions to the prevailing circumstances, acquiring a better picture of the circumstances and actions available should improve the odds of navigating the environment successfully – making survival and flourishing more likely. So it is that learning and education in general can be appraised as an answer to the primal challenges of life, an idea elegantly expressed by Immordino-Yang and Damasio:

"The more people develop and educate themselves, the more they refine their behavioural and cognitive options. In fact, one could argue that the chief purpose of education is to cultivate children's building repertoires of cognitive strategies and options, helping them to recognize the complexity of situations and to respond in increasingly flexible, sophisticated and creative ways."[31]

They go on to hypothesize about the connections between emotions, abstract rational thought and ethics, seeing this last as combining emotional and rational processing at the highest level. All of this emotional and cognitive action in the process of human life happens in a social and cultural context, which imparts its own effect. Specifically, they speculate that "it may be through emotional route that the social influences of culture come to shape learning, thought and behaviour". Emotions, in their elemental roughness, remain central drivers of humanity. Yet, rational high reasoning remains a possibility, even if it cannot fully exist without emotions, nor alone account for guiding human behaviour.

EMOTION, EMOTIONAL THOUGHT AND COGNITION AS STYLIZED BY IMMORDINO-YANG AND DAMASIO

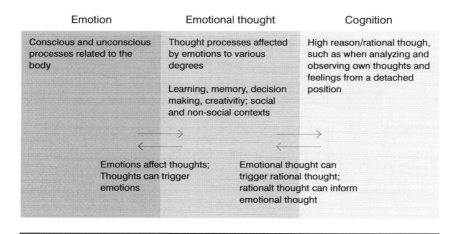

Emotion	Emotional thought	Cognition
Conscious and unconscious processes related to the body	Thought processes affected by emotions to various degrees	High reason/rational though, such as when analyzing and observing own thoughts and feelings from a detached position
	Learning, memory, decision making, creativitiy; social and non-social contexts	
	Emotions affect thoughts; Thoughts can trigger emotions	Emotional thought can trigger rational thought; rationalt thought can inform emotional thought

31   We feel, therefore we learn: the relevance of affective and social neuroscience to education. Immordino-Yang, Mary; Damasio, Antonio. *Emotions, learning, and the brain*. Norton Professional Books, 2016

TRUST AS AN INSTANCE OF EMOTION-BASED LEARNING

Having achieved a measure of enlightenment through to the efforts of our industrious affective neuroscientists, let us now return to trust and how it is built: from assessing the other based on our perceptions of ability, benevolence and integrity, and then observing their behaviour to adjust our estimate of trustworthiness in the course of our interactions. This is obviously a dynamic learning process, a context where our emotions are in play. Should our trust be broken, we fail to get what we hoped for and a negative emotional experience follows. This in turn leads us to revise our assessment, so that we are less likely to trust the source of disappointment later on. From the findings about emotions and learning, we may hypothesize that the evolution of the trust relationship appears likely to be underpinned by the same emotional factors as learning in general. Broken trust might be said to be a social equivalent of a hand on a hot stove – a painful experience altering future behaviour.

The subconscious nature of many of the guiding emotions is likely replicated in our assessments of trust. It seems not only that the unconscious emotions providing rough guidance to approach or avoid something are involved in the ABI assessments themselves, but also that the ABI assessments are probably often of a similar unconscious sort to many of the emotional cues. When meeting a new person, how often do you go through a conscious thought process about whether you can trust them? Often you might do that, but you also frequently just immediately know that you can or cannot trust this particular person. In these cases the assessment was completed subconsciously.

As for the mirror neurons empowering our social learning and ability to empathize, it is apparent that they are of fundamental importance in enabling trust to exist in the first place. Trust is a social phenomenon – you can't have trust without a counterparty, whether it is another person or an institution. Evaluating trustworthiness involves by necessity trying to understand and internalize motivations and capacities for action (through the prism of ability, benevolence and integrity) in others, which is exactly what mirror neurons are all about. But when we talk about abilities as skills and knowledge, and benevolence, behaviour and values composing integrity, we are talking about categories of things that are by themselves fundamentally dependent on mirror neurons for their existence. Many of our skills and much of our knowledge depend on being able to observe others and internally model what is going on, and then imitate what we have seen. This is achieved with mirror neurons. Active benevolence towards others is made possible by the fact that we can somehow understand other people's situations and feelings – empathize with them, in other words – which is again the job of mirror neurons. And it is difficult to imagine social values and behavioural standards without the capacity to step virtually into other people's shoes with the assistance of mirror neurons.

In other words, mirror neurons, which are at the root of many aspects of sociability in general, seem essential not only for making it possible to assess the trustworthiness of others but also for the existence of the antecedent elements of trust itself.

The two systems governing our attention, one towards the external environment and the other towards free association and introspection, also seem to be directly involved in trust formation. You certainly need to be aware of the external environment to make the necessary trust-related observations. On the other hand, the internally oriented default mode is the locus for pattern recognition and moral judgements, which are also necessary for establishing trust. One needs to evaluate the record of past behaviour to extrapolate what the future might look like from a trust perspective; and a capacity for moral judgements is in turn indispensable for evaluating benevolence and integrity.

The interpersonal and generalized ends of the trust spectrum provide grounds for further speculation about the functions of the two attention systems. During outward attention we observe and recognize the developments in interpersonal trust situations (or vis-a-vis a specific institution we are engaging with), but then it would seem it is in the free association of the default mode where we make more global and general inferences based on what we have witnessed, influencing our generalized trust. Furthermore, if default mode is responsible for our general ethical processing (conscious or not), including weighing our values, it seems that this is also where we establish at least some of the standards that affect our trust assessments.

Of course, trust involves much else besides, starting from the senses that give us our observations to begin with.

There is a multipolar interplay between emotions, learning, values and trust, each playing off the others, a system of forces approaching the three-body problem of physics in its inscrutability. Emotions steer us along our path of learning in life, and on the way values act as signposts, affecting what we believe is good or bad and thus linking to our emotional responses, which themselves are at the very bottom of our impulses to avoid or approach something. Through it all we learn from our experiences, manifesting as evolving emotional predispositions, new values and capacity for trust assessments. Finally, value congruence is relevant for the trust that is necessary for much of our learning. Although we know from personal experience that all this is true and really does happen in life, measuring the exact forces of causes and the resulting proportions of effects is nigh on impossible.

We may assume that the trust process is governed largely, if not fully, by the same biological factors as learning in general. From here it follows that trust as a social phenomenon has clear biological origins in our bodily sensations and brain functionality.

The direct physical basis of trust is broadened by experiments involving the hormone oxytocin, a chemical tentatively shown to cause higher levels of trust in people, or at least restore it from low levels, though the claims are not quite universally accepted.[32] Oxytocin is produced by the hypothalamus in our brain, and has been implicated in the promotion of various social emotions such as attachment and bonding, as well as helping with the inference of mental states of others and with reducing anxiety and depression. It seems natural that if the hormone increases sociability and the ability to understand others, while reducing feelings related to fear and avoidance, one side effect would be increased trust.

With its impacts on social emotions, oxytocin has also been connected with the regulation of resting-state brain processes, affecting the operating of our inward attention system that is essential for our moral judgements and ethical thinking. However, the research here is in its early stages, and the results have been mixed, showing for example age- and gender-related differences in the effects of oxytocin on brain region connectivity – with young women being affected by nasally administered oxytocin with increased connectivity between brain regions, while other groups showed no significant change.[33] Likewise, evidence exists pointing towards differences in trust between men and women, but the results have been so variable that the full picture remains cloudy and unfocused.

---

32   Oxytocin as Treatment for Social Cognition, Not There Yet. Erdozain, Amaia M; Peñagari-kano, Olga. *Frontiers in Psychiatry*, January 2020.

33   For example: Oxytocin's Effect on Resting-State Functional Connectivity Varies by Age and Sex. Ebner, Natalie; Chen, Huaihou; Porges, Eric; Lin, Tian; Fischer, Håkan; Feifel, David; Cohen, Ronald. *Psychoneuroendocrinology*, July 2016.

TRUST-BASED KNOWLEDGE IN ACTION

To demonstrate the real-life dynamics of trust, learning and knowledge, let us shift our attention to issues relevant to the present world. As mentioned previously, trust is potentially less of an issue when we are dealing with issues of minor consequence that are not controversial or values-linked. In other words when both we and our counter-party have smaller stakes in play, we care less about the outcome and thus are less demanding with our trust. But if we are engaged with things more personally important, socially impactful, yet abstract and difficult to verify – such as is the case with theories of society or economic policies – the issue of trust in knowledge rises in importance. Here we also find a seeming contradiction, in that abstract matters relating to religion, politics or values, which may not have a direct impact on one's wellbeing as it unfolds in the present, can nonetheless assume the importance and

US CLIMATE CHANGE VIEWS

% of voters by party affiliation who say that 'Climate Change' should be a top priority for the US president and Congress

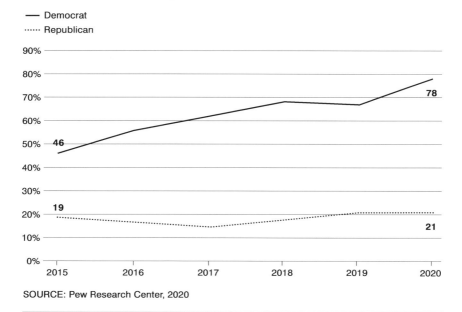

SOURCE: Pew Research Center, 2020

character of a life-and-death issue. This can be assumed to spring from the facts that despite not necessarily having anything to do with immediate material circumstances, the values or moral judgements being contested often comprise things that have been identified as the ultimate good in life, and may also be related to perceptions about survival in the long term. Religions with their promises of a glorious afterlife epitomize this dichotomy between the present reality and a potential future.

A striking example can be found in attitudes towards climate change at the different ends of the political spectrum – an issue of massive contemporary relevance. Pew Research Center has long polled the American people for their views on the topic, providing the results by party affiliation. The outcome has been consistent over years: a clear division between the Democrats and the Republicans in views on climate change. Equivalent results have been confirmed in Europe between parties on the left and right, indicating that the situation in the US is not merely a local peculiarity. Pew's report on the topic released in February 2020 provides an excellent example of this disparity. It finds that over the years the environment and climate change have risen to rival jobs and the economy as the top

TRUST IN CLIMATE SCIENTISTS BY POLITICAL AFFILIATION IN THE US.

% of U.S. adults agreeing with: "Climate scientists can be trusted a lot to give full and accurate info on causes of climate change"

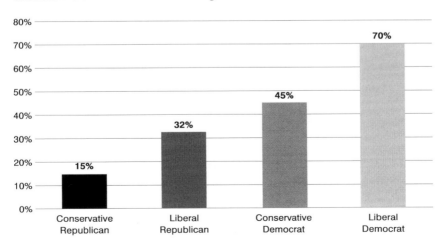

SOURCE: The Politics of Climate. Pew Research Center, October, 2016.

priorities on US citizens' political agenda. But although these topics have become increasingly important, the clear divide between party affiliation has persisted. In 2020 85% of Democrat voters considered the environment as a top priority, and 78% of them gave the same answer on the topic of climate change. By contrast, of Republican voters only 39% and 21% prioritized the same topics.[34]

In another study from 2016, Pew researchers asked Democrats and Republicans whether they agreed with the statement "Climate scientists can be trusted a lot to give full and accurate info on causes of climate change." Fifteen percent of conservative and 32% of moderate Republicans agreed with the statement, whereas 45% of moderate and 70% of liberal Democrats agreed, again highlighting the persistent differences in perception.[35]

Of course trusting a *lot* (as the question words it) is asking a lot, but the variance in answers is striking. This marked disparity has caused wonder among many and raised questions over its origins. Why do different people, who presumably have access to the same data, draw such different conclusions? It can be speculated that the results could reflect different levels of generalized trust, fundamentally different views about how many "top priorities" there can be for a state and to what extent scientists can be trusted to give full and accurate information on any subject, rather than differences over the importance and meaning of climate change itself. In other words, we might be seeing a difference in how people read the questions in the first place. Or perhaps it is a genuine expression of different values between the left and right in the context of the climate issue. Many explanations may be found, but one specific theory is especially relevant to our investigation of trust.

To answer the questions arising from the clashing perspectives on the same climate data, many environmentalists have proposed possible reasons why conservatives are unwilling or unable to trust climate-related science. In their article *The influence of political ideology on trust in science*, a group of American researchers posed the question: how do conservatives and liberals (liberals in the US roughly corresponding the left in Europe) vary in their trust in both production science and climate impact science? In the course of their answer, the researchers invoked and explained the anti-reflexivity thesis, which they summarized as follows:

34   *As Economic Concerns Recede, Environmental Protection Rises on the Public's Policy Agenda*. Pew Research Center, February 2020.
35   *The Politics of Climate*. Pew Research Center, October, 2016.

"The Anti-Reflexivity Thesis hypothesizes that some sectors of society mobilize to defend the industrial capitalist order from the claims of environmentalists and some environmental scientists that the current economic system causes serious ecological and public health problems. The Anti-Reflexivity Thesis expects that conservatives will report significantly less trust in, and support for, science that identifies environmental and public health impacts of economic production (i.e., impact science) than liberals. It also expects that conservatives will report a similar or greater level of trust in, and support for, science that provides new inventions or innovations for economic production (i.e., production science) than liberals."[36]

So the thesis is premised on the assumptions that trust in different types of research is linked to particular political orientations in connection with a degree of self-interest; and by extension that it is specifically the conservatives who are the principal beneficiaries of the capitalist system. These views can be easily reconciled with our understanding of the factors of trust. Political orientation is tightly linked to values that form an important part of integrity. Financial interests for their part relate to both values as integrity and how we perceive others' actions as being good or bad for us, thus also linking to benevolence. In this case the key benevolence-related contradiction arises from the assumption that climate and environmental regulation can be thought of as complicating and costly for the industrial interests that are presumably close to the conservatives' hearts. The researchers summarize their findings with the following claim:

"Analysing data from a recent survey experiment with 798 adults recruited from the US general public, our results confirm the expectations of the Anti-Reflexivity Thesis. Conservatives report less trust in impact scientists but greater trust in production scientists than their liberal counterparts."[37]

The results, along with others such as those from Pew, serve to highlight the very real impact our values have on our trust. Trust in turn influences our tendency to select and accept information as legitimate knowledge. Operating in this example through the channels of integrity (political values) and benevolence (economic self-interest), our trusting facility guides us towards scepticism or acceptance. These timely exam-

36 The influence of political ideology on trust in science. McCright, Aaron; Dentzman, Katherine; Charters, Meghan; Dietz, Thomas. *Environmental Research Letters* 8, 2013.

37 The Influence of Political Ideology on Trust in Science. McCright, Aaron M.; Dentzman, Katherine; Charters, Meghan; Dietz, Thomas. *Environmental Research Letters* 8, 2013.

ples give vivid evidence of how trust is directly involved in our concepts of true knowledge. If our trust is in disagreement with the facts, so much the worse for the facts. The specific example here highlights the role of values, but the other constituents of trust are also constantly evoked in arguments and debates everywhere when questioning whether the particular source of information has the ability or knowledge confirming they actually know what they are talking about and, more worryingly, increasingly often whether they are "good" or "bad" people, with us or against us.

Climate change is but one example of an issue where a dramatic and persistent difference in readiness to accede to certain complex aspects of knowledge can be found between people based on their values and ability to trust the source of information. Other obvious divides of a similar magnitude are around issues such as the economy, the role of the state in general, immigration, sexuality and gender.

Equipped with our understanding about the role of trust in knowledge, let us conclude by looking back to the middle ages and the start of this chapter. Step, for a moment, into the shoes of a private citizen in medieval Europe. It is the high time of the Christian church and papal authority reigns supreme. Now someone comes up to you, claiming many esoteric things – that the earth is far older than a mere 6,000 years, and is actually but a small and insignificant speck in an unfathomably large universe; that man is descended from monkeys; that there are no such things as god or eternal life. After shocking you with such heresies, they proceed to provide arguments that appear disturbingly solid. Contending with these outrageous claims requires you to entertain notions endangering your entire worldview. From a trust perspective, the outlandish perspectives presented are completely at odds with your understanding of cosmology, and a total mismatch with your established set of knowledge. Thus, in light of your prior understanding, based on strict adherence to the Bible, perhaps lightly flavoured with the ancients, the claims advanced with scientific argumentation may appear non-sensical, making for a low rating in your ability-based assessment. If religion plays an important part in your life and identity, as is highly likely in medieval Europe, the statements contradicting the basis of your existence can easily seem hostile, netting a poor score on benevolence. If your life is ordered along religious values and lines of thought, the arguments are also coming from a completely different set of values and standards of behaviour (in relation to knowledge, at least), making it difficult to see eye to eye on the integrity part of trust.

Given all this, it is no wonder that the adoption of the presently dominant scientific worldview was a laborious process taking hundreds of years of incremental baby steps. It effectively entailed going against and dismantling the deepest foundations upon which society was built, and constructing them anew from new materials. A task whose architects could not rely on a profusion of trust from their compatriots for its completion. These examples strive to illustrate our challenges with new information, as they arose yesterday, as they are met today and as they will be faced again tomorrow.

The medieval example also highlights a difficult and paradoxical aspect of trust and human relations more generally: the issue of subjective experience and actual intent. If someone experiences a claim as hostile, such as the clergyman facing scientific claims about aspects of the universe, how does this relate to the estimation of benevolence of the interlocutor? A daring claim about the earth orbiting the sun rather than the other way around can certainly be made without threat or hostile intent. Indeed it can even be made in a warm, friendly and polite manner. If it is, why or how would someone then make a (subconsciously or not) non-benevolent assessment? Here we find that the subjective trust experience may be completely different from the actual intent of the other party. Indeed the scientist here may have the best intentions, and think very highly of their compatriot. And both may even consciously understand this. Yet the assault from the new information to the foundations of the recipient's beliefs and worldview may be such that rather than meeting the challenge of revisiting the foundations of personal knowledge and belief, they shut down and refuse to trust. In this situation the distrust or trust arises from the contents of the message and the subjective meaning it carries. Likewise we might encounter someone who says things that are very agreeable to us, yet something about their character or way of being alerts us towards distrust.

Our distinct perspectives of reality are the products of our different backgrounds and unique lived experiences. Into the process of individuation, trust adds its own twist. Being able to trust a particular claim is essential for our learning and knowledge; and learning and knowledge are things we can't do without. From here it can be conjectured that our idiosyncrasies lead each of us to different sets of knowledge, a process moderated by the operations of our trusting facility. The resulting variety of views is a natural reflection of the vast richness of our different lives. The divergence in views towards climate science is one prominent example of this process, showing how those most concerned with the costs of action tend to distrust such knowledge, whereas others with less skin in the game have no qualms with the results.

If climate science is not in line with your material interests, that does not mean it is false. Yet we are imperfect human beings, guided by our emotions and trusting apparatus, which are not necessarily interested in actual truths. And so we turn away from the disagreeable. It must be assumed that similar mechanics of distrust of unfortunate information are at work in lesser and greater degrees throughout our lives and societies, touching many issues besides climate change.

We must also be clear that not all information or interpretations are worthy of the designation "knowledge", and many things we may believe or think can have only the thinnest coupling to the true state of affairs. If trust guides our actual knowledge, we can expect it to do the same for the broader categories of beliefs and ideas not in full satisfaction of the accepted definition of knowledge.

Likewise, it is worth reiterating that the many-sided nature of reality and experience means that much knowledge reflects only a portion of some greater issue, rather than the full picture. The emphasis put by some on the costs of climate action and by others on the risks of inaction both reflect actual factual knowledge. More commonly this emphasis on one set of facts to the exclusion of others is almost a defining feature of political life in general.

Human capacity for thought is blessed and cursed with limitations. As a consequence, simultaneously holding multiple perspectives on a subject, which might bring us closer to full understanding, is a feat of incredible difficulty. Thus, we are often stuck with holding one piece of truth and disallowing other parts of it. Perhaps it makes our lives simpler and easier, but in effect we are blinkering ourselves in the face of full reality. Understanding trust and its role in learning and knowledge shows us why.

First of all, we must rely on trust to create and learn new knowledge, as the examples from the day-to-day work of science showed. Yet at the same time the trusting facility, with its suboperations around ability, benevolence and integrity, also limits our ability to freely consider new ideas and notions by disinclining us towards that which is not immediately agreeable. This is the paradox of trust in knowledge. It is a necessary component for much of our knowledge, but also a limiting factor. Given that the world is full of misinformation and our ability to handle data is finite, a strong filtering function is absolutely needed. Thus, we are endowed by nature with the regulating function of trust.

With all this in mind, it is not so surprising to find Europeans, and practically everyone, no matter their origin, resisting challenging ideas and knowledge in the past. The fight is basically built in and essentially eternal. Of this the disagreement over the reality and gravity of climate change is merely one contemporary manifestation, though perhaps the most prominent.

TRUST, KNOWLEDGE AND SOCIETY

"Without truth, no trust; without trust, no society. Truth and trust create a world we can share."

RABBI LORD JONATHAN SACKS, *MORALITY*

With the split in attitudes to climate science, the impacts of trust on knowledge and society at large came into sharp focus. The diverging approaches to knowledge are in turn grounded in our ability to trust. As we have seen, that ability, as well as an individual's capacity for relationships in general, grows from influences such as family and social backgrounds and early trust experiences. The networks of social capital represent fully grown fruits of trust-enabled connectivity. Besides their relationship to trust, the commonality between views on climate change, knowledge and human relations in general is that all of these occur in the context of a wider society. Trust regulates behaviour towards another party, being a built-in mechanism of risk-assessment in cooperative contexts. Springing from this inherent quality, its highest-order impacts can be expected to transcend everyday face-to-face interactions and manifest at the societal level. We will therefore now turn to speculative musings about the three inseparable friends: trust, knowledge and society.

So, let us stop peering at the individual celestial bodies of trust and knowledge, and see if we can predict some movement in the solar system of society.

Among the defining features of an open society are broad toleration for citizens' expressions of their ideas, coupled with rights to actively promote agendas privately found worthwhile. This combination of free speech and behaviour enables such a society to interact with a greater set of knowledge possessed by its citizens, compared with a closed society limiting expression. As a consequence, the free society is presumably better informed and therefore able to align with the actual realities of its citizens and the surrounding world, which should be to the benefit of the people. On the other end of the freedom of expression spectrum an ideologically or otherwise closed society, such as the Soviet Union of the past, depends on a narrower set of knowledge (as in socially expressible and acceptable views and behaviour, or information) in navigating the times. In effect ideological and other limitations on what can and cannot be said, and how citizens can conduct their lives, constrain opportunities for citizens and the state in answering various challenges as they arise, by restricting debate and alternatives for action. This narrower suite of problem-solving strategies may over time lead to an increasing likelihood of suboptimal outcomes and failure.

This is not to say all ideas and information should be freely expressible. Information about the construction of nuclear or biological weapons, for example, is best kept outside common knowledge, for the safety of everyone. Likewise, some ideas can be very toxic and lead to disastrous outcomes, and should therefore be guarded against. This too we know from the record of history. Yet it is also noteworthy that ideas deemed dangerous or heretical can often be exactly what is needed. Again, we can turn to the example provided by the Soviet Union.

The Union of Soviet Socialist Republics stood as a bulwark against the presumed exploitation meted out by the imperialist capitalist countries against workers in their own countries and abroad. As a part of this anti-capitalist stance, the bourgeoisie – the owners of private enterprises large and small – were stripped of their companies and sent to gulags for re-education and fates far worse. In this ideological environment expressing interest in or arguing about the merits of private ownership, free economic behaviour and western economic ideas in general became a practical impossibility. These were imperialist capitalist ideas, against which the whole of the state and its official ideology were arrayed. Yet it was the absence of private economic initiative and the price signals of a free market guiding resource allocation – hallmarks of capitalist economies – that led to the stagnation and collapse of the Soviet economy, taking the state down with it. In short, the very ideas that might have saved the system, not to mention massively improve the material wellbeing of the people, were denied as heresy.

Noting these developments in the Soviet Union, the Chinese communists ditched their rigid orthodoxy and quickly started adopting capitalist ideas with the spectacular success we see today.

We may therefore claim that freedom of thought and expression are not merely good and desirable for the private individual as a means of achieving a safe and authentic life, but are also beneficial for society more broadly. By increasing the amount of information available and alternatives for action, free expression improves the potential for adaptation that is necessary as times change and challenges arise. These are perhaps the underlying evolutionary functions, or advantages, freedom bestows on individuals and societies. As a downside we may perceive at least the resulting profusion of diverse interests and perspectives, which possibly make decision making, coordination of interests and behaviour more difficult. Certainly all societies, whatever the type, face these challenges. Yet an environment of freedom appears to intensify these issues, if only because there are more interests and ideas out in the open to take into account in public administration and decision making.

To harness the inherent opportunities and compensate for the challenges of free speech and action, we assume free societies place a special emphasis on institutions and arrangements enabling citizens to channel their interests, views and activities in peaceful and productive ways. Therefore, it is no surprise that parliaments and senates, markets and private companies, organizations of civil society, widespread education and strong legal systems all prosper in free countries. It is not that these institutions are unique to these societies. But is undeniable that many of them, whether of ancient or modern origin, have been pioneered in relative freedom, and it is in these circumstances that their functioning seems to reach heights not seen elsewhere.

Incidentally, these institutions also support trust in society, and in turn rely on it.

Collective meaning-making is one of the ways trust is achieved. Common ideas, concepts and perspectives result in more unified values and behavioural standards – essential ingredients of trust. The most obvious example is the universal education system providing a mostly common curriculum for all students, handily imparting a common set of skills, knowledge and ways to perceive the world in the process. A similar feat is achieved through the free press and democratic institutions. In reflecting on pressing issues, merits and problems are argued for and against. This happens in the free press, as well as between politicians and parties. Over time, common positions are staked out, turn into policies and thence harden into stable, common understandings. A key difference in the meaning-making between the educational system and the deliberative one is perhaps time perspective. The educational system promotes established ideas and knowledge, whereas politics and the media are the playgrounds where new ideas take shape. All the same, all of these institutions take part in the meaning-making that forms a pillar of trust assessments within the society.

By imparting skills and knowledge the educational system also builds up the trust-relevant abilities among the population. Recall that ability was one of the dimensions of trust assessment. We might therefore assume that a skilled society is also a trusting society, relative to an unskilled one.

This view has broader implications for the relationship between trust and sociability in general, which we will cover in more detail later on.

Private property and the freedom to pursue economic interests release productivity and creativity, paving the way to a persistent flow of economic growth. From a trust perspective this is an awesome achievement. First, the escape from absolute poverty and subsistence economy must have made the world seem a much more benevolent place in general, helping generalized trust from the benevolence perspective. Second, the growing economy has also supplied a growing number of opportunities to satisfy the endless variety of personal talents and ambitions. This has transformed the logic of wealth accumulation. Cooperation to create (in the context of a start-up, for example) has become more rewarding than competition to possess the scarce resources available that marked the zero-sum logic of the old no-growth regimes. Recall that the riches of ancient empires rested to a large degree on plunder and slaves. In a world where innovation and economic growth are possible, more benevolent – more trusting – approaches to living become real.

Another central ingredient for sustaining an orderly and trusting society is a legal system that lends recourse in grievances and is perceived by the citizens as fair and functional. By providing a measure of security and predictability, legal institutions reduce the risks of cooperation, thereby promoting more of it. Laws also codify and declare the values and behavioural standards of a society, contributing to meaning-making and providing a basis for trust assessments.

A common thread between these institutions in free societies is that they are not monolithic, but open, mutable and reflective of the needs and worries of the broader society. Think of the evolving laws and the ever-changing political landscape with its rising and falling values, politicians and parties, for example. This relative openness and responsiveness enable the feedback loop of the trust process, from evaluation to observation and adjustment of behaviour. This process between people and institutions in a society allows trust to be maintained and created over time. Information about changing circumstances is allowed to be expressed, and institutions take it into account in their operation, should the pressure be strong enough. Thus, change is effected in society and institutions, providing grounds for trust reassessment. Trust can be impacted between citizens, towards the institutions themselves or at the general level. As we saw, particular trust experiences tend to impact generalized trust, and the other way around.

Notice that, as we discussed in the previous chapter, plain data and information turn into actual believed knowledge with trust. Therefore, we may assume that the responsiveness of an open society can only be maintained as long as it can broadly come to terms with the information provided from different segments of society – in other words, as long as there is enough trust to believe the various claims made. If there is no trust in the claims being made, it will not become actual knowledge and remain unaddressed. Obviously not every claim has a basis in truth and reality, and the chaff needs to be separated from the wheat. But the more generalized trust there is, the more easily even difficult subjects will be taken into consideration and subjected to serious scrutiny. Challenging and difficult ideas will by default be less trusted, if they pose a challenge to the existing state of affairs. As such robust generalized trust between competing political parties, between the governing and the governed, and among people in general is necessary to bridge the gap to common knowledge. This point is especially pertinent in light of the documented declines in trust in the west.

Contrast the openness and responsiveness of institutions in free societies with authoritarian ones. The Soviet Union fell because it was incapable of admitting the failures of its economic system and adjust accordingly. Economic ideas and knowledge that would have saved it were shut out, and the people who might have had the courage to exhibit critical thinking were driven out or locked up. It is not really surprising that this happened. After all, western capitalist ideas and values were a comprehensive contradiction to the ideas and values of the Soviet state. Acceding to their worth would have meant at least a tacit admission of the false premises the whole Soviet apparatus was built on. From a trust antecedent perspective, it is obvious why the challenge to values and concepts of self-interest and benevolence posed by the western ideas was so severe to those relying on the continuation of the Soviet system.

As a consequence of the Soviet reluctance, problems and failures cropped up. Everyone knew the system didn't work, but no one was able to do anything about it. The feedback loop of trust was blocked in the sense that, publicly, there was little the citizens were able to do to alter the policies of the proletarian tyranny, which might have resulted in renewed trust creation. The only real options were either to submit or to flee to the other side of the iron curtain. Privately, they then lost trust in the system, which eventually led to its collapse.

In an environment where the trust process is blocked, trust cannot be created, and will slowly wither with every unaddressed grievance and problem. Ultimately the whole system will lose its credibility in the eyes of the citizens. This cycle of failure, blocked adjustment leading to lack of trust, which eventually results in system breakdown, is a tale as old as time, replicated in states and societies across time and place. Acknowledging the role of trust in this process, its impact in knowledge and its feedback process helps us gain a new perspective on the success and failure of states and societies. Generally, trust is involved in a strange mutual tension between ideological conformity, knowledge and freedom. Ideological uniformity implies higher trust among the like-minded, but this conformity can also lead to resistance of competing ideas and knowledge, which are in turn essential for freedom and societal error correction – also central for the trust process.

When it comes to trust creation, the evidence of recent centuries points towards the primacy of freedom and error correction over the totalizing impulses of ideological conformity. European history since the renaissance can be described in many ways. One way is as an ascent and triumph of institutions enabling the feedback loop of trust.

Taking stock of Europe around AD 1400, we find that it was mostly an illiterate, poor place, in the control of the church and nobility. But from these humble beginnings scientific and technological innovation paved the way towards the new, leading to the upheavals of the reformation and the Thirty Years' War, and the eventual dilution of absolute monarchies towards greater and greater power-sharing. As the sea-borne exploration of the world got under way, joint stock companies were formed to take advantage of the economic opportunities awaiting in the new worlds. The universities began to break free from their religious moorings, and literacy rates started to improve in tandem with the number of books printed. As the grip of religion loosened, new secular humanist ideas arose and supplied the intellectual basis for the nascent democratic order. In the course of this centuries-long transformation from the medieval to the modern and post-modern worlds, a host of new institutions sprang up. As we will see, besides their many other merits these institutions were also a boon for trust.

KNOWLEDGE, EDUCATION AND TRUST SINCE THE RENAISSANCE

At the time Gutenberg was busy building his printing press, the Catholic Church stood as the pre-eminent source of intellectual, spiritual and ideological legitimacy and power in Europe, and the small number of universities remained tightly tied to their scholastic and religious origins. Despite these seemingly undisturbed waters, the currents of thought had changed dramatically, and the ship of the intellect was already drifting towards a new course.

The renaissance geniuses in Italy had begun to look for new shores of undiscovered knowledge, and were soon joined in their efforts by the rest of Europe. In the midst of this new intellectual exploration, Gutenberg's printing press supercharged the process of information dissemination by dramatically reducing the cost and effort required to create printed works, and its immediate consequences seem in many ways to be echoed in our experiences with the internet today. Book production became much cheaper and, as a consequence, the availability of books exploded. This helped spread existing works far wider, and encouraged the production of new works. Among the most printed books was of course the Bible, and the details of its story help us illustrate the revolution in relationship to knowledge that occurred during those centuries.

As odd as it sounds to modern ears, especially given the importance of the Church in the medieval world, most of the biblical texts and often the sermons in churches were in Latin – a language incomprehensible to the vast majority of people. The one most important, most sacred, thing in society – religion – was in large parts off-limits to the detailed scrutiny of the greater public thanks to the Latin language barrier. In the 16th century, with the mass printing of Bibles, things began to change, however. Bibles became widely available at reasonable prices and, more importantly, they were finally widely translated into the vernacular languages the European peoples actually used in their everyday lives. The language revolution was not limited to the book itself, and church services held in Latin began to be converted as well. For the first time the public gained access to the foundational texts and speeches in a form they could comprehensively understand and study. It is no surprise that these changes were accompanied by a wave of new interpretations, new sects and denominations, most profoundly resulting in the reformation and the Protestant church.

With these developments the Roman Catholic Church effectively lost its monopoly on the Bible, on the interpretation of its contents and consequently on the religion itself. The printing press and the concurrent developments broke the tight information control the Church had, and people became free to make up their own minds about correct religious practices – and started to organize accordingly.

Although the changes in religious institutions were perhaps of foremost importance during the 16th and 17th centuries, as evidenced by the wars of religion at that time, they were but one part of a broader movement. The process of information liberalization from previously strictly regulated systems that brought revolution to religious life was repeated in many shapes and forms – for example, in sciences.

The most accessible manifestation of the new world of ubiquitous printed information was of course the newspaper. Handwritten periodic publications had already started appearing in Venice and Germany during the 16th century, mostly catering for specialist commercial interests or covering happenings in foreign countries. With the advent of printed versions, first appearing in Germany in 1605, the age of the newspaper got its proper start. The modern broadsheet form we recognize today was pioneered almost immediately after, with the Dutch paper *Courante uyt Italien, Duytslandt*, &c in 1618, focusing on foreign news. But why is all this so important for our interest in trust?

By spreading information and news to the public, newspapers greatly expanded citizens' minds. Whether it was commercial information about the latest trade fairs or about political developments in neighbouring countries, the papers offered knowledge that had previously been limited to a much smaller circulation. But early on the press was heavily censored, and consequently matters unpleasant to the state did not enter the discussion. Over time calls for freedom of the press won out, and the newspaper transformed into a true arena of societal debate. The latest gaffe by a government minister, turmoil in the markets, the optimal form of the economy – more or less everything under the sun was fair game. This meant that grievances or new ideas could be aired publicly and circulated widely, with very real hopes of affecting policy, all thanks to the platforms provided by newspapers. Even today it is common for a scandal broken by the media, of which the press remains an important part, to seal the fate of a government or a political party ahead of elections. The power of the press grew to such a degree that it acquired an unofficial distinction as the fourth estate, in addition to the traditional triumvirate of clergy, nobility and commoners.

The platform for expression provided by a free press, and power derived from it, have profound implications for trust. First of all the information disseminated by books, newspapers, magazines and publications of all manner helped spread and develop knowledge, understanding and values across the population. These obviously map into the ability, benevolence and integrity assessments we make in trust situations. By reaching wide audiences newspapers create communities of readers who have a common grounding on how to engage with topics they have read about in those papers. Competing publications may offer alternative perspectives, creating the grounds for a lively debate but also a divergence in worldviews and trust assessments. All the same, a thriving ecosystem of free press should ultimately help develop trust because it functions as a channel of the trust feedback loop. Various issues and problems can be aired, which may then result in further debate and potentially even broad societal reform. If the original problems are satisfactorily resolved along the way, it can be presumed that this dynamic would be helpful in building trust in the system (if not in the particular targets of the original criticism), as those yearning for change notice with satisfaction that the system has delivered their wishes. Of course, we must also assume that this holds only as long as the changes made do not make other people significantly worse off, so as to offset the positive effects. Freedom of the press is thus a cornerstone of trust in society.

Scientific journals represented another novel form of printed knowledge. The first ones published were the *Journal des Savants* in France, and the *Philosophical Transactions* by the Royal Society in the UK, both appearing for the first time in 1665. These pioneering journals were soon joined by a growing number of similar publications across the European world. Unlike newspapers, with their more pedestrian orientation, these journals focused on scientific topics, often presenting ground-breaking research and findings. Together with the gradual development of universities and the establishment of independent scientific institutions (such as the Royal Society), the scientific journals were but one practical way to cultivate and deliver the fruits of the new approach to the systematic creation of knowledge, today referred to as the scientific method.

The universities of Europe grew mostly from the earlier monastic and cathedral schools across the continent. Thanks to their extensive couplings to the church and religion, universities retained their strongly religious character at the time of the renaissance. This meant that the curriculum was strongly tied to theology, and the natural sciences such as astronomy were interpreted in accordance with biblical truths. The Copernican revolution began to challenge all this and, slowly but surely, over centuries, the universities found themselves increasingly dedicated to the advancement of empirical science instead of debating theological interpretations. The number of academic subjects increased with the advance of knowledge, and the subjects themselves changed towards the forms we recognize today. Alchemy gave way to chemistry. A high-water mark in this institutional evolution was reached with the creation of the modern research university, embodied in the principles of Berlin's Humboldt University established in 1809. The university, founded by Wilhelm von Humboldt, championed the idea that high-level research and education should go together, with a holistic and comprehensive curriculum of arts and sciences giving a deep grounding in civilization; and all of this complemented by academic freedom allowing staff and students to focus on the subjects of their keenest personal interest. Academic freedom also meant that religious, market and state interests and biases should not be allowed to hinder the pursuit of truth and knowledge. In short, Humboldt provided the model for the modern university – a model that has in recent decades been increasingly eclipsed, as ideological and market interests have effectively taken over many universities.

Alongside the universities a number of independent and state-sponsored research institutions developed, the earliest of which became known as academies of science. The first and foremost of these was the still-operating Royal Society, founded in 1660. The basic idea of these academies was to provide support to science and scientists. To this end, they published journals, offered lodgings, meeting rooms and libraries and funded the research of their members. In addition, an increasingly important function was to promote science and provide advice to the government and other bodies. Over time the academies of science were joined with other private bodies, associations and foundations all seeking to provide similar services to scientists and artists alike, across the many fields of knowledge and creativity.

As research and development efforts were identified as a key source of economic competitiveness among firms, in tandem with the maturation of the capitalist economy, market-driven research laboratories started sprouting in firms in the 19th century. These institutions, like the famous Bell Laboratories, which was the birthplace for the transistor and laser alike, added their practically oriented voice to the choir singing the glory of science.

Alongside these developments the growth and increasing sophistication of the economy increased the demand for a skilled and educated workforce. Likewise, the revolution in printing made texts ubiquitous and thereby incentivized reading and writing skills, because they could now be used far more often and far more profitably than previously. And finally, the enlightenment with its political demands saw a more educated citizenry as a requirement for the realization of a democratic self-governing population. In the cross-pressure of these influences, mass primary education was gradually expanded in Europe, first starting slowly in the 18th century, but then gathering pace in the 19th, until nearly universal literacy was reached in the 20th century in the western world. Similarly, the number of universities grew considerably.

As we can see, since the renaissance and the printing press there has been ongoing growth in institutions creating and disseminating knowledge. This seems a natural consequence of the explosion in the number of books and papers, economic imperatives and the new habits of mind that drove the scientific and political revolutions. Universities, academies, research journals, schools and the like all rode on the wave unleashed by the printing press, the scientific method, the capitalist economy and the enlightenment.

Coming back to trust, we briefly discussed how newspapers allowed opinions and views to be voiced, which in turn granted the citizenry a new measure of power in societal affairs, with presumably trust-enhancing consequences. This ability to affect things is bound to increase trust if it bestows agency in relation to the state and society, turning the citizen from a passive to an active participant in society. These in turn give potential for the improvement of circumstances. The mere fact of being better informed than previously enables one to participate to a higher degree, and the arena for action provided by the various papers and other institutions accentuates this capacity further.

The burgeoning constellation of universities, academies and research journals resulted in a massive upgrade in our collective and individual knowledge-creation and sense-making abilities. In effect the new institutions replicated for scientific knowledge much the same impact books and newspapers did for general societal discourse: they formed a web of interrelated institutions that enabled a many-voiced discourse about all the subjects they touched. Empirical methods were used to acquire new findings, and theories about possible explanations were debated. Scientific journals spread ideas and findings, which in turn lit up minds elsewhere, who then responded with their own insights in new articles. The scientific ecosystem provided a system of knowledge that was far more robust than its medieval predecessor. Instead of strict biblical truths, deviation from which was heresy, we now had a self-correcting process, where failure, mistake and stepwise progress were to be expected on the way to real knowledge. Whereas before there had been a rigid Rome-centred hierarchy of infallible truth and knowledge, and very little in the way of actual challenges to them, thanks to censorship, general poverty and backwardness, we now had a widely distributed iterative self-correcting process, and with it the admission that perhaps not all, or even most, questions about the nature of the world and existence had been settled. We can say, therefore, that the scientific revolution was also a revolution in intellectual honesty.

The monolith of religious doctrine was shattered, and blind faith opened up to a vision of an empirically sensible world. An incredible step was taken from a worldview where things were generally thought to be fundamentally beyond human understanding and control, to one where the senses and the intellect were seen as the guides to mastering our environment and the laws of nature for the improvement of mankind. Increasing comprehension of causes and consequences brought about an unstoppable flow of new insights and innovations, which in turn provided a growing body of evidence supporting the new perspective. This change, slow and centuries in the making, had profound consequences for trust in society.

One way the new scientific paradigm, and all it entailed, helped create trust was by making things tractable in a way never before seen. As an example, let us think of the practice of medicine. Before the 19th century, in a tradition going back to esteemed ancient sources, most disease was thought to be the result of imbalances in bodily fluids or "humours" – or of "miasma", polluted air. The compound microscope developed during the Dutch golden age paved the way for observations of various animalcules, or micro-organisms in the present language, too small to observe with the naked eye. Slowly, the understanding of bacteria, viruses and other animalcules accumulated, and so the germ theory of disease evolved. Connections were established between diseases and the presence of micro-organisms, and this understanding was used to create working cures for many diseases such as smallpox and tuberculosis.

The emergence of increasing numbers of successful solutions to health problems has undoubtedly increased trust in doctors and the medical arts. The many quacks and charlatans from earlier centuries were replaced by professionals administering far more accurate diagnoses and actually effective treatments. Recall the formula of the trust feedback loop: assessment – cooperation – observation – adjustment. The medications afforded by the new scientific approaches must have increased the relative and absolute number of positive experiences, observations and subsequent trust adjustments, thereby generating trust not only towards particular doctors and their drugs, but over time towards the profession and science of medicine in general as well.

Similar progressively positive developments have occurred across the sciences and society, as the fruits of scientific labour have been harvested. Chemists did not find a way to turn lead into gold, but they did discover dyes and fertilizers, innovations that brought riches to many. Physicists taught new ways to understand motion in the heavens and on the ground, while astronomers armed with their telescopes looked further than ever before to find a night sky full of wonders.

All this science-based understanding must also have led to a general increase in trust. The discoveries made, and the practical applications they enabled, showed time and again the effectiveness of the scientific method and the institutions supporting it, generating massive amounts of trust for them. When it became possible to admit and correct failures, trust in the answers given also increased. This has enabled the scientific mindset to largely supersede the earlier religious modes of thought. Indeed, today when people need to be convinced of something, it is common to cite research or bring a prominent scientist specializing in the subject to comment and lend weight to the claims being made. Scientists are trusted because they are perceived to have, in a trust assessment sense, superior credibility in the realm of ability in their given field.

Thinking again about the trust assessment framework, the better you can understand (assess) the behaviour of your counterparty, the easier you find it to adjust your behaviour in relation to them – and trust. In effect the scientific revolution made it far easier for us to relate to the world in general, because everything became easier to understand.

As a result of the improvements in education, literacy, practical skills and knowledge, people must also have gradually found each other more interesting company and capable collaborators, which by itself would affect trust assessments and the propensity to get together and cooperate. There is simply more to be had when your interlocutors and co-workers have more to share in terms of skills and knowledge. Imagine going back to a time where most people were illiterate and unskilled. How readily would you take their advice over your own? How many start-ups might be founded among people with little in the way of applicable skills and knowledge? Advanced skills, knowledge and capabilities are very helpful in fostering trust and cooperation.

The institutions we have discussed here not only promoted massive progress in knowledge and material prosperity, but also provided an ecosystem in which issues could be explored, mistakes corrected and real discoveries made, and trust could grow. In practice this has of course been a far more tortuous and difficult path than the idealized picture given here. For example, in science it is often joked that "progress is made one funeral at a time" – implying that new ideas are rarely adopted by those already holding older concepts, but as a generational process. Yet over the course of centuries, the trend of dynamic adaptation has held.

The process of dynamic iteration that marked the new knowledge regime, and enabled the functioning of the trust feedback loop, was not confined to science and universities. Indeed, institutional developments enabling similar modes of self-correcting operation occurred in the realms of politics and the economy as well.

LIMITED LIABILITY AND THE MODERN CORPORATION – THE ENGINES OF CAPITALIST ECONOMIC DEVELOPMENT

The formation of the British and Dutch East India Companies, in 1600 and 1602 respectively, heralded the dawning of a new age of capitalism. In more practical terms, the two companies represented the first steps in organizational innovation that continues to this day, combining limited liability and joint shareholding.[38] Both of these practices, joint stock companies and various forms of liability limitations, had existed previously to some degree – with guilds and religious organizations, for example. But the combination of these two with explicit for-profit commercial purposes was an innovation with far-reaching consequences. Limited liability clauses free a company's directors and shareholders from personal responsibility for its debts and other liabilities. Today, limited liability refers especially to the arrangements between the holders of equity and debt in the case of insolvency. Liability limitations have the practical effect of reducing the personal financial risk of those participating in the organization's activities and setting a floor to the losses one can incur from an investment gone sour (the equity invested, but not more). Joint stock shareholding for its part enabled the mass participation of investors in various commercial ventures. Together, the new legal practices and organizational forms shaped by them spurred an ever-continuing crescendo of economic activity.

In conjunction with the formation of the Dutch East India Company, the company's shares and bonds were offered for public trading on the Amsterdam Bourse. Although trading in stocks and bonds did exist before this, the Amsterdam stock exchange provided the first "modern" context for stock trading. For the over thousand initial investors in the Dutch East India Company, the ability to trade the shares publicly

---

38   A New Understanding of the History of Limited Liability: An Invitation for Theoretical Reframing. Harris, Ron. *Journal of Institutional Economics*, 2020, 16.

offered several advantages. First, the value of the asset became more firmly and transparently established with the public price of the share. This had the second-order effect of increasing trust among those interested in participating in financing such ventures, and thereby acquiring shares. More importantly, the ability to turn those investments back into cash at short notice, handily provided by the constantly available trading opportunity, further reduced the risks of participating in these ventures. Should a shareholder require funds quickly for other purposes, it became possible to realize the value of their shares in an orderly fashion at the stock exchange. This is certainly possible with privately held shares as well, but a public setting with a vast number of potential buyers and sellers makes things much easier, practical and therefore attractive.

With the founding of the East India Companies, we arrive at a critical juncture in the development of the capitalist economic regime. These were the first large-scale companies – they dominated international trade and made fantastic fortunes in the process. To be sure, they were in many ways very different from the companies of our present day. For example, they employed private armed forces, for conquest and protection alike, and often acted as direct representatives of their national governments in foreign lands. But the fact that the European trading companies were able to conquer distant lands and establish outposts so successfully that they turned into full-blown empires speaks volumes about the efficiency and ability to get things done unleashed by economic incentives and the new organizational forms.

The significance of the innovations in corporate form can hardly be understated. Nicholas Murray Butler, the president of Columbia University at the time, gave a speech to the Chamber of Commerce of the State of New York in 1911 about the subject that is worth quoting at length:[39]

"I weigh my words, when I say that in my judgment the limited liability corporation is the greatest single discovery of modern times, whether you judge it by its social, by its ethical, by its industrial or, in the long run, – after we understand it and know how to use it, – by its political, effects. Even steam and electricity are far less important than the limited liability corporation, and they would be reduced to comparative impotence without it.

"Now, what is this limited liability corporation? It is simply a device by which a large number of individuals may share in an undertaking without

---

39   *Politics and Economics*. Butler, Nicholas Murray. 143rd Annual Banquet of the Chamber of
     Commerce of the State of New York. New York: Press of the Chamber of Commerce, 1911.
     Pages 43–56.

risking in that undertaking more than they voluntarily and individually assume. It substitutes cooperation on a large scale for individual, cut-throat, parochial, competition. It makes possible huge economy in production and in trading. It means the steadier employment of labour at an increased wage. It means the modern provision of industrial insurance, of care for disability, old age and widowhood. It means — and this is vital to a body like this – it means the only possible engine for carrying on international trade on a scale commensurate with modern needs and opportunities."

Now that is quite the set of impacts, offering poignant evidence of how legal and organizational innovations can guide the path societies take.

When it comes to trust in society, these developments were equally earth-shaking. Although we cannot say that the evolving limited liability corporation underpinning the larger movement towards capitalism had a direct impact on the general level of trust, there were certainly second-order effects. As Butler highlighted, the corporate form reduced the risks of investing and working for such firms, thereby encouraging investing and cooperation for economic purposes. The additional risk-reduction provided by the stock market further sweetened the proposition of taking a chance with the new companies.

Recall the discussion in the first chapter of this book about trust's basic features. One of them is that trust is sensitive to the gravity of the issue at hand, and the bar for trust is set higher when more is at stake. Significant amounts of money for investors, and employment for those working in the new companies, no doubt place among the weightier matters. Things being so, the innovations in corporate form and financial risk-reduction effectively lowered the bar for trusting others and cooperating, by removing significant parts of the risks involved. This meant that the level of trust that existed suddenly went further in terms of satisfying the threshold of cooperation. As such, it is not surprising that over time the East India companies grew to become the largest organizations known, aside from the national militaries and the supernational Christian churches.

We may also speculate that the experience gained from these new ventures seeded trust between those who had taken part. At any rate, trust grows (or withers) with repeated cooperation and observation. Presumably the risk-reducing advantages of these new organizational forms brought together many people who would not otherwise have collaborated, leading to new trust and new ventures as outgrowths of the first experiences. It is certainly common now for old colleagues to strike out together and found a new start-up. The seeds for these kinds of collaborative offshoots spread further afield than ever before with the help of the first modern companies in the

17th century. Of course, people had always done things with the people they already knew and trusted, but the new environment expanded these opportunities further, as larger companies brought together more and more people.

Those who might otherwise have been farmers or solitary craftsmen – working in realms of lesser cooperation – suddenly found themselves drawn to large and complex organizations, which expanded their social circles significantly. This socially expanding effect of corporate employment is certainly very familiar to almost everyone today – so much so, that the familiarity perhaps makes it difficult to appreciate its impact. But the contrast is massive between the fully grown company-based modern economy and the medieval economy where organizations were very small, and most were working the fields or small-time craftspeople.

As stock exchanges and company employment proliferated further, most prominently in the 19th century, the feedback loop of trust found new expressions. The ease of public share trading helped investors who had lost their trust in the venture to divest from the trade, whether that loss of trust was due to the investor's negative perception of the management quality and choices, or the outlook of the market. Nevertheless, the ability to sell lends an opportunity to cease the relationship between the shareholder and the company. If alternative employment is readily available, the same applies to the company's employees. As such the development of these institutions, and the vibrant economy they brought about, in its own way enabled an economic variant of the feedback loop of trust, of trusting, observing and adjusting behaviour to suit one's needs. The flexibility of the system afforded yet again a measure of risk-reduction by providing escapes from undesirable situations.

As the limited liability corporation became a widely and easily available form of organizing economic interest, it transformed the way people express themselves economically. Whatever the desired goal, from running a club, a dance school or a website with commercial dimensions, the various corporate forms provide the relevant framework of self-actualization to a very broad degree.

The rise of the modern corporation was further strengthened by the birth of modern accounting and banking practices. Sound accounting practices are essential in providing reliability and transparency on the actual performance of a company, and so are highly important for anyone investing in or otherwise relying on it. Being able to ascertain the health of a firm from its accounts is first and foremost a trust-enhancing tool. It is no surprise that accounting developed hand in hand with banking, because banks are among those with the keenest interest in using the information provided by accounting. Banking for its own part provided the necessary financing for profitable projects and ideas, thereby fostering economic development.

Another significant development, which coincided with the triumph of the modern business corporation, was the gradual end of the old merchant and craft guilds. The guilds had over time turned into rather insular institutions, having for example in many places made positions hereditary, and being in general against innovations in mass production to preserve and enhance the value of their own high artisanship – they had turned into closed-off, self-interested institutions extracting monopolistic profits and acting against the general public and consumer good. The dynamic new corporations open for anyone's investment that replaced them were an improvement in many respects.

Perhaps the most profound outcome of the virtuous circle of economic development was that collaboration became more profitable than it had previously been, for states and citizens alike. This encouraged productive behaviours over violent extraction.

Economic strength had always been essential for states' military success, but before the advent of economic growth wealth differences between nations had been fairly small. With sustained growth, wealthy and advanced nations could attain immense advantages over less developed nations, as evidenced by the European empires. Therefore, it became essential for any state wishing to remain competitive to focus on fostering economic growth. Domestically, this meant developing the institutions and infrastructure in place of the wasteful displays of wealth and might that had long been the staples of kings and emperors. The expansion of education and construction of canals, roads, railroads and the like provide concrete examples. On the high seas, the period was marked by the increased pacification of international shipping lanes by the European maritime powers, dramatically reducing piracy and thereby facilitating even more profitable trade. Overseas, the unfortunate side effect of economic competition was the capture of third countries – the colonies – to be used as raw-material sources and new markets to sell to.

Citizens of states enjoying the fruits of economic development may have made a positive distinction between their own governments, credibly focusing on developing the nation for the better (at least on occasion) economically, and foreign ones where rulers' self-interest more often manifested in extravagant palaces and other signs of personal enrichment at the expense of the people. This comparative view and the increasing wealth of the citizens themselves are likely to have lent the economically progressive states and their governments an extra measure of trust. More importantly, spreading economic security itself brought about security of the mind –

relieving the anxieties that accompany poverty. Put otherwise, those who are well off economically will have a more benign view of their circumstances and the world: in trust parlance, a more benevolent – more trusting – view of people and things. Hence, economic prosperity can help spread benevolence and trust across a society. The economic innovations and institutions pioneered since the renaissance were instrumental in achieving just that.

NEW POLITICAL AND LEGAL INSTITUTIONS

All these profound changes eventually found their culmination in the age of enlightenment during the 17th and 18th centuries. With the onset of the enlightenment human rights were conceived in the place of religious ordinances, and human sciences such as economics found individual forms separate from moral philosophy. At the same time, new ideas for politics and political rights arose, the realization of which in turn required new institutions.

Central to the new politics of the enlightenment was the apotheosis of democracy. And soon enough, instructed by the thinkers of the age, the first steps towards modern democratic governments and institutions were taken with the American and French revolutions. These revolutions were a starting point for a progressive series of reforms aiming to realize the enlightenment ideal of democracy and equal rights between citizens. Privileges of the nobility, such as tax exemptions, were stripped away. Slavery, although it was not practised in western Europe, was still ongoing in America and much of the rest of the world, until it was abolished by enlightenment ideals. Political rights were slowly expanded, first for a limited number of men, and gradually to everyone regardless of their background. In the 20th century women gained equal rights with men in practically every endeavour imaginable. As a consequence of these changes, people gained equal status before the law regardless of who they were. The authority and legitimacy of the state came to rest with the approval of the people.

In the course of this development new institutions such as parliaments and senates were established and often continued and expanded the work of the previous less representative and less active ones, like the estates general.

The unifying principle across all of these legal and institutional reforms was the reduction and equalization of power distances between people, the empowerment of the common people versus the aristocracy and, later on, the empowerment of women versus men. As we know, power

distance is a factor for trust and distrust, because distance implies opportunities for abuse and divergent interests in general. These equalizing
reforms reduced power distance, and thereby over time created grounds
for a more trusting society. Certainly, in the short term the reforms were
highly contentious and often accompanied by revolutions, but in the long
run likely created a positive impact.

New democratic regimes also predictably enhanced the functioning of
the trust feedback loop by making the processing and resolution of various
interests arising in the population their main business. Kings and governors
have always had to pay at least some measure of attention to their subjects'
wishes, but the democratic states with freedom of expression took this to
new heights. When the citizens' approval is the source of power, the system
tends to produce outcomes that generate approval from the citizens (for reasons right and wrong). As long as the interests of the citizens are not self-de-
structive, mutually exclusive or of an existential nature that makes yielding
impossible, the game of give and take that is party politics can continue to
function – and if the solutions provided yield net improvements in society's
happiness and quality of life, the result should also be growing trust.

Finally, the reforms in political and legal institutions since the enlightenment have often improved the transparency of governance and politics,
and reduced corruption across the public and private sectors alike. Once
again, if the citizens are better informed about the process of governance,
which should result from transparency, they are better able to align their
demands and expectations of the state, again with consequences that in
the long-term should be supportive of trust. With less corruption, they can
be more confident about the fairness of the treatment they receive, and
how their taxes are spent.

Free, fair, transparent and participatory governance and politics may
often seem contentious and divisive, but as long as the differences are
bridgeable, they provide fertile soil for the growth of trust.

INSTITUTIONS IN THE WEST AND IN THE SOVIET UNION

The institutions of knowledge, economy and politics have all undergone
massive evolutions in western countries since the renaissance. Change
is of course the norm over the centuries, no matter what. But a common
denominator with the changes we've been discussing is that, inspired
by new ideas since the renaissance, they all opened up institutions to

far wider input than before and became more responsive to it than their predecessors. In short, institutions became far more effective processors of information, economic incentives and political interests. The feedback loop of trust was allowed to function with an efficiency never before seen. This empowered the citizens and participants in these systems, which over time led to continued flourishing of trust in the west. The present demands for greater recognition among minority ethnic and sexual groups seem to appear in a continuum with these historical developments.

To be sure, this summary glosses over the many fits and stops, revolts and revolutions, that happened along the path to these more inclusive and representative institutions. In large part the developments were driven by evolving ideological positions and attendant demands for reform. When the demands were not met fast enough or in an adequate manner, distrust eventually broke into outright rebellion.

We see evidence of the proclaimed triumph of trust in the generally high levels of interpersonal and generalized trust in the western countries, the vitality of civil societies and the vibrancy of economic and intellectual organizations. As trust is the essential ingredient of cooperation, it is no surprise that with the advent of the new institutions the west was able to create international business corporations with personnel numbers and sophistication rivalling those of armies and religious orders. Likewise, the political reforms brought with them mass movements, political parties and interest groups of every kind. In short, growing trust enabled growing cooperation across society, which was the backbone of improving social conditions at home and a fundamental source of western advantage during its years of global ascendancy.

Against this backdrop we can again return to the Soviet experience. While western institutions over time from the renaissance became more responsive to society's needs, the Soviet state did the exact opposite and effectively shut down the trust feedback loop. Freedom of expression, never a Russian forte to begin with, was further curtailed. Politically, there was only the communist option available. For a while the Soviet Union managed to advance economically by applying scientific and technological innovations. But suppressing the market mechanisms removed the essential price signals and motivating incentives from the economy, and stagnated it. In the process trust eroded, and once it was lost decisively enough, the whole system finally collapsed on itself.

The success of the open western institutions contrasts well with the Soviet counterexample and highlights their role in building trust in society.

The core issue from a trust perspective is to create institutions able to process information and react constructively to the needs that arise. Institutions such as these empower their constituent citizens and stakeholders, offer opportunities for improvement and thereby create trust. Keeping all this in mind, the statistics of trust decline in recent decades seem especially worrying, and raise a question about the health of our institutions today.

TRUST, FREEDOM AND KNOWLEDGE

As we've seen, by providing a setting for the functioning of the trust feedback loop, the institutions of a free society can help build trust. The operations of the trusting facility shepherd our ability to take new information into account and cooperate to create prosperity, knowledge and wellbeing. All of this seems to imply the potential existence of a virtuous circle whereby institutions allowing freedom of expression and action may help build trust over the long run, which would in turn enable us to weigh different viewpoints and new data more openly than before, also improving trust among those holding the previously marginalized views.

To some extent this appears supported by the record of history – at least since the medieval times there has been a general trend towards more freedom, more trust and a greater ability to engage with all sorts of information, and the empowerment of various groups within society. Yet it is also clear that many issues remain controversial and difficult if not impossible to have a dispassionate or civilized discussion about. The declines in trust seen in statistics help explain why the recent decades have seen divisions heating up, resulting from ever more divergent worldviews and interests.

A positive implication of all this is that there may be much to be won in terms of healing the present polarizations if we can find a way to build more trust in society. Before digging deep into an analysis of the problems and solutions the west faces, let us conclude our discussion about the interplay of trust and knowledge in a free society, which serves to ground the subsequent analysis of contemporary issues.

In free societies the importance of trust is pronounced for several reasons: some degree of it is necessary for the peaceful coordination of the many diverse and often to some degree mutually exclusive interests that can be freely promoted. Whether in private organizations or in the political forum, interests need to be aligned without resorting to force and coercion. In the process of interest coordination, we need to take into account the multitude of views present in the populace if we hope to maintain a free and just society. Trust helps reconcile differences and lend the benefit of doubt to others' claims.

Contemporary free societies are furthermore marked by extensive power-sharing in many forms. Voting and other political rights, broad economic redistribution policies, education and free social services, equality before the law and so on level out the playing field and spread power and opportunities across society, evening social circumstances to some extent. This has the practical impact of reducing power distances among people, which is conducive to trust. In other words, free and equal societies generate trust not only by allowing the trust feedback loop to operate, but also by limiting excessive power distances between people.

Of course, we must note that too much equalizing between people has an opposite effect, as underscored by the exodus of people following the institution of excessive wealth taxes by the socialist President Hollande in France in 2012. People voted with their feet in response, and soon after the measure was dropped.

In contrast with free and relatively equal societies, those with fewer freedoms and gross inequalities can be expected to be less trustful. In other words where the operating of the trust feedback loop is obstructed and power distances are greater, trust is bound to be scarce. In the absence of trust, societies like this have to employ more coercion and rougher methods to ensure cooperation and coordination. The example of the Soviet Union, and authoritarian regimes in general, corroborates this view.

In one way or another, behaviours in constrained circumstances will be different from what they would be in an environment of full freedom. The most obvious examples can be summoned from the most extreme situations of compulsion, such as imprisonment or slavery. When one's actions and circumstances are fully controlled by others, trust plays no part in the relationship and the situation is likely such that one would do everything to escape from it. Often these sorts of cases represent an effectively antagonistic relationship between the individual and the state and its representatives, an antithesis of trust. Naturally every society requires its members to adhere to some set of rules, and then enforces those rules. But in free societies these rules tend to be less limiting, and their enforcement more humane and fairer.

As a consequence of governing at the people's consent, free societies tend to be, by necessity as much as by built-in ethos, relatively open-handed with information and transparent about the functioning of many key institutions. These features have historically lent further support to trust in such societies. Provision of information services like public libraries, coupled with greater transparency of governance in general, naturally empower citizens in their dealings with each other, and with the state, generating trust.

Democracy as a form of governance implies by definition a measure of trust among citizens, because each is prepared to surrender among the rest an equivalent opportunity to influence the matters of state and society. With this act the people of a democratic state implicitly admit that their fellow citizens may have claims and views equivalent in importance and worth to their own. Whether this idea has arisen from humane enlightenment or successfully prosecuted self-interest of the previously powerless, it represents a remarkable investment of trust among the people. Considering that evidence of the self-serving nature of humankind has never been in short supply, and that in every state groups and individuals will jostle to influence affairs to improve their own relative positions, democracy springs from a remarkable act of courage and good faith.

Whereas free societies tend to be marked by relative openness, power-sharing and representative governance, non-free societies tend to be ruled by a group that is suspicious and distrustful of the rest and uses its powers to forcibly maintain its superior position – a form of rule most of the time repaid with equally strong distrust from the rest of the populace.

Freedom of thought and action are especially relevant in the pursuit of new knowledge. Trust is necessary for the operation of the various institutions and interpersonal cooperation at the very base of contemporary knowledge production. Such institutions certainly can and do exist in low-trust environments; but they are enhanced in their function by the presence of high trust. This view, espoused by the philosopher John Hardwig, is corroborated by empirical evidence in various contexts.[40]

A closed society enforcing strict ideological boundaries on debate and research tacitly admits that there exist views and knowledge that are incompatible with or dangerous to the existence of such an order. In effect, just as some people might hesitate to admit things contrary to their own interests, so too with leaders, parties and states. When we think of ideologies and totalitarian regimes alike, they often seek to impose very strict values, interpretations or social structures. From a trust perspective we may assume these efforts will fail sooner or later, as the strict norms inevitably

---

40   For example: Trust and Innovation: Evidence from CEOs' Early-life Experience. Kong, Dongmin; Zhao, Ying; Liu, Shasha. *Journal of Corporate Finance*, volume 69, August 2021. Mediation Effects of Trust and Contracts on Knowledge-sharing and Product Innovation: Evidence from the European Machine Tool Industry. Charterina, Jon; Landeta, Jon; Basterretxea, Imanol. *European Journal of Innovation Management*, 2018.

come into conflict with changing circumstances and the multidimensional nature of life and humanity. Imposing boundaries on acceptable speech and action effectively shuts down information flow in society and disrupts the feedback loop of the trust adjustment process, leading to its eventual collapse.

A rough analogy to the free flow of information and the operations of the trust feedback loop can be found in the sphere of economics. A generally held observation from basic economics is that the greater and more balanced the number of buyers and sellers for a given product in a freely operating market, the closer the price comes to the "correct" value and the smoother the trading. When buying or selling, producing or consuming are constrained in some artificial fashion, suboptimal outcomes tend to follow.

A classic example of a disequilibrium in the stock market illustrates the issue perfectly. If buyers for a share disappear, for whatever reason, the consequence will be that the price of the asset will collapse as the number of people wanting to sell the share vastly outnumbers those willing to buy. In this case the sellers are forced to dramatically drop the asking price to find interested buyers. The resulting crash in the price of the share in this circumstance might have nothing to do with the underlying profitability or outlook of the company itself. This is common in times of stock market panics, but the same dynamics can surface across the economy, wherever there is buying and selling going on. The other side of the phenomenon can be seen when the number of willing buyers greatly exceeds those looking to sell, without any material change in the prospects of the company, leading to quickly rising prices. In both of these situations the price of the share tends to become unmoored from the actual economic fundamentals such as the performance of the company. In normal balanced trading circumstances with a good number of buyers and sellers the price tends to converge accurately with the underlying fundamentals of value and future outlook. These are common features of demand, supply and price discovery.

The analogy here is that the buyers and sellers correspond to the multitude of opinions society allows expression of. Allowing many voices leads to a more nuanced account of the varied interests of the populace, whereas limitations give rise to disequilibriums not unlike the price distortions in the market when one party is excessively benefiting at the expense of others. As such, totalizing ideologies or political movements are an attempt to make permanent some narrowly favourable set of circumstances in the marketplace of thought, which would not exist with balanced trading of ideas. So we could perceive a similarity between limitations of production (such as in a monopoly) and limitations of thought (such as in a totalitarian ideology); both lead to overall welfare below potential, to the excess benefit of some privileged group.

Indeed, free markets are in many ways analogous to free speech. Real-life experience has shown both need some regulation to avoid abuse and extreme outcomes; and the question of where to set the limits requires constant debate and deliberation. More fundamentally it is difficult to see how a free society with free speech and thought could exist without a free economy or the free ability to invest one's efforts and money. Both also rely on and benefit from trust to reach their full potential.

Of course, the analogy is rough and applies only up to a point; as long as everyone follows good practices, there appears to be little downside to a profusion of participants in the markets, with different perspectives on the value of items traded. In the space of trust and society, a proliferation of values, skills, income inequalities, identities and competing groups – all following the rule of law – might on the other hand lead to a disintegration of trust. This would seem like a potential consequence when trust is constructed from commonalities among the dimensions of ability, benevolence and integrity. Yet the operating of the trust process, with its trust-related observations relying on availability of information, and consequent adjustments of cooperation relying on freedom of action, will function best when everyone can freely express their ideas and selves in an authentic and genuine manner without fear or censure.

Emotions are found at the bottom of our rational behaviour and capacity for learning in general. Various biases in information processing are employed to manage our self-trust, and thus colour the way we select and react to new information. When it comes to our concept of knowledge, how we create and engage with new ideas is largely mediated by our capacity for trust. We might hypothesize that the conscious and unconscious emotional cues guiding our learning also modulate the biases we have, and from there our higher-level trust and ways of learning and engaging with information. Hence the insights about emotions and trust in learning together point us towards a new biologically grounded understanding and theory of knowledge.

The working of our trusting facility lends us a natural disposition towards arguments we find beneficial for ourselves, and in alignment with our values and standards of knowledge and behaviour. This means trust, although it is necessary for new knowledge, paradoxically also guides us towards the already known and accepted and leaves us hesitant about things contradictory to our existing benefit or values. This limitation is unfortunate, but the ways trust seems to interact with knowledge readily align with the record of history and common understanding of human behaviour. A more nuanced and comprehensive understanding of how trust and information interact should be a boon for our capacity to overcome difficulties in mutual comprehension.

A trust-based theory of knowledge also seems able to bridge the gap between traditional concepts of knowledge and the postmodern perspectivist theories, even providing vindication for them by showing how we are led to emphasize and accept different knowledge. The greatest lesson is surely the understanding of how we may naturally come to different points of view, each often representing an aspect of a greater whole, and that each may have merit.

TRUST AND SOCIAL CAPITAL

Social capital is a term commonly used in public discussion, mostly as a broad reference to various enabling social structures: family networks, commonly held values, work and leisure groups and so on – in general anything helping us cooperate, either as individuals or as members of larger groups. The want of precision in the everyday use of the concept has naturally led to its widespread use in all sorts of contexts, leaving the term in a bit of a haze. This conceptual mist also exists on the academic side of the discussion. Perhaps as an outcome of the many broad and loose definitions, social capital is thought to be important for many reasons, and in many different circumstances.

At the very roots of the concept's development, in a 1916 formulation social capital was used to describe the goodwill, mutual sympathy and social intercourse that make for flourishing and successful communities.[41] In the 1960s Jane Jacobs referred to the term while articulating the importance of networks and social connections in the local governance of great cities and their neighbourhoods.[42] The Harvard professor and political scientist Robert Putnam described social capital broadly, as "The social connections and the attendant norms and trust, which enable the partici-

---

41   The Rural School Community Center. Hanifan, L. J. *The Annals of the American Academy of Political and Social Science*, September, 1916, Vol. 67, New Possibilities in Education.
42   *The Death and Life of Great American Cities*. Jacobs, Jane. Random House, 1961.

pants to act together more effectively to pursue shared objectives".[43] John Brehm and Wendy Rahn on the other hand saw social capital as "the web of cooperative relationships between citizens that facilitates the resolution of collective action problems".[44] The main difference from Putnam's definition is the focus on relationships and problem solving and the exclusion of norms and trust. These definitions emphasizing social connections, capacity for collective action, trust and norms as the basis of social capital originate from the 1990s and, as can be expected, the number of definitions has multiplied since then.

The definitions all orbit the centre of gravity that is society itself. This is what gives the concept its importance. For example, Francis Fukuyama, who thought social capital an informal norm promoting cooperation, saw it as the essential foundation upholding stable liberal democracy.[45] Social capital is seen as the key ingredient for successful communities, whether at the level of the local community or the federal state. This is agnostic of the positive or negative connotations; even a criminal gang is thought to manifest a type of social capital, which just happens to be bad for the wider society. The concept has also been widely studied in business and economics. As an example, it is seen to contribute to the creation of the intellectual capital that powers economic development. All in all there can be no doubt that the stakes are high and the topics major when we are talking about social capital and its associated benefits. It is also noteworthy, and very much as expected, that the perceived benefits of social capital are highly similar to those articulated for trust. Trust is often claimed as a source, a part of or a consequence of social capital.

Out of the mist of definitions Janine Nahapiet and Sumantra Ghoshal, two London-based researchers, condensed three dimensions to group the core characteristics of social capital: structural, cognitive and relational. As with everything concerning social capital, the categories are broad, with varying definitions in different sources, and of course have considerable interrelations. In the article introducing the three-dimensional approach Nahapiet and Ghoshal focused on how social capital supports the creation of intellectual capital. Despite the cerebral context, their categorization

---

43   *Making Democracy Work. Civic traditions in modern Italy.* Putnam, Robert. Princeton University Press, 1994.
44   Individual-Level Evidence for the Causes and Consequences of Social Capital. Brehm, John; Rahm, Wendy, *American Journal of Political Science* Vol. 41, No. 3, July 1997.
45   Social capital, civil society and development. Fukuyama, Francis. *Third World Quarterly* 22, February 2001.

has gained wider support and helps us refine our understanding of both social capital and more importantly trust itself, as will be demonstrated in the following pages.[46]

STRUCTURAL	COGNITIVE	RELATIONAL
Social structure	Shared understandings	Nature and quality of relationships
• Network ties and configuration • Roles, rules, precedents, and procedures • Appropriable organizations	• Shared language,codes, and narratives • Shared values, attitudes, and beliefs • Shared goals, purpose, and vision	• Trust and trustworthiness • Norms and sanctions • Obligations and expectations • Identity and identification

Dimensions of social capital, adapted from Janine Nahapiet & Sumantra Ghoshal and Tristan Claridge at www.socialcapitalresearch.com.[47]

The *structural dimension* refers to perhaps the most tangible and easily quantifiable aspects of social capital. Network ties represent the contacts and connections in the system, whether looking at an individual person and their circle of friends and acquaintances, or at the level of the entire system with its universe of interactions. The importance of network ties can be confirmed with a quick bit of self-reflection: who you know affects what you know, often when you know and what kind of referrals, chances and opportunities come your way. This corresponds perhaps most closely to the common understanding of social capital in general. Network configuration on the other hand is about the density, connectivity and hierarchy of the network ties, all areas of importance when analyzing the functionality of the given system. Appropriable organization may sound curious. And indeed, it might not be the first thing to come to mind when thinking about social capital. It refers to the existence of organizations enabling the development and transferability of social capital between one setting and another. An obvious example here is the

46   Social Capital, Intellectual Capital and the Organizational Advantage. Nahapiet, Janine; Ghoshal, Sumantra. *Academy of Management Review*, 1998, Vol. 23
47   www.socialcapitalresearch.com/structural-cognitive-relational-social-capital

university. As a side effect of studying, one probably develops numerous new friendships and connections, many of whom are highly valuable in contexts other than the partying that can be a central university activity. The result is thus more than the degree that validates one as a respectable member of society worth employing elsewhere. Thus, the institution of study produces social capital that is transferable between time and place, settings and organizations.

Cognitive social capital is divided into shared language and narratives, shared values, attitudes and beliefs, and finally shared goals, purpose and vision. The argument of Nahapiet and Ghoshal essentially boils down to the fact that unless we understand each other, in which common language and shared concepts offer substantial assistance, creating social capital is very difficult. That seems a fair claim. Without shared values and beliefs we are unlikely to have shared goals, purpose and vision. Without shared goals, we are more likely to be in disagreement and competition, rather than in cooperation. All views very much understandable.

The relational dimension of social capital consists of trust, norms, obligations and identification.[48] If the structural dimension addresses the most readily quantifiable parts of the phenomenon, the relational dimension may be thought to reflect the more qualitative forms of social capital. In practice this means the motivation behind the formation and content of the network ties within the system under observation. Trust is seen as the foundation for cooperation and, thus by promoting engagement, as an essential component of social capital. Norms for their part represent social (rather than individual) control of acceptable activities. By guiding activities, norms also affect how social capital manifests. Obligations and expectations represent mutual "credit" between people, promises of and expectations about behaviour. Though separated in this context from trust, it is clear the two go hand in hand. Finally, identification, as in seeing oneself as part of some group, generates social capital by encouraging sharing, learning and creation within the reference group. The presence of distinct identities may also act as a barrier between different groups.

From the theories and definitions of social capital, including those covered here, it is difficult to differentiate between social capital itself and what causes it. Most often these two are happily mixed. If social capital refers in general to social connections and capacity for collective

---

48   Social Capital, Intellectual Capital and the Organizational Advantage. Nahapiet, Janine; Ghoshal, Sumantra. *Academy of Management Review*, 1998, Volume 23.

action, does it mean that more or less everything that affects our sociability can be thought of as a source of social capital? So it seems. Indeed, as the website socialcapitalresearch.com puts it: "The sources of social capital potentially relate to virtually every aspect of human existence." The site also provides a handy list of some commonly cited factors for social capital, replicated here:[49]

EXAMPLES OF COMMONLY CITED SOURCES OF SOCIAL CAPITAL

- History and culture
- Economic inequalities and social class
- Ethnic and social heterogeneity
- Social structures and hierarchy
- Legal and law enforcement systems
- Economic and political systems including formalized institutional relationships and structures
- Labour market trends
- Size and nature of the Welfare State
- The strength and characteristics of civil society
- Scale of social organisa,tions
- The built environment including transport and urban design
- Residential mobility
- Television and digital technologies
- The farnily
- Education
- Individual values and beliefs
- Religion and religious organisation

SOURCE: Tristan Claridge, www.socialcapitalresearch.com

Everything and anything from history and culture to the family and digital technologies can influence social capital. Moreover, it is easy to argue the case for the items on the list. These things really do affect how people conduct their lives and interact with others. Not quite content with the extent of the list, the article proceeds to complement it by adding thoughts around biology, psychology and morality as even deeper sources.

---

49   www.socialcapitalresearch.com/sources-of-social-capital

The problem is, as long as almost anything can explain social capital, establishing cause and effect will be difficult. And without a clear view of causality, functional real-life tools to nurture the benefits associated with social capital remain out of reach.

TRUST AS THE FUNDAMENTAL SOURCE OF SOCIAL CAPITAL

Given the great tradition of competing definitions for social capital, and the topic's high relevance for this treatise on trust, let's add a pinch of flavour and stir the pot once more.

I propose an interpretation of the relationship between trust and social capital, which should clarify and alleviate the problems of cause and effect, making social capital and its benefits more tractable. Rather than being part of social capital, the central claim here is that trust is the primary cause of social capital, and the accumulated social capital with its connections, institutions and capacity for collective action may be seen as the product of trust. The forms of social capital manifested are dependent on the level and types of trust present in a society. We shall proceed to substantiate these claims by reviewing the relationships between trust and its antecedents as we understand them, and how the various definitions of social capital tie into our framework of trust. Ultimately this examination should help us generate a more practical understanding of how further trust can be built, and as a consequence how social capital can be deepened.

First, let us review the three dimensions of social capital expounded by Nahapiet and Ghoshal in light of our understanding of trust and its antecedents. We find that they can easily be interpreted through our ABI framework. The structural dimension with its network ties and configuration of connections between people can quite obviously be thought of as outcomes and forms of cooperation, and therefore something largely growing from trust, which is most of the time an absolute necessity for voluntary cooperation and thus a condition for many such network ties. The other part of the structural dimension of social capital is "rules, roles, precedents and procedures". This aspect of social capital seems quite at home under the integrity heading of our trust framework, with its focus on values and behavioural standards. It is also easy to imagine that knowledge of rules, roles and procedures may be a necessary part of the ability to fulfil trust-related promises, therefore showing up in that part of the trust assessment as well.

In the cognitive part of Nahapiet and Ghoshal's grouping we find shared languages, codes and narratives. The capacity for mutual understanding afforded by shared language is clearly necessary for cooperation, so is perhaps the most fundamental ability consideration in trust. Codes or narratives can be thought of as more finely grained versions of the fundamental requirement of communication in cooperation. Yet narratives shape and are shaped by the values and worldviews we hold, linking them to some extent to the value-based integrity dimension of trust assessments. Shared values, attitudes and beliefs, another part of Nahapiet and Ghoshal's cognitive dimension of social capital, are then full-on components of the integrity part of trust. Finally, there are shared goals, purpose and vision. These can relate to anything from values strived for to material prosperity (the creation or redistribution of it) yearned for and political movements fought for. As such they might be thought to play out in both the integrity and benevolence parts of trust.

The third and final part of Nahapiet and Ghoshal's framework, the relational dimension of social capital, has components going nearly every way within our concept of trust. First, they thought trust itself was a part of the relational dimension of social capital. We would argue that here is a misconception of causality, and that social capital is effectively built from trust, not that trust is a part of social capital. To be frank, the picture is a bit more nuanced than that, which we will cover shortly. Norms and sanctions here go directly under integrity. One is not liable to trust another who does not abide by the same basic norms or who fails to act within the confines of the law one approves of. Obligations and expectations are in turn again seen to depict trust itself in many ways, which, as we recall, has an element of expectation. As the last part we have identity and identification, which may initially seem a curious subject to place within the trust framework. Identity is obviously something that can be based on things such as values and worldview, vocation and professional interests or perhaps geographical location and ethnicity. What all these have in common is that they construct a dividing line between something that is considered a part of the self, and the rest that is not included. As such identity and identification as sources of social capital can be thought to channel into trust and, from there, social capital, by influencing assessments of integrity (recall the impact of values and behaviour on trust) and benevolence (who is friendly and good for me – probably someone who shares identity and identification with me).

Here we must pause to acknowledge reality. Although the preceding paragraphs and much of the text throughout this book might imply it, we do not make trust assessments on the virginal canvas of a tabula rasa. Instead we have grown up in certain countries, in certain cultures, in certain families, all of which, and much more, affect our assessments about who and what to trust. The factors affecting our trust evaluations are highly dependent on and affected by the environments we grow up in. Trust and the social capital growing out of it shape the present and the future society, but are themselves coloured by the past. So, the future is affected by the past. Not a radical idea in itself, but worth stressing once again.

The influence of the past in the present is prominently on display in the "sources of social capital" table we saw in the previous chapter. Family, education, religion, various institutions and so on were identified as sources of social capital. My argument is that these, and many other things on the list, are indeed sources of social capital, but in a broader sense than is commonly understood. While these things teach and foster cooperation by bringing people together through example and custom, they also form the context and environment impacting our trust assessments. These pre-trust contextual factors are a key addition to our unfolding model of trust and social capital.

Coming back to the list of sources of social capital, many items are simultaneously not only contextual or environmental factors, but clearly also outcomes of trust and social capital. We are born into our countries, which already have their histories and cultures (claimed sources of social capital); yet the very same histories and cultures pre-dispose people and nations to certain ways of trusting and guide the present creation of new ways of being and relating, and thus responses to various challenges as they arise – the cultural and political evolution of a nation.

Again, the past affects the present, which builds the future. Yet this perspective is often missing from formulations of trust and social capital, at least explicitly.

The preceding discussion can be concretized into a more complete picture of the dynamics between the society at large, trust and its outcome social capital. Every unit of evaluation, whether an individual, society or a state, has some set of pre-existing circumstances forming the context or environment for cooperation and trust decisions – its history and all it entails. Trust for its part plays the central role in coordinating behaviour and actions with or towards others, manifesting in different forms of organizational and social being. These fruits of trust-based cooperation show up concretely as social capital, as the organizations of civil society, entrepreneurial networks and the endless number of ways people come together. Or, in a negative case, in breaking down of various ties. The evolving forms of cooperation in turn form a new scene for new trust decisions, returning the cycle to its beginning.

The cycle of trust and social outcomes is presented in the below chart. The contextual factors form the environment for trust, which in turn affects the extent of cooperation in society.

This shows that social capital resulting from trust is split into three levels. First we have the voluntary human connections and civil society. Next, the formal institutions of the state, including the law and the judicial system, and the economy. Finally, we have the idea space of goals, narratives and values and politics. This is of course a relatively arbitrary grouping, and in practice all are tightly interconnected, rather than separate monolithic blocks. And given the myriad and evolving forms of

TRUST, SOCIAL CAPITAL AND SOCIAL DEVELOPMENT

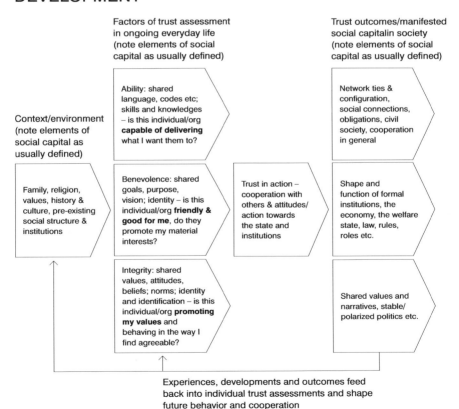

Factors of trust assessment in ongoing everyday life (note elements of social capital as usually defined)

Trust outcomes/manifested social capitalin society (note elements of social capital as usually defined)

Context/environment (note elements of social capital as usually defined)

Ability: shared language, codes etc; skills and knowledges – is this individual/org **capable of delivering** what I want them to?

Network ties & configuration, social connections, obligations, civil society, cooperation in general

Family, religion, values, history & culture, pre-existing social structure & institutions

Benevolence: shared goals, purpose, vision; identity – is this individual/org **friendly & good for me**, do they promote my material interests?

Trust in action – cooperation with others & attitudes/ action towards the state and institutions

Shape and function of formal institutions, the economy, the welfare state, law, rules, roles etc.

Integrity: shared values, attitudes, beliefs; norms; identity and identification – is this individual/org **promoting my values** and behaving in the way I find agreeable?

Shared values and narratives, stable/ polarized politics etc.

Experiences, developments and outcomes feed back into individual trust assessments and shape future behavior and cooperation

cooperation, the dimensions listed are not exhaustive. Note that the many items variously associated with social capital as its sources, hallmarks or outcomes can be found on different parts of the chart. What we bring to the table here is a dynamic causal description of the development of social capital, based on trust.

Looking at this framework we can note that the pre-trust contextual environment represents the existing history and reality – something we cannot change. This existing environment conditions our perceptions of the world, shapes the values we hold (which are not immutable, however) and the standards of behaviour we assume as normal, also influencing our personal interests. From this starting point, trust reflects our relationship to other people, society and state with its institutions, with our assessment of them guiding our behaviour in the present and the future. The actions undertaken in the present recreate the world, which turns into the new context for new trust assessments in the future.

As an example, we may think of climate activists. They perceive a threat to the climate, which remains unaddressed by the present level of action, and seek to alter the course of our societies to mitigate the threat. To effect the necessary actions they collaborate with others who share their worries, and thereby align on important trust-central values and perceived mutual interests. The original drive for action derives from distrust of the state and other actors and their efforts to tackle the perceived problem. Trust in others who share the worries then forms the basis for collective action. It is thereby not just trust, but also the lack of it, which can motivate cooperation. By collaborating and taking action they create new social capital in the form of new networks and organizations, and inevitably alter society's institutions, values and narratives.

Other similar examples include anti-immigration parties concerned with the preservation of their own cultures and communities, and the sexual rights movements so successful in recent decades. All of these movements share similarities in the way they perceive threats or problems creating severe distrust in the status quo, and mobilize with like-minded people to effect change. Values, shared interests and identities act through trust and result in new forms of social capital shaping and making communities.

The impact trust has on cooperation is not a black-and-white, yes-or-no thing, but an issue of a million shades of grey. On an individual level low or uncertain trust might often manifest as a limited interaction, instead of a full-blown no. Then over time, depending on the outcome, the cooperation might be deepened or cut short. Think of the growth of a new friendship, with its increasing levels of trust and mutual reliance. Across the whole society this means that even at the lowest levels of trust there will of course always be some cooperation, but that it will be more limited than in circumstances of high trust. In between we find gradual development showing up in a million ways, in the prevalence of social clubs, sports associations, political groups and the like. An essential regulating factor is the extent to which the legal system and the powers governing a given country actually allow for such activities, which are themselves perhaps causes and expressions of the generalized trust present in the country. Nor can we forget the most indispensable support sustaining the development of any nation, its people and organizations – namely internal peace and stability. Certainly, companies and voluntary associations thrive in the trusting stability of peace, not under the duress of chaos and war. At the same time, it is also trust that helps maintain stability, and without a necessary level of trust a country can fall into chaos and civil strife. What all this means is that trust brings about a sliding scale of interactions; and the lack of it can also seed cooperation, as happens at the birth of revolutionary movements. And where trust appears, so does social capital, as its more tangible expression.

Nearly everything worthwhile in life is achieved in concert with other people. The banquet of social life nourishes us with play, partnership and love. Connecting with others is an intrinsic good, towards which trust paves the way. At work we collaborate with others to produce the material resources we need. Trust is grease in the wheels of the economy, enriching the teamwork and specialization we depend on. In the realm of politics, we negotiate our way in the world with others based on our values and interests. In all of these activities we join with others and form clubs, associations, teams, companies and political parties to achieve our desired ends. These organizations and their scope and functioning in turn reflect our collective capacity for action, and the degree to which we find common interests with other people. Given that so many valuable things are achieved together, and that these actions often yield external benefits to the rest of society, it makes sense to promote the creation of trust and social capital.

Deeper and more extensive trust in society allows for more finely grained forms of cooperation to appear, lifting social capital to greater heights. Manifestations of high trust and social capital include thriving civil society, a vital economic sphere and well-functioning institutions of governance that are appreciated and respected by the citizens. Most importantly, high trust and social capital help keep a society happy and internally stable. This might explain why the countries with the highest trust scores tend to sit on top of rankings of wellbeing and success.

The features of trust and social capital also allow us to hypothesize about why democratic forms of government have historically started small, whether in ancient Athens, republican Rome or the maritime republics of renaissance Italy. These were small tightly knit populations who managed to transcend their larger contemporaries in artistic and scientific achievements, and in economic and military performance. The reasons for their success were certainly many, but it must be noted that they were critically bolstered by an environment far better suited for the flourishing of trust and social capital than that found in larger rivals such as the monarchic Persian empire of Xerxes. These early democracies had a strong sense of community and a culture fostering strong fellow-feeling, as well as relative economic sophistication with its attendant material wellbeing, which also helped equip these communities militarily. These factors together may have made power-sharing arrangements far more palatable, and thus realistic propositions. When there is strong internal alignment and high trust within a community, allowing differences of opinion and perspective becomes less divisive and daunting. Indeed, evidence shows that proto-democratic and communal forms of governance were common in smaller tribal societies – for example, among the various Germanic groups outside the borders of the Roman empire. Of course, there were many small tribes, poleis and groups in the ancient world, and most did not develop into Athens, Rome or anything close. The argument here is that the small size of the community is not by itself a condition for success and the development of trust or democracy, but it certainly helps, because upholding common values, standards of behaviour and feelings of mutual benevolence tends to be much easier for a small community than for one that is larger in population and geographically more spread out. Perhaps a key challenge for a growing community is to maintain trust and thus avoid splintering and breakdown. In the absence of supporting trust, imperial coercion by military power seems to be a common, unattractive, alternative.

As trust is about willingness to cooperate, it is of course an indispensable aid for any common cause or project undertaken by free will – all such efforts by definition rely on cooperation. In collective endeavours a smaller community may have a relative advantage over a larger one because its population, being fewer people in a smaller area, means it is likely to be more cohesive thanks to the closeness inherent in its dimensions. Here we assume the physical closeness will be replicated in the values and standards of behaviour held, as well as in mutual feelings of benevolence among the closer-knit group who likely belong to the same tribe or nation. Given the close proximity of a small group, the transmission of information, values and worldviews would likely be faster and remain more aligned than in a larger, more spread out and more heterogenous group. These things potentially empower smaller groups with higher trust and higher relative capacity for cooperation, compared with larger units. While this might have been true among tribes and nascent nations of the ancient world, it applies just the same today – for example, in the workplace. It is a common observation that small close-knit high-trust teams can often achieve excellence and rapid results in a manner that is impossible for larger groups. The key here is that although the larger group tends to have advantages in many areas thanks to its size (say, the number of soldiers in its army), the smaller one can have its own benefits too, in potentially higher trust and easier coordination for example. In a contest between two groups these are of course but some of the variables in play, and the final result tends to depend on the interplay of multiple factors.

The role of trust in economic development

"Virtually every commercial transaction has within itself an element of trust, certainly any transaction conducted over a period of time. It can be plausibly argued that much of the economic backwardness in the world can be explained by the lack of mutual confidence."

KENNETH ARROW, ECONOMIST AND NOBELIST[50]

---

50   Arrow won the Nobel memorial prize in economic sciences in 1972, together with John Hicks. The quote is from the article "Gifts and Exchanges", published in *Philosophy & Public Affairs*, Volume 1, No. 4, 1972.

WHETHER YOU'RE BUYING a book online or getting hired for a new job, almost all transactions in the sphere of economy are fundamentally questions of trust. One can hardly have a thriving one-person economy. And so, you have to act in concert with others to fulfil your economic interests. In practice, however, it is not a given that you are ready to provide your money and payment details to some unknown company over a website in return for a promise of a product you want at the time you specify. Taking the leap and offering your sensitive information is an act of trust, just as hiring a new employee is. You are acting in the expectation, trust, that you will not get fooled, scammed or worse. If the element of trust in these examples is self-evident, so is the fact that to be able to perform acts like these is absolutely essential for the functioning of the economy and society at large.

But how does trust really affect economic activity and conversely how does economic activity affect trust, and what are the implications of these and other key questions in the area? This is where we will be heading next in our quest to understand trust.

HOW ECONOMISTS APPROACH TRUST – A HELICOPTER VIEW

Although the value of trust was understood early on in the field of economics, it was long considered too nebulous and, to make things worse, difficult to approach empirically. This in turn led to a relative paucity of attention on the subject. With the development of new research methods and data sources, such as experimental economics and a broader array of social surveys, these troubles have started to yield, and since the turn of the millennium both empirical and theoretical understandings of the subject have progressed considerably.[51]

Before turning to issues of trust, let us consider briefly how economists view economic output and growth itself, and where these wonderful things come from. Economic output means all the material and immaterial things, like the physical computer and the software this text is written with, that we produce through our efforts, aided by the tools and machines we've designed. Economic growth refers to the typically annually calculated

---

51   Trust, Growth and Well-being: New Evidence and Policy Implications. Alhgan, Yann; and Cahuc, Pierre. *IZA DP* No. 7464, June, 2013.

increase in the productivity of our efforts. The importance of economic growth stems from the simple fact that it has driven dramatic rises in living standards across the globe. Being able to generate more and more outputs from our limited resources has made us better off in nearly every way imaginable. The benefits are not limited to the physical sphere of life. The material wellbeing springing from economic development has no doubt strongly contributed to the internal peace and stability of our societies and sponsored the flourishing of art and culture.

To be clear, the underlying assumption throughout this book is that we should be interested in maintaining and developing our material wellbeing, buttressed by the process of economic progress, while at the same time being mindful of the limitations imposed by climate change and the natural world.

The question of how to formally describe economic growth was prominently addressed by Robert Solow in the 1950s, and his neoclassical growth model can be seen as the foundation upon which the current models of economic growth are built. The basic logic of the model is very simple: economic output is the fruit of human labour and the capital stock enabling the production, both affected by the technologies available. Economic growth results from an increase in the inputs of labour or capital, or from technological progress enabling more efficient utilization of the inputs. Savings accumulate capital that can in turn be invested in production-enabling machinery. The development of new technologies provides new ways to use the resources available. Likewise, education can improve the productivity of labour, and therefore drive increases in economic output. However, the Solow model does not itself explain what ultimately drives change in inputs like savings or the labour force, or the development of new technologies. These weaknesses are what more recent economic growth models have addressed by considering more deeply the nature of innovation and the drivers of (or hindrances to) both capital investments and technological development.[52] Population growth adding to the supply of human labour cannot perpetually sustain productivity growth by itself. Similarly, the marginal productivity of new factories and other physical manifestations of capital drops off in the absence of new demand and innovations – it doesn't pay to build a new production site if the existing ones aren't already fully used. Therefore, in the long run it is the development of new science, new ideas, new technologies and new creations springing from them that undergirds the continued growth of productivity and economic prosperity.

---

52   A Contribution to the Theory of Economic Growth. Solow, Robert M. *The Quarterly Journal of Economics*, Volume 70, No. 1, 1956.

In simplified terms, then, economic output is the result of human labour using the capital stock with the technologies they possess. How does trust link into all this? Directly and indirectly, according to economists. The direct contribution comes from the fact that trust is seen to lower transaction costs in various ways, which means that more is left for productive investments, leading to higher growth. Indirect contributions to growth may follow the direct contribution by, for example, leading to a phenomenon where in the presence of lower transaction costs there isn't simply a bit more money left for productive purposes, but the investment itself becomes more attractive – thus increasing the rate of productive investment. An equally important indirect contribution to growth may be expected to come from the presumably positive effect trust may have on the functioning of social institutions, which in turn affect labour, capital and technology.[53]

If we turn our attention to the basic model of economic growth based on labour, capital and technology, keeping in mind trust's association with lower transaction costs,[54] it seems likely that higher trust could be associated with higher rates of investment. There is at least some measure of empirical support for this from the venture capital industry.[55] A number of studies also suggest that there are grounds to believe that higher trust is also a positive factor for education and technological development.[56]

To better illustrate the direct and indirect contributions to growth let us turn to the frictious world of principals and agents.

PRINCIPALS, AGENTS AND TRUST

Would you give your money into the care of a relatively unknown person and trust them not to abuse the opportunity? This is the essence behind a set of questions explored under the names of the principal–agent problem, or the agency problem. The basic structure of the problem consists

---

53   Social Trust and Economic Growth. Bjørnskov, Christian. *Oxford Handbook of Social and Political Trust* 2017.

54   For example, The Role of Trustworthiness in Reducing Transaction Costs and Improving Performance: Empirical Evidence from the United States, Japan, and Korea. Dyer, Jeffrey; Chu, Wujin. *Organization Science* Vol. 14, No. 1, 2003.

55   For example, The Importance of Trust for Investment: Evidence from Venture Capital. Bottazzi; Da Rin; Hellmann. *The Review of Financial Studies*, Volume 29, Issue 9, September 2016.

56   Social Trust and the Growth of Schooling. Bjørnskov, Christian. *Economics of Education Review*, 28, 2009; and Social capital, innovation and growth: Evidence from Europe. Akçomak, I.Semih; Ter Weel, Bas. *European Economic Review*, 53, 2009.

of a situation where the actors have a contract to cooperate while holding differing private interests. What makes the agency problem a good reference point for our enquiry into the economic dimension of trust is the fact that similar dynamics of trust are present almost everywhere, from the workplace to the relationship between citizens and elected politicians or the private saver and their money manager.

The classic example is of a business owner (principal), who needs to employ personnel (agents) to manage the business. The business owner has the incentive to maximize their own benefit, which in turn translates into objectives such as minimizing costs such as salaries and maximizing the value of the business. The personnel, on the other hand, have the opposite incentives to maximize their own pay and private benefits from the business and potentially to minimize the effort they need to exert in return for their pay. Anyone who ever slacked off at work can surely relate. Therefore, as a result of the misalignment of interests, the main question for the business owner becomes how to ensure that the people hired will act in accordance with the owner's interests.[57]

The implications of the agency problem are far-reaching. First, it clarifies how under diverging interests the actors may seek to exploit each other. This has been corroborated by numerous studies, showing for example that executive use of corporate jets is far more prevalent in companies with laxer owner oversight,[58] and can indeed be confirmed simply by observing the behaviour of our fellow human beings. Second, it implies that to mend the situation the principal has to do something to influence the agents to act in an agreeable way in line with the principal's interests. In practice this means that the principal has to expend resources to create appropriate employment contracts and subsequently monitor and control the agents' behaviour. The point is to create structures that seek to align the principal's and the agents' incentives. This is of course why stock options and bonuses exist as a form of compensation, bringing us to the fact that resolving the agency problem, even if only partially, is costly. Finally, the more the principal can trust the agents, the less they need to spend resources on evaluating each potential hire and ensuring they act in the right way after the fact, implying that trust may have the virtue of reducing the costs of addressing the principal–agent problem. This can be thought of as an example of the direct effects that trust may have in supporting wellbeing and prosperity.

57   The Economic Theory of Agency: The Principal's Problem. Ross, Stephen. *American Economic Review*, 63(2), February 1973.

58   Agency Problems in Public Firms: Evidence from Corporate Jets in Leveraged Buyouts. Edgerton, Jesse. *The Journal of Finance*, Volume 67, No. 6, December 2012.

The efforts to align interests between the shareholding principal and the employed agent tend to be most pronounced at the top of the corporate hierarchy. This is understandable because the risks of misbehaviour are highest among the managers who have the greatest ability to appropriate resources from the firm or otherwise cause havoc for the shareholding principal. The numerous scandals involving out-of-control CEOs and plummeting share prices attest to this, while it is rare for a line-employee to be found to be the cause of troubles at similar scale. Thus, the greater the risk, the greater the value of compliance from the principal as shown by the compensation and incentive systems awarded at the top. All this implies that the value of trust also peaks at the top. The more the principal can trust the agents to behave in an agreeable way, the lesser the need to expend resources to secure and monitor their activities, inducing the principal to look for agents who give the impression of trustworthiness.

To appear trustworthy is therefore an advantage for the person looking for employment (as is obvious to anyone with a modicum of exposure to the real world). From this it follows that it pays for the jobseeker to acquire some evidence of their trustworthy qualities. This corroboration usually comes in the form of various degrees, professional qualifications or references to previous achievements and expertise, all conveniently summed up in the victory lap of virtue that is the curriculum vitae. In addition to actual evidence the next best thing is to invest in impression management. The way one suits up for the interview in accordance with the unwritten rules of the position acts to promote the image that the applicant has at least some inkling of what is expected of them, exemplified by the hipster cool at the marketing company or the more formal flavour at the London white-shoe law firm. The dress-up is of course to ease the hiring manager's toss-up: even if the candidate turns out to be a mess-up, at least they look like they know what's up.

The importance of credentials in modern society stems from the fact that the history of a person's behaviour, expressing their trustworthiness, is difficult if not impossible to accurately verify. This difficulty raises the value of universally recognized and provable achievements, such as education, which act as beacons of trustworthiness in the dark of an otherwise unknown personal history. In a tribal society where everyone knows everyone, and is aware of the full history of a person's behaviour, these kinds of trust-enhancing signifiers would be meaningless. But in a large and complex society their value as signs of capability and trustworthiness is high. Therefore, the value of trustworthiness, approximated by recognized achievements, encourages investment in education for the private individual. This happens to have the wonderful side effect that the private interest in education comes with a host of unintended positive consequences for wider society, including lower crime rates, more efficient state institutions and new ideas and innovation that often result in higher productivity and material wellbeing.[59] The positive externalities of education are of course a prime example of the indirect social contributions stemming from trust-related incentives.

Trust therefore becomes increasingly valuable in a complex society as a way to mitigate costs related to the agency problem, which arise in many contexts. From an economic perspective, trust's value is further augmented by its other positive indirect consequences. The principal–agent issue occurs in many contexts other than a business-owning principal hiring agents to manage the business – such as the relationship between the voter and the elected politician or the investor and the money manager. The cost-mitigating impact of trust should therefore be widely felt, not just in the sphere of the economy, but also in the operation of public institutions and society in general. If trust reduces the principal's need to monitor and control the agents, it may be expected that high trust enables less hierarchy and more autonomous behaviour in organizations. Empirical evidence supports the connection between trust and autonomy. Furthermore, trust seems to lead to increased willingness to share sensitive information, and openness to being more vulnerable towards one's co-workers. Tentative connections have also been made between trust and greater engagement at work.[60] As the information economy of the 21st century appears to favour independent code smiths, specialized experts and knowledge-creating scholars, high trust seems essential to sustain such roles without excessive monitoring and controlling costs.

TRUST, INNOVATION AND INVESTING

The economies of the 21st century are marked by the intensifying importance of knowledge and data in all aspects of operations. This can be seen as an evolution from earlier ages where things such as pure human labour, industrial processes or fossil fuels were the principal drivers of the

---

59   The External Benefits of Education. McMahon, Walter. *International Encyclopedia of Education*, 2010.
60   Volitional Trust, Autonomy Satisfaction, and Engagement at Work. Heyns, Marita; Rothmann, Sebastiaan. *Psychological Reports* 2018, Volume 121(1).

economic engine. Against this backdrop there is a concomitantly intensi-fying demand for an educated workforce, often working autonomously in narrow fields of high expertise. We might expect such circumstances to amplify the agency problems, as performance monitoring becomes more difficult. This in turn might increase the opportunities for and odds of misbehaviour by the agents, working perhaps by themselves on a task or subject they alone in the organization fully comprehend. Given these characteristics of the dawning environment, we may expect trust to become increasingly valuable, alongside growing efforts to monitor, con-trol and more finely incentivize employees in general. These outcomes seem to be natural consequences of the new situation.

We have already explored the importance of trust in the creation of knowledge, science and the dissemination of new ideas. In line with these findings, it is no surprise that trust is a key factor in the more practically oriented research and development efforts going on at companies around the globe. Yet we can expand our understanding by delving deeper into the findings around innovation and trust in the context of the economy. Doing so helps us gain a more granular understanding of how trust impacts our practical efforts in creating the new.

Innovation is often pictured as something achieved by a lone genius, tinkering away in an obscure laboratory – until the proverbial bulb lights above their head and a breakthrough is made. Certainly this happens, but in the context of the present-day economy it is of course mostly a roman-tic and outdated perception. Among the larger companies huge budgets, armies of research and development personnel and masses of market insights are all employed in the search for the critical innovations that are necessary to defend and develop competitive advantages. Yet some-thing of the older image remains. Start-ups do tend to be small and lean, often labouring in teams of just a few people around an insight they seek to monetize. It is often these smallest and newest companies that are at the forefront of innovation, while the corporate giants nurture proven crafts developed during some preceding generation of opportunities. The start-up ecosystem is supported by venture capital financing. The venture capitalists, whether private angel investors, big institutions or state bod-ies, provide the necessary financing for the early-stage companies looking to create something new. The hope is that some day the losses of initial development turn into explosive growth, profit and sky-high returns for the investment. In the process, the venture capitalists are willing to suffer even extended periods of losses and cash burn. What is essential for the investors is trust in the idea and the team executing the business plan.

A group of researchers explored how trust impacts venture capital investments in 15 European countries. To start off they noted a positive correlation between the share of people reporting high generalized trust and the relative size of the venture capital industry among the countries. The more generalized trust there is, the more venture capital there is to go around. This general observation was followed by the major focus of the study, where the researchers looked at how the relative level of generalized trust in one country towards another (e.g. how many Brits think the Germans are highly trustworthy) affects venture capital investments between the countries. The first finding is that the higher the relative trust of the target company's home country, the more likely are investments. The researchers postulated that the generalized trust exhibited often acts as a proxy in the absence of more accurate knowledge of the target company and its personnel. Alternatively, lack of trust in general (a high level of sentiments such as "the French/British are not trustworthy" for the eternally acrimonious pair across the channel) will generally act as a hindrance to investment interests. Given trust's role in facilitating cooperation in general, this seems in line with expectations.

While higher trust was significantly related to the propensity to invest, curiously enough it also had a slight negative connection with good outcomes for those investments. Likewise trust seemed to be negatively correlated with investments from larger and more internationally experienced venture capitalists. It may be guessed that for the more sophisticated venture capitalists investment decisions are more robustly based on other relevant factors than generalized trust in the country of the target company, which might have a distracting effect for a less seasoned money manager. Other findings show that trust is positively associated with earlier-stage deals, while syndicating (sharing) the deals with other investors decreases as trust goes higher. The assumption here is that the higher the trust, the more valuable the deal is seen to be, thus lowering the interest in having other investors take part.[61]

Generalized trust is relevant for the willingness to provide financing for the high-risk start-ups that drive innovation, but not necessarily for profitable outcomes. This appears credible based both on our understanding of trust and on the characteristics of investing in general. Too little trust inhibits cooperation, yet too much of it can lead to folly. For an investor some base level of trust certainly needs to be met, and a good

---

61   The Importance of Trust for Investment: Evidence from Venture Capital. Bottazzi, Laura; Da Rin, Marco; Hellmann, Thomas. *The Review of Financial Studies*, Volume 29, Issue 9, September 2016

amount of it seems to be an attractor. Too much trust in the founders of a start-up may lead the investor to ignore other relevant information, perhaps signalling trouble. It is indeed common in business for a board of directors highly trustful of their CEO to tolerate problems and warning signs far longer than would be warranted, thanks to their trust. To be fair, the same dynamic extends to nearly all areas of human interaction. In the case of investments and innovation, trust makes investors more eager to fund start-ups bringing new life and ideas to the economy. If a country is interested in attracting international venture capital for its start-ups and innovation activities, other countries having high generalized trust in yours should be the first places to go looking.

Start-ups and venture capitalists certainly do their best to drive and finance innovation, but what about the actual work going on inside companies? A group of Finnish researchers presented evidence that trust within an organization is positively linked to innovation in all its forms, whether it is about products, processes, behavioural or strategic matters, explaining between 15 and 35% of the variance in innovativeness. The researchers concluded by remarking that developing institutional trust might be considered an important strategic question for companies.[62]

Elsewhere, trust seems to be essential for knowledge-sharing and a factor for innovation cooperation between buyers and suppliers in the machine tools industry.[63] Among companies in Germany, the introduction of trust-based working-hour practices (in contrast to rigidly regulated work hours) was found to make such firms "12–15% more likely to improve products and 6–7% more likely to undertake process innovation".[64] Trust is an important ingredient enhancing innovative activities, aiding the supply of new ideas, processes and products. It is also essential for the uptake of the new ideas and products created. For example, a study from Taiwan revealed that trust-based integrity and competence (going under the heading of ability in our concept of trust) are essential factors predicting the adoption of mobile banking services.[65]

62   The Role of Trust in Organisational Innovativeness. Blomqvist, Kirsimarja; Ellonen, Riikka; Puumalainen, Kaisu. *European Journal of Innovation Management*, April 2008.

63   Mediation Effects of Trust and Contracts on Knowledge-sharing and Product Innovation: Evidence from the European Machine Tool Industry. Charterina, Jon; Landeta, Jon; Basterrextea, Imanol. *European Journal of Innovation Management*, Volume 21, No. 2, 2018.

64   Trust-Based Work Time and Innovation: Evidence from Firm-Level Data. Godart, Olivier; Görg, Holger; Hanley, Aoife. *ILR Review*, 2017.

65   An Empirical Investigation of Mobile Banking Adoption: The Effect of Innovation Attributes and Knowledge-based Trust. Lin, Hsiu-Fen. *International Journal of Information Management*, Volume 31, Issue 3, June 2011.

All this empirical evidence chisels out the finer details in the shape of trust's relationship to innovation and economic activity. As you would expect, this relationship appears close and highly impactful. However, it is not simply a matter of "the more trust the better". In many cases, as with trust in general, too much of it can lead to problems. This duality of trust is highlighted by studies indicating the impact of trust is at first highly beneficial, but as trust keeps increasing the incremental advantages diminish. The benefits for innovation purposes seem to peak at a moderate or high level of trust and stay flat and sometimes even slightly decrease from this point onwards, as high trust turns excessive. Too much trust might, for example, reduce the critical thinking and analysis essential for innovation, high quality and performance.[66]

The practical ways trust facilitates innovation, as shown here, highlight yet again how trust impacts economic development. From its fundamental role in knowledge, to the smaller-scale impacts in the practical works of innovation, trust is a significant component enabling the advance of science, knowledge and technology that is the foundation of our material prosperity and economic development. Trust alone will not be enough – new ideas backed by investments to realize them are the backbone of growth. And too much trust may even be worse than just the right – moderate to high – amount of it.

TRUST AND FINANCE

Trust is important for all business, but especially so in the world of banking and finance. Let us illustrate this by thinking briefly about banking as a business.

Simplifying things quite a bit, banks' core business is about matching those with excess savings with those who have uses for money but don't have enough savings for those uses.

Banks provide a service to their customers by offering a safe and easily accessible place to hold their wealth. On top of this practical concern, the deposits in regular bank accounts may yield a small amount of interest for

---

66 On the downsides of trust in innovation: Why Too Much Trust Is Death to Innovation. Bidault, Francis; Castello, Alessio. *MIT Sloan Management Review*, June 2010. The Dark Side of Trust: The Benefits, Costs and Optimal Levels of Trust for Innovation Performance. Molina-Morales, Xavier; Martínez-Fernández, Teresa M.; Torlòa, Vanina Jasmine. *Long Range Planning*, Volume 44, Issue 2, April 2011.

account holders, giving another reason to store wealth at the bank. Should the savers have more appetite for risk, higher returns are available through various investment products. On the other side of these services, banks use the money entrusted to them by lending some of it out with interest to other customers in need of money.

Savers and account holders will of course periodically want to withdraw some of their balance. Banks therefore need available reserves of money to accommodate the withdrawals, which in turn acts as a limiting factor on outward lending operations. In normal circumstances the scale of withdrawals can be quite accurately predicted, giving banks an idea of how much to hold in reserve. Armed with an understanding of the correct level of reserves for withdrawals, banks can then plan their lending operations based on the available funds.

From this combination of activities, we arrive at the fundamental source of the banks' profits, namely the difference between the interest income from lending and the interest paid for deposits. This is the classic core of banking. Today, banks of course do much more besides, and a large part of their income and profit comes from various fees and other transaction-related sources. The monetary regime governing the financial system as a whole has also changed, from being backed by precious metals to the current fiat system, which has freed up credit and money creation to a new degree.

Looking more closely at the determination of interest paid for deposits and charged for loans illuminates the role of trust in economic life. Because banks promise to their customers that their holdings are available for withdrawal at any time (for typical checking accounts), the risk of loss for depositors is small – the cash is effectively lost only if the bank itself becomes insolvent and unable to dispense the money it owes to the depositor. As a reflection of the low risk and continuous availability of the money, the compensating interest for the depositor is also low.

Now think about the situation when a bank is considering a 20-year mortgage requested by a prospective customer. The bank will recoup its investment over 20 years, in contrast with the constant availability of the deposit. This is of course predicated on the customer's ability to pay back in the first place. Therefore, the bank will be interested not only in the present wealth and income of the customer, but also in their employment histories and how they might cope in the case of unemployment, or should interest rates increase dramatically. Given that the debt relationship is to be for 20 years, the likelihood of adverse events is not insignificant. And since we are talking about a mortgage, the bank will be keen to understand the future prospects of the property itself, because it will probably be used as collateral for the debt. These sorts of considerations will weigh on the bank's willingness to lend, and what it will consider the appropriate amount of debt the customer is able to service and carry.

All this put together means the bank has a much higher risk of losing its money in this situation compared with the depositor who effectively has constant access to their funds. This higher risk on the bank's behalf will of course need to be compensated for. The price of money is the interest paid, including an extra margin the bank will add to reflect its customer-specific risk-assessment. Because the risk of default is much higher over 20 years than with the always-available deposit, so too are the interest and margin paid for the mortgage compared with the liquid deposit.

The bank is thus engaging in a game of chance with the 20-year mortgage, where the return on the investment in the individual customer is uncertain. The higher the income, present wealth and perceived reliability of the customer in relation to the scope of the transaction at hand, the less likely the bank will be to estimate an unwanted outcome. In these circumstances the bank will be happy to lend a hand, and its money, to finance the customer's property purchase at a moderate price (that is, interest and margin on the loan). If the likelihood of a negative outcome is deemed higher, the principal loan available may be smaller, with a higher margin to offset the less auspicious odds of recovery and profitable transaction.

When a bank is assessing a request for a mortgage (or any other financing), the major question it asks itself is: how much do we trust the client to pay us back? The answer determines whether the transaction will happen and, if so, under which terms.

The present income, existing wealth and an agreeable work history will signal to the bank that the customer has the resources to honour their commitment and a track record of having done so in the past. These markers of trustworthiness shine easily through the lenses of our ability, benevolence and integrity framework. Does the customer have the income to actually pay back? If yes, then that clearly counts as ability to honour the commitment proposed. Does the customer have a work history testifying to their character as a dependable person, and not as a con artist? If yes, then they score on the integrity and benevolence tests of trust. It might seem naive to think things such as values and character matter in the cold world of profit-maximizing finance, but they really do to some extent. Values of responsibility and productivity go hand in hand with profit-based incentives.

Think about the present drive for environmental action. Many banks have stated that they will no longer finance companies involved in coal and oil production, for instance. There is strong pressure for this coming from society and the personnel working in the banks. So, it is very plausible that banks would take such a stand on genuinely held values alone.

Yet there is also a relevant business case for this action. The bank may with good reason believe businesses based on selling fossil fuels will be in serious jeopardy in the future. Certainly, the changing social mores and necessities of climate action will not aid these companies. In fact, the impact will be the contrary, calling into question the very existence of these businesses. Equipped with these observations the bank may then expect the room for operation to be narrowing for these companies, potentially impairing their revenues and profits in the process. The banks have identified the risk for themselves under these circumstances, namely that the debt-service capability of these companies seems more likely to diminish than increase. This will affect their calculations about margins charged and willingness to lend. If the outlook is dire enough, the banks may well decide the risk is not worth taking, and cease financing these companies altogether.

And so we find that a union of profit-mindedness and climate concerns can yield the same results as a pure "do-gooder" value-based approach. Of course, this also cuts to the real meat of the climate change issue – namely that should climate change be left unaddressed, and the risks associated with it turn out to be real, the outcomes for social stability and business activity in general will likely be very negative. As such, addressing the issue should be top of mind for every serious capitalist. The main problems preventing effective action seem to stem from high up-front costs with not much in terms of payoffs combined with the pervasive short-term orientation present in the markets and the west in general. Thus, the necessary incentive structures are not quite in place for an orderly adaptation.

These observations also serve to highlight the close connections between values and utility. Although they dress it up in language of equity and fairness, those favouring more income redistribution are rarely on the paying side, but rather on the benefiting side. Likewise, it is no wonder that it is specifically the wealthy and successful who promote lighter taxes and lesser regulation in general – often employing the fairness and equity arguments from another perspective. The same applies to many things. Scratch a bit off the surface of beautiful language about virtues and moral goodness, and beneath you will often find material and other benefits, or opposition to some disadvantageous state of affairs. Values are indeed about things that have real and tangible value to us, even if this tends to get clouded by high-minded ideals. Therefore, it is to be expected that foresighted capitalists and green activists alike should increasingly discover common ground for climate action. Values, trust and economic interests are highly interlinked. As trust is fundamentally about taking the risk of relying on another party to act in your interest, such as paying back the debt they owe, we can appreciate lending relationships as economic exemplars of trust in action.

If we switch back to the customer's perspective, we will note that the more trust- and creditworthy they appear to the bank, the greater their consequent access to financing is. This has profound importance for the individual customer. On the back of their existing assets and high cash flow for debt service, they can secure more financing at a cheaper rate. This in turn means that this person has far greater opportunities to maintain and further augment their wealth. They pay relatively less for the debt they hold, and have access to more of it, which together mean they will be able to profitably realize a larger array of investments than their less creditworthy peers. All of this applies to individuals, companies and countries alike. Should we assume that the set of available investments are fully equivalent between two individuals, or countries for that matter, then the party with better access to financing will be able to realize higher returns for their investments. Over time this advantage obviously results in greater wealth.

These advantages are not restricted to the financial world. Imagine two people are applying for a job, or perhaps running for president of their country. Keeping all other variables equal, you would probably bet that the candidate who better aligns with the voters or the hiring manager on the dimensions of trust will win out. Being trustworthy pays off, economically and socially.

Coming back to the investment opportunities determined by interest rates and the availability of financing, perhaps the most obvious sign of trust in the markets comes from the interest rates paid by different countries for their debt. Germany is famed for its financial discipline, and as a sign of investors' trust pays the lowest interest rates for its federal debt instruments. Its chief European peers such as the UK, France and Italy, all of which have similarly large and liquid debt markets, have to pay higher rates because the markets' trust in them seems slightly less solid. The smallest and less financially well-off countries are in the weakest, and most expensive, position.

The European debt crisis that followed the great financial crisis illustrated this harsh reality in a harrowing financial drama. Greece's public finances were deeply questioned by the markets, resulting in a much higher cost of debt, making things all the more difficult for the country. Given the perceived inflexibilities of the eurozone, the problems spread to other countries thought financially weak as the whole system began to wobble. Throughout the troubles, Germany's and other stable countries' situations remained nonetheless untroubled, as can be seen from the following graph.

EUROPEAN 10 YEAR BOND YIELDS, %

━ Germany
⋯⋯ Greece
■■■ Italy

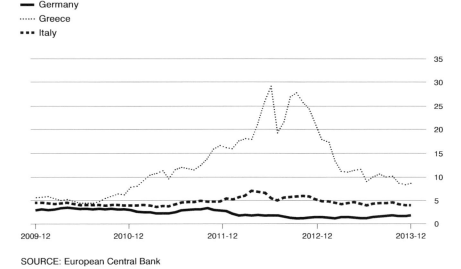

SOURCE: European Central Bank

To be sure, the Greek crisis was a special situation, and factors such as the existing level of debt, stable social and governmental conditions and an existing track record of honouring obligations affect the interest demanded by investors for their money. Yet all of these could also be viewed as impacting the three-dimensional prism of trust.

Coming back to present challenges, we might rightly assume that European countries all need to make significant investments to upgrade their infrastructures to accommodate a less polluting and greener future, funded by national debt. The cost of these investments is the interest paid to investors funding the debt by the countries. For the Germans the cost would be lowest, because they enjoy the greatest trust among investors. If the payoffs for such investments are equivalent for each country, then the undertaking would be most profitable for the Germans. Of course, the irony is that in the real world the Germans have proven to be so married to their financial discipline that they have refused to take debt to fund new investments even in the present environment where the cost would be close to zero. The fact that trust is reflected in the cost of money, as we have seen from our discussion about the individual debtor and sovereign European states, is remarkable. It allows us to draw further parallels between the functions of interest rates in general, and trust with its broader social implications.

In investment theory the value of an investment can be calculated as the present value of future cash flows. In practice this means that future cash flows are forecast, and their present value is estimated using a discount factor, an interest rate expressing the time value of money. The time value reflects the fact that €100 received today is preferable to €100 received 10 years from now. Money available right now can be used profitably so that it may yield a return. All else being equal the further out from the present a sum of money is earned, the less valuable it is in the present.

Investors rate their potential investments by comparing these sorts of calculations. The most lucrative investments are those that yield the greatest relative present value and annualized return for their money. The present value can increase either by having greater cash flows in the future or by having a lower interest rate as a discount factor.

The equity investor, keen to maximize the return on their investment, will be happy if they can be more trustful of the prospects of the company they are investing in – with the result that they may use a lower discount rate and thus achieve higher present value and return for the case. In short, higher trust will make an investment more attractive.

The debt investor who above everything else desires the security that their capital is safely returned for a modest interest payment will find trust equally essential when choosing to park their money. As with the German example, it makes them more secure in their trust that they will one day get their money back, with a fair reward in the form of the interest received.

While trust is always important for investors of all stripes, its value becomes especially visible during economic crises. The common reaction in times of declining market values is a flight to safety, between asset classes and within them. In the arena of debt, we find that money is moved from riskier countries to perceived safe havens such as debt issues from the US, Germany or Japan. Interest earned becomes secondary to securing the repayment of the principal itself. In equity markets professional investors tend to cycle their funds away from assets in greatest jeopardy towards businesses operating in more stable industries. The same reactions extend to currencies, with more exotic ones easily being shunned and the most liquid and secure dollars, euros and Swiss francs and the like gaining. To paint a fuller picture of trust's role in crises, let us turn to historical experiences in the banking sector.

FINANCIAL CRISES

It is the banking system that proves the most acute example of the value of trust in times of economic upheaval. For banks, trust is the anchor that holds the institution firm in rough weather. Without it, the ship would soon find itself on the rocks should the winds turn stormy.

To be more precise, financial crises involving bank failures are among the most devastating economic events known to humanity and economist alike. They differ from regular downturns in their severity, breadth and long-term consequences. As examples, think of the great recession starting in 1929 or the financial crisis of 2007–2008. Neither were small matters, nor were they quickly forgotten. And their impacts are still felt and remembered.

To understand why financial crises precipitated by bank failures are so destructive, let us return to the relationship between the average depositor and the bank. The checking account holder has their money deposited at the bank, typically available for withdrawal more or less at all times through ATMs and bank branches and usable with credit cards, digital wallets and net banking services.

In normal times one does not need to question the security and availability of the funds at the bank. Ultimately the safety of a deposit depends on the financial health of the bank. In other words, the availability of the deposit is in question only when there is a perceived risk of imminent default, whereby the bank would be unable to honour its commitment to the depositor. Consequently, much banking regulation aims at reducing the risks of bank default and, should it happen, at minimizing the loss of depositor assets. For example, many states and central banks have in place universal guarantee schemes for bank deposits. Under the prevailing EU rules at least €100,000 for every depositor is guaranteed – in the event of default a sum of at least €100,000 is recoverable for every depositor. For institutional clients, the sum and the guarantee is mostly insignificant, but for the average individual customer it can mean good coverage.

Now assume you know your bank is on the brink of collapse, and you hold significant wealth in its accounts. What would you do? The obvious answer is to withdraw all your money at once, before the bank embarks on its trip to the abyss. As it happens, every client of the bank will be going through the same thoughts at the same time, precipitating what is known as a bank run. As everyone tries to get their savings out of the bank at the same time, the bank's reserves and capacity to service the withdrawals run dry at the worst possible moment, pushing the already teetering bank off the cliff. The great recession started in 1929 with the crash of Wall Street shares. The global economy was already hobbled by the effects of the crash when the Austrian bank Creditanstalt faced a bank run in 1931 and collapsed, which initiated a banking crisis in Europe, turning the global recession from bad to worse.

In olden times bank runs were mostly events between private individuals and the bank. Today, corporate clients and short-term funding arrangements between banks play a much larger role. The global financial crisis of 2007–2008 saw a string of bankruptcies reflecting the interconnected nature of the modern global financial system. Like its predecessor in 1929, this crisis was precipitated by a decline in asset values. This time the culprit was real estate, which had been propped up by low interest rates, lax lending standards and excessive securitization mainly in the form of repackaged mortgages and derivatives based on them. When real estate prices in the US started going down (which was thought impossible), those caught with real estate assets and their derivatives were soon in trouble. The market rout turned into a full-blown crisis when Lehman Brothers, a leading Wall Street investment bank, went bankrupt thanks to its holdings of now toxic subprime assets.

What happened was that the crash of real estate prices, and with it the values of assets deriving from them, led to massive losses for the banks and investment companies holding them. To cut their exposure, everyone wanted to get out of the holdings at the same time – meaning the market was inundated with sellers, and buyers were nowhere to be found. This dynamic crashed the values of the assets even further. These developments led to market participants becoming very cautious towards parties they knew or suspected to hold the damaged assets, a natural consequence of perceiving the risks arising from the steep fall in asset values. This wariness froze the so-called inter-bank lending markets, which banks and financial institutions used for short-term funding among themselves to satisfy their immediate liquidity needs.

The seizure of the interbank lending market, of which Lehman was a casualty and a further accelerator, sent shockwaves throughout the whole financial system, raising the prospect of a wholesale meltdown of the banking sector. With trust between banks – and towards them by others – gone, the whole system was jeopardized, and the economy along with it. What makes the financial sector so important is the fact that the rest of the economy is wholly dependent on its continued functioning. Payments need to be made, debt taken and serviced, and so on, all of which depends on the financial institutions. If these basic functions become stressed or imperilled, the problems will quickly spread everywhere. This elemental connection between finance and the rest of the economy is what makes financial crises so devastating, compared with crises centred on other parts of the economy.

The common thread with bank failures across time is the disappearance of trust leading to bank runs, or to sudden droughts of short-term liquidity as happened in 2008.

TRUST AND TRANSACTION COSTS

Trust in nations' commitments to upholding their promises is a central factor for sovereign interest rates and trust itself could be thought to have characteristics of an interest rate, given that the degree of its presence affects the availability and cost of money, business and investment opportunities quite broadly.

To be sure, without trust any complex and risky business endeavour will fail to get off the ground. If the prospective partners for a start-up do not trust each other enough, the company will stay in the realm of ideas rather than becoming a reality. If customers fail to trust the company, the prospects of sales will be dimmer than in circumstances of high trust. Perhaps trust is in large part behind the magic of brand value, where brand reputation is the practical expression of trust earned through good customer experiences over time. It is certainly difficult to think of high brand value existing without a considerable level of trust in terms of product quality and reliability, although trust can't quite accommodate the special cool that is often at the core of a brand.

Another way to perceive trust's gatekeeper-like nature is as a transaction cost.

Transaction costs show up in many shapes and forms in nearly every corner of the economy. They are the costs arising from participating in a trade, but not consisting of the price of the product being traded. The cost can be incurred by the buyer or the seller, the consumer or the product-offering company, or even within a company in its internal transactions. As an example, think of the fees brokers charge for buying and selling shares on their platforms. The share has its price, on top of which the broker takes its own fee, which tends to be a very small percentage of the overall transaction value. For the buyer of the share these costs are the price of participation, rather than the price of the product itself. Should transaction costs be too high relative to the product itself, they can easily hinder or dissuade the prospective buyer from the transaction altogether.

How does this relate to trust, then? Trust is about cooperation, the beginning of which is preceded by a decision whether to engage with another party empowered with the potential to harm or disappoint you in some way. The decision to cooperate, or not, is made on the back of an ability, benevolence and integrity evaluation of the counterparty, made with conscious effort or in an intuitive instant, weighing the prospects of a good or a bad outcome. This appraisal is affected by contextual things such as the gravity of the matter at hand and the individual's intrinsic propensity to trust stemming from their unique background. In making the evaluation, the costs and benefits of cooperation and potential adverse outcomes are estimated at some level.

We cannot usually be sure how much trust is really warranted, and at any rate we know that circumstances can change over time, opening the door to undesirable alterations in the relationship. That being so, we find ourselves in an ongoing fog of uncertainty about the trustworthiness of the other. To manage this ever-present uncertainty and to maintain trust, many practical tools have been developed to monitor and control our trusting relationships. When significant amounts of money are at stake, the questions of trust and monitoring become all the more relevant.

We may think of the various rules, formal and informal, that guide behaviour in society as trust-enhancing tools. Think of the biblical commandments: thou shalt not murder, thou shalt not commit adultery, thou shalt not steal. Rules such as these make the social environment predictable and less dangerous and provide the fertile soil for trust to flourish. If we take citizenship as the price of admission to a given society with its multitude of benefits, keeping one's behaviour within the confines of its written and unwritten rules might be thought of as a kind of necessary transaction cost requiring adjustment in behaviour and values.

When it comes to the rules of trust governing a society, I received an illuminating example in my youth while spending some time working in London. The experience was marked by many observations about peculiar local practices that in hindsight perhaps derived from differences in general levels of trust between Britain and my native Finland. From getting employed to renting an apartment, the transactions required the production of a substantial amount of evidence and backing materials such as several years' worth of salary and address histories. This was presumably first to prove I am who I claim to be, and second to give evidence of trustworthiness in general. Often there were third party businesses handling the diligence process, obviously at a cost to the company doing the hiring, for example. Background checks of similarly extensive scope were, and remain, mostly unheard of in Finland.

These experiences aptly highlight the transaction costs arising from the need to assess trustworthiness. No doubt the company doing the background check charged fees for its services. The contrast between the UK and much lighter-touch Finland seems likely at least to some degree to result from differences between generally less and more trusting societies. In other words, thanks to a greater degree of generalized trust, companies in Finland may be able to do their hiring with lower costs than their peers in Britain. This hypothesis is of course dependent on the assumption that after hiring the personnel misbehave at roughly equivalent rates in Britain and Finland, and that Finland does not suffer from a meaningfully larger number of bad apples thanks to laxer background checks during hiring – offsetting the initial savings through costs incurred later.

Ascertaining the trustworthiness of potential employees is important for every company but the principle also applies increasingly to customers and suppliers. When it comes to suppliers, ensuring that they comply with standards of good business practices, or use desired sustainable materials, has become an important reputational matter – for example, ensuring that no supplier uses child labour. External consultants are often used to design or inspect supply chains to these ends, again entailing a form of transaction cost in the absence of concrete trust.

Banks are especially interested in their own clients' trustworthiness and compliance with established norms and standards. To control for the risks arising from customers' activities, banks use various 'know your customer' checks requiring clients to disclose information deemed relevant by the banks. Various anti-money-laundering policies in turn seek to ensure that a bank's accounts or money lent are not used to circulate funds of illegal origin. All of these policies put together mean that the compliance functions in banks have ballooned in recent decades, as have their costs. The Copenhagen-based Danske Bank was hit by a money laundering scandal revealed in 2018 and was subsequently hit by fines and legal claims totalling over a billion US dollars. Following the news the bank's share price halved, erasing billions of shareholders' wealth. A few years after the case, in its 2020 annual report, the bank reported 4.1 billion Danish kroner, or about US $700 million, worth of costs related to compliance, financial crime prevention and ongoing handling of the case.

The Danske Bank case is but one of the many such cases in the banking industry, and again displays the monitoring and controlling costs banks incur on the side of the main business. Whether a company is selecting a new employee or a new customer, both situations have the potential for what is known in the economic literature as the "lemons problem".

TRUST AND THE LEMONS PROBLEM

The lemons problem is a concept in economics introduced by George Akerlof in a 1970 paper about the information asymmetries between buyers and sellers in a market, and how they reflect in the quality and prices of products being traded.

The main finding of the paper is that the presence of significant information asymmetries results in considerable deviations from what would be optimal market outcomes. For example, the seller of a used car knows much more about the actual quality of their car than the buyer showing interest in it. And so an unscrupulous seller will from time to time manage to sell their car to a buyer who will afterwards be bitterly disappointed, when the real, poor, condition of the car becomes evident. They bought a "lemon", a poor product with a bitter price far higher than was merited. Because of situations like this, savvy buyers are unwilling to pay full price for actually good products ("peaches") – because they know they do not have the necessary information to verify the quality of the product beforehand and must take into account the unfortunate possibility of ending up with a lemon.[67]

It is worth noting that the side with more information is often at a distinct advantage in a given trade. Insider trading of shares, which was once commonplace but today is heavily regulated and often illegal, provides an excellent example. People who have inside information about a company's situation, which is not publicly known, can trade the share to their advantage before the information becomes public. As the information is finally revealed to the public and the share price adjusts accordingly, those who had previously traded the share based on inside information tend to profit greatly. This is an example of the value of information in markets in general, but is not an instance of the lemons problem, because it does not deal with differences in product quality. A share is a share, no matter how you trade it.

But, coming back to the lemons problem, as a consequence of the information asymmetry between the buyer and seller in the used car market, Akerlof predicted that sellers of actually good quality cars would be less willing to participate, because they feel they do not get the full value for their product. The incentives for sellers with poor-quality vehicles

---

67   The Market for 'Lemons': Quality Uncertainty and the Market Mechanism. Akerlof, George. *The Quarterly Journal of Economics*, Volume 84, No. 3, August 1970.

are reversed, on the other hand, because they are able to get a relatively high price for their product. These incentives combined can thus lead to a market with few high-quality sellers, but an abundance of poor-quality products. The buyers may be expected to note this development, and over time adjust down their willingness to pay, further driving out quality sellers and steepening the downward spiral in market conditions. In extreme cases, Akerlof claimed, the information asymmetries enabling abusive practices could lead to markets effectively ceasing to function.

The origin of the whole problem is of course the fact that people will abuse superior information, should they possess it. Akerlof himself described the lemons problem as an example of the economic costs of dishonesty – good products are driven out by the bad, dishonest sellers gain excess benefit at the cost of buyers and high-quality sellers, and in the end the whole market may fail. In short, the whole society is worse off. All as the consequence of opportunistic dishonesty afforded by information asymmetry.

To be fair, empirical evidence is mixed when it comes to the real-world impacts of the lemons problem. Sometimes evidence of welfare losses in line with the theory is found in one study or industry but is then disconfirmed by another study on another market. Yet it is plainly true and obvious that people do make use – sometimes not quite fairly – of their information advantages when buying and selling things. And it is just as true that those dealings do have consequences. Just ask the shareholders of Enron, or the victims of Bernie Madoff, who were effectively sold lemons instead of the peaches they were promised. Indeed, at its extreme end the lemons problem describes nothing if not fraud.

And here we can of course make a connection to trust.

In essence the unfortunate purchase of a lemon constitutes a breach of trust. The buyer realizes they have been fooled, and the product that they received was not what they expected, and the seller was perhaps well aware of the fact. As Akerlof noted, if the lemons problem is especially bad, the market may fail and cease to function. The breakdown of cooperation is of course a definitive sign of a lack of trust between the market participants.

One of the basic findings about trust in the beginning of this book included power distance, which has been found to be negatively correlated with trust. The greater the power distance, the less trust there is generally found between two parties. The lemons problem might be considered an example of this, where the information asymmetry represents a kind of power distance. So perhaps we might expect the lemons problem to be most severe in fully unregulated, wild and obscure frontier markets where information asymmetries and power distances can be expected to be largest. And on the contrary end of the spectrum highly developed markets with widely available information about the products and established practices, complemented by the presence of various consumer protections and appeal opportunities, should suffer less from the lemons problem. The degree to which interaction is regular must have a significant impact on the behaviour of market participants. An anonymous market of one-off spot transactions seems more liable to abusive action than markets where the parties expect continuous interaction and reputation matters.

If we imagine a market where trust is high between buyers and sellers, this implies that the buyers cannot have been seriously betrayed or disappointed by the sellers, meaning the lemons problem cannot be a serious issue in such a market.

Not surprisingly, dishonesty, as exemplified by the lemons problem, does not make for trust. In the marketplace this means trust is more likely to flourish in conditions where the abuses arising from informational asymmetries are curtailed by thoughtful policies, widespread information and established good practices, where the negative impacts of power distance are mitigated.

SECULAR STAGNATION

By this point the window on trust's importance in economic life has been scrubbed clean of most obscuring grime, and we can shift our attention from the contours of the immediate landscape and begin to ponder the more hypothetical features of the revealed ecosystem.

We have found trust to be a relevant factor for economic growth thanks to its many impacts on cooperation, institutional functionality, interest rates, investing, transaction costs and so on. With this in mind, let us circle back to economic growth.

Since the great financial crisis there has been a curious resurgence of a concept that originated in the aftermath of the great depression in the 1930s. Prominent economists such as Paul Krugman, Lawrence Summers and Robert J. Gordon among others have expressed renewed concerns about a "secular stagnation", referring to an observed and persistent downward trend in economic growth rates in the US and elsewhere, starting (according to some) during or after the 1990s or after the financial crisis of 2007–2008. In short, economic growth since the 1990s has not been nearly as robust as it was from 1945 to 2000, and this phenomenon has been dubbed the "secular stagnation".

SECULAR STAGNATION AND THE DECLINE IN AVERAGE GROWTH RATES

Annual GDP growth in the developed economies, 1971–2016. CEO-to-worker compensation ratio, 1965–2018

▬ Non-crisis average growth
•••• Annual GDP growth

Percentage

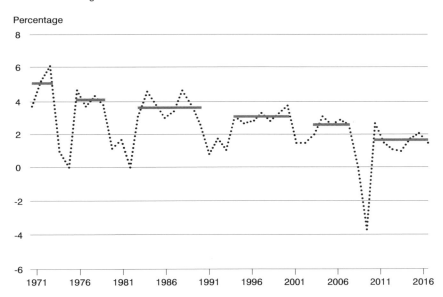

SOURCE: www.un.org/development/desa/dpad/publication/development-issues-no-9-low-growth-with-limited-policy-options-secular-stagnation-causes-consequences-and-cures

Several very credible explanations have been offered for this lacklustre growth, including demographic decline, lack of demand and dearth of investments thanks to the increasingly intangible nature of the information economy, and the decline in the number of significant technological innovations that drive growth, relative to previous times.[68] However, none of the explanations that I have seen take into account the simultaneous decline in trust, as reported in the statistics at the outset of this book. Although the reasons listed by Summers and others are by themselves enough to account for a slowdown in growth, it is striking that based on our understanding of trust, the decline in trust would also be expected to show up as a depressed growth rate.

---

68   For example, Larry Summers' article on the topic: www.imf.org/external/pubs/ft/fandd/2020/03/larry-summers-on-secular-stagnation.htm

Although a trust-based account cannot explain the decline in interest rates (rather, interest rates might be expected to have gone up with the decline in trust), nor the variations in levels of trust and growth between the US, Europe and Japan, for example, it could certainly explain a secular decline in investments and increase in various monitoring and control costs – both of which would be poison for long-term growth. Likewise, because trust is linked to innovation and knowledge creation, the decline of it may well have made our research and development efforts less effective.

That would lead us to hypothesize that in addition to the other theories on the cause of secular stagnation, the decline in trust may be a significant factor. While this is all hypothesizing with very light evidence, based on the theory at our disposal a long decline in trust should act as a drag on growth. Food for thought to economists interested in exploring trust and growth.

It is nonetheless abundantly clear that whatever economic growth we have had, the fruits of it have not been shared equally among the population. Income inequality is increasingly a topic of attention, and there seems to be a clear consensus that it needs to be addressed somehow. But how does it relate to trust?

INCOME INEQUALITY

When thinking about trust and economic inequality, the immediate reaction is that of course the two are opposing forces and thus negatively correlated: higher inequality should lead to lower trust, and lower trust to higher inequality, whereas high trust should support moderate or low inequality. When it comes to second-order effects, income inequality easily leads to diverging, even opposing, economic and other interests among the population. The rich will want to minimize taxes to preserve their wealth, while the poor will want to raise them to secure wealth transfers for themselves, and so on. This of course has consequences for the basis of our operating model of trust. The outcome of increasingly different economic situations seems to be that it takes people further apart in their trust assessments, especially in the benevolence and integrity dimensions, leading to lower trust. And if trust is very low, then it might be expected that citizens will not care much about the fates of each other, with dire consequences. Even if they are not outright abusing each other, they might be unwilling to sponsor much in the way of public services and wealth transfers through taxation, in turn leading to even higher income inequality. As material interests drift apart, so does trust; as trust evaporates, so does care for others' interests.

There is indeed a lot of truth to this interpretation, but the picture is slightly more nuanced than expected. Digging once again into the research helps us see why. The negative relationship between trust and income inequality has in general found much empirical support in the past few decades. A more detailed study by the Scandinavian duo of Andreas Bergh and Christian Bjørnskov shines light on the finer details of the two-way interactions.[69]

To begin with, some of their more basic observations concern the general levels of trust among different sets of countries, drawn from their overall sample of 89 nations. Nordic countries and monarchies seemed to be associated with higher trust, while those with a communist history or strong religious component were found to be less trusting on average (though elsewhere at least Protestant religious traditions have been connected with higher levels of trust).

When it comes to inequality, Bergh and Bjørnskov made a surprising finding: trust seems to be more robustly related to pretax and pre-redistribution inequality, rather than post-tax and post-redistribution inequality. Moreover, their results indicated that an increase in trust decreases pre-tax inequality quite clearly among nations, whereas lower pre-tax inequality has a more modest positive feedback effect on trust. Could it be that trust precedes the welfare state rather than resulting from welfare policies?

In response to their findings, the authors brought up collective action problems created by the provision of free services by the welfare state. Welfare policies such as lavish unemployment benefits, free healthcare and free university studies can be expected to result in various incentives for free-riding in the society, where people consume services without contributing to funding them through work, saving and tax-paying. These incentive structures should in theory lead to lower labour market participation rates, excessive reliance on welfare benefits and broad efficiency losses for the economy. All of these put together would imply that states with high degrees of welfare policies should be clearly less wealthy than their peers. Yet this is not what we observe in real life.

With regards to the collective action problems, Bergh and Bjørnskov referred to their fellow Scandinavian, Peter Nannestad, who had previously proposed high trust as the solution to these apparent collective action problems.[70] To quote Nannestad: "Because the universal welfare

69   Trust, Welfare States and Income Equality: Sorting out the Causality. Bergh, Andreas; Bjørnskov, Christian. *European Journal of Political Economy*, Volume 35, September 2014.

70   What Have We Learned from Generalized Trust, if anything? Nannestad, Peter. *Annual Review of Political Science*, 2008.

states are also high-trust countries, it is tempting to hypothesize that it is their high level of generalized trust that has enabled them to solve the collective action dilemma created by their welfare systems. People contribute their share because they (justifiably) trust that others will do the same and will not abuse the system. Thus, generalized trust is what makes the universal welfare system sustainable and allows equality to coexist with wealth."

Bergh and Bjørnskov interpreted their results as empirical confirmation of Nannestad's hypothesis. Indeed they refer to empirical evidence supporting the notion that it is historical levels of trust that explain the sizes of the welfare states in the present, not the other way around. Welfare states can be supported if citizens find each other trustworthy and free-riding is not perceived as a serious issue. Trust and trustworthy behaviour are what make welfare states sustainable.

But welfare states are about redistribution. Yet when we are concerned about the impacts of income inequality on trust, we should be focusing on pre-tax income inequality, as Bergh and Bjørnskov demonstrated. What this means in essence is a focus on the development of incomes and economic fortunes between different segments of the population – the things driving differential income development.

In a sense the finding that it is pre-tax incomes that matter most is understandable. This is because it corresponds well to the common observation that people are actually less concerned by the exact amounts they earn, but are very much irritated or amused by their friends', neighbours' and competitors' earnings relative to their own. In other words, it is more about status, ranking and pecking orders than actual levels of material wealth.

Luckily for our present study, income inequality is something that yields itself easily to measurement and documentation. Therefore, let us see what the data says about incomes, so as to see the dynamics between Bergh and Bjørnskov's claims on the one hand and general societal developments on the other. This should pave the way for at least a partial understanding of why we see trust measures declining in the west.

A classic example of pre-tax income inequality is the ratio of CEO pay to average worker's salary. In 2018 the average CEO in the US earned a salary that was 278 times the pay of the typical worker in their companies. For comparison, the wage ratio was only 20 to 1 in the US in 1965.[71] Predictably, the pay ratio gap seems to be narrower in Europe.

---

71   www.epi.org/publication/ceo-compensation-2018 – CEO compensation

CEO COMPENSATION RELATIVE TO TYPICAL WORKER, US

CEOs make 278 times as much as typical workers. CEO-to-worker compensation ratio, 1965–2018

▬ CEO-to-worker compensation ratio based on options realized
···· CEO-to-worker compensation ratio based on options granted

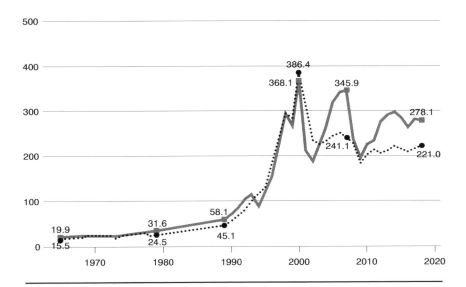

The trend in CEO to worker pay ratio points in the direction of strong divergence in pre-tax incomes, which we found to be toxic for trust. But CEOs are only the very top of the pyramid, and in any case a very small portion of the population. A more comprehensive picture is needed.

The World Inequality Report, by a group of renowned economists, offers a comprehensive look into the evolution of income shares between different groups around the world. The overall development is striking, with pre-tax incomes diverging clearly over time between the high-earners and low-earners. In other words, it seems the fruits of economic progress are distributed unevenly, no matter where you live. But this overall impression hides great variations between regions. Europe seems to be the most equal continent, whereas Africa, the Middle East, Brazil and India are among the most unequal.[72] Since our interest lies mainly with the western countries, we will focus our enquiry on Europe and the US.

72 World Inequality Report, 2018: wid.world/document/world-inequality-report-2018-english

The following graph presents the shares of national pre-tax income going to the top 1% and bottom 50% of wage earners between 1980 and 2016. The top 1% took home about 11% of all income in 1980, but by 2016 their share had risen to over 20%. In a contrary development, the bottom 50% of wage earners had a bit over 20% of all income in 1980, but by 2016 only about 13%. In real wage terms the bottom 50% had experienced practically no growth in incomes, whereas the incomes at the top had grown strongly. In other words, the pre-tax income inequality in the US has increased considerably over the past decades.

TOP 1% VS. BOTTOM 50% NATIONAL INCOME SHARES IN THE US, 1980–2016: DIVERGING INCOME INEQUALITY TRAJECTORIES

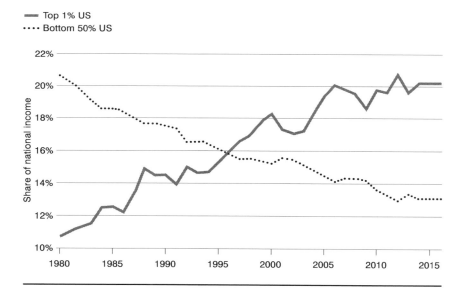

The picture is quite different for Europe. The initial shares of income for both the top 1% and bottom 50% start out in 1980 at about the same levels as in the US. The subsequent development is markedly different, however. Whereas there is a modest increase in income inequality, with the top 1% income share increasing by about two percentage points and the bottom 50% share decreasing by the same amount, the overall picture is remarkably stable.

TOP 1% VS. BOTTOM 50% NATIONAL INCOME SHARES IN WESTERN EUROPE, 1980–2016: DIVERGING INCOME INEQUALITY TRAJECTORIES

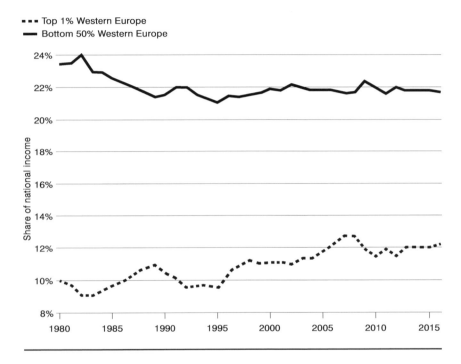

As income inequality is on the rise, and dramatically so in the US, it is no surprise that trust may be eroding at the same time. It is what we should expect based on academic literature. People are seeing their fortunes and material wellbeing diverge, which in turn leads to a widening gulf in interests and values. And then, common ground becomes harder and harder to find. As for the reasons for diverging fortunes at the top and bottom of the income pyramid, let's briefly mention a few candidates. On the basis of the results provided by Bergh and Bjørnskov, it was specifically pre-tax income inequality that was most robustly related to trust, or the lack of it. Diverging pre-tax incomes mean that the salaries on the ends of the spectrum are drifting further and further apart. Thinking about it economically, this may hint at diverging productivity and demand for jobs in different segments of the economy. These differing prospects are naturally reflected in the way these jobs are compensated.

Silicon Valley, with its starting salaries for programmers fresh out of school in the hundreds of thousands, attests to this. The increasing demands for stock market performance have probably driven both the exploding salaries for CEOs and their continuously shortening tenures. Shareholders want returns for their investment in the stock, and as a result companies compete for those perceived to bring the best value growth for shareholders. And if that performance does not seem to materialize quickly enough, it does not take long to change the captain of the ship. At the same time manufacturing jobs have been shipped overseas and many tasks have been essentially automated away, reducing the demand for a vast array of jobs. These are but some of the influences leading to differing prospects and incomes for different segments of the workforce.

In the parting words of their excellent article Bergh and Bjørnskov made an extremely interesting observation: "Given the evidence that social trust reduces the various forms of rent-seeking, it is probably a good idea to examine the relationship between trust and elite rent-grabbing in the private sector."[73] Rent-seeking can refer to the excess returns monopolists, asset owners and elite decision makers can derive from abusing their power.

As it happens, there is strong evidence that both the US and European economies have become more and more concentrated in the past decades.[74] The less competition there is, the greater the rent-seeking opportunities and the profits. It is remarkable that many of the largest and most profitable companies in the present, such as Amazon, Google or Facebook, are all effectively monopolies. Likewise, a group of friendly CEOs sitting on the boards of each other's companies and deciding on outsized raises for themselves would for example fit the definition of rent-seeking.

It is obvious that incomes and the economy have a material impact on trust. Structural economic changes and rent-seeking offer small glimpses of the fuller picture on the interactions between economics, income inequality and trust in recent decades. We will continue untangling the knot in a later part of this book with a more thorough discussion of the many economy-related influences on trust in the west.

73   Trust, Welfare States and Income Equality: Sorting out the Causality. Bergh, Andreas; Bjørnskov, Christian. *European Journal of Political Economy*, Volume 35, September 2014.
74   *Industry Concentration in Europe and North America*. Bajgar, Matej; Berlingieriu, Giuseppe; Calligaris, Sara; Criscuolo, Chiara; Timmis, Jonathan. OECD Productivity Working Papers, January 2019, No. 18.

EQUALITY OF OUTCOMES AND EQUALITY OF OPPORTUNITIES

The research on income inequality and trust might give the impression that inequality is the bane of trust in general. Of course, the relationship between the two is far more nuanced than that. The often competing concepts of equality of opportunity and equality of outcome offer an apt arena for analyzing the issue.

Severe income inequality could be thought to split interests and realities between people, leading to deteriorating trust. Another way to articulate the same idea is to note that higher income inequality increases the power distance between people, as wealth and income inevitably manifest as power over others, to the detriment of trust. As we find that trust is significantly related to skills, knowledge and education, common values, behaviours and interests and a sense of benevolence between people, high income inequality can be a negative factor for all these. An understandable outcome of these observations would be to consider them as arguments for equality of outcome – in other words, arguments for equalizing things like educational opportunities and income, regardless of individual merit. While there is some truth in this, a quick analysis shows that excessive equalization would be a disaster for trust.

Signifiers of excellence, such as school marks or variable salaries, help us identify ability – a factor of trust. Should signals such as these be turned off through equalization efforts, perhaps by abolishing grades or equalizing salaries, we would effectively be stumbling in the dark when it comes to individual abilities. This in turn would make it much more difficult to trust, because information about others would be diminished. If someone performs at a much higher level than their peers, yet is rewarded the same, it hardly feels fair or benevolent and can easily lead to a collapse of trust in the system.

In the real world the problem is that signifiers like grades or salary can often be divorced from actual ability to a considerable degree. But they are accurate just as often, and even fuzzy information can be better than no information.

Authoritarian regimes imposing strict regulations on values and expressible views similarly shut down information about genuine thoughts and interests, making it more difficult to know what people really think and feel, again diluting the ability to trust. Someone who is forced to confess values alien to them is likewise bound to become an enemy of this system, again destroying trust.

Thus, excessive equalization of outcomes is bound to end in a collapse of trust, because it makes assessing and acting on the factors of trust, ability, benevolence and integrity, that much harder; and would lead to the exploitation and suffering of many, who would cease to support such arrangements. The common desire to equalize and impose uniformity probably stems from the need to make one's environment ideal to oneself, and often from a purely selfish will to improve one's own situation at the expense of others. In the process of enforcing strict equalizing limitations, the dynamic adjustment that is necessary for trust is shut down. Perhaps the ubiquitous equalizing desire can be seen as a dark side or overreach of the normally positive trust-enhancing qualities that can arise from alignment on the factors of ability, benevolence and integrity.

From a trust perspective we might say that large inequalities are a recipe for disaster, just as excessive equalization is. The golden path lies between the two poles, where people find enough in common with each other and their inherent differences have enough room to bloom.

In light of these reflections on equality of outcome, equality of opportunity shows up as a more agreeable concept. This is an idea rooted in the working world and its selection processes for jobs and roles. In short, the basic gist of it is that hiring should be free from discrimination irrelevant to the task at hand. The only things that should matter are the relevant qualities for the role in question, such as experience and education. This purpose-fit line of thought has since spread further across our societies. A fair and equal selection process is one that should lead to selecting the best people for the positions available, because previously biasing factors such as gender, race, wealth or social status have in theory been driven out of the process. In short, equality of opportunity should then place people in positions that best match their abilities, and represents a mindset that should appeal broadly to people's sense of benevolence and integrity, because the majority can be expected to be on the benefiting side of the arrangement. The losing side, those previously exceptionally advantaged by privileges, might of course feel otherwise.

In sum, promoting equality of opportunity should increase trust if it results in the best matches between ability and position, improving the quality of outcomes. Likewise, it is an agreeable and benevolent philosophy towards all ambitious persons, regardless of their background. Equality of opportunity admits different outcomes for different people, in response to their deeds, ambitions and abilities. It does this by providing a fair and equal playground for people's varied talents to flourish in. Well, ideally at least. But even if reality is always a bit more complex than this, the outcome of equality of opportunity should be a society that can more flexibly adjust to the inherent diversity of talents and interests found in any population, also giving trust a hand.

In practice equalizing opportunities requires some measure of equalizing of outcomes. The levelling of the playing field is mostly achieved through state action, such as by providing universal access to education. States operate on taxation that often, but not always, acts to decrease the post-tax income inequalities. Indeed, the equalization of opportunities, such as by providing access to education, will also tend to lead to a degree of equalization of outcomes, because success becomes more widely distributed across the population. At the moment there seems to be much conflation between equalization of opportunities and outcomes, because the prevailing mood tends to interpret all differences in outcomes as indicators of oppression and denied opportunity. In reality it seems that it is difficult to establish the degree to which differences arise out of biases or inherent and cultural characteristics. It must be remembered that in a perfectly fair and equal system it is precisely inherent differences in abilities and interests that will come to dominate outcomes.

When it comes to trust and inequality, too much inequality is bad, but so is stamping out all difference. Thus we must dance on a tightrope and avoid pitfalls on both sides. Inequalities, wealth and income distribution are also at the heart of politics, with parties competing over whose money to spend on whose benefit. The successful exercise of political power in turns rests on the legitimacy of rule, the perception that it is justified. These are some of the topics we will be turning to next.

Political and social implications of trust

"It may be observed, that provinces amid the vicissitudes to which they are subject, pass from order into confusion, and afterward recur to a state of order again; for the nature of mundane affairs not allowing them to continue in an even course, when they have arrived at their greatest perfection, they soon begin to decline. In the same manner, having been reduced by disorder, and sunk to their utmost state of depression, unable to descend lower, they, of necessity, reascend; and thus from good they gradually decline to evil, and from evil again return to good. The reason is, that valor produces peace; peace, repose; repose, disorder; disorder, ruin; so from disorder order springs; from order virtue, and from this, glory and good fortune."

MACHIAVELLI, *HISTORY OF FLORENCE AND THE AFFAIRS OF ITALY*

MACHIAVELLI'S CLAIM OF oscillation between order and ruin was grounded in his review of the history of Europe and Italy from the fall of the Western Roman Empire up to his day. The evidence he found furnished him with an insight into the development of states and communities, the verity of which has been underscored again and again in the centuries succeeding him. European history, with its wars embroiling the continent or parts of it at regular intervals, not to mention the even longer historical cycles between empire and anarchy, offers an inexhaustible record of the dance between wisdom and virtue, error and evil. States and governments are hobbled by war and competition at regular intervals, but they may fall just as well in peacetime. Whether a political unit can avoid collapsing upon itself is a question of legitimacy, of the consent that forms a central pillar upholding the system.

TRUST AND LEGITIMACY

By now it should be no surprise that trust, being connected to many things social, provides an opportunity for novel interpretations in connection with the concept of political legitimacy. Whether based on a mandate from heaven, strange women lying in ponds distributing swords or popular consent, legitimacy as it is commonly understood refers to the acceptance and justification of political authority. Legitimacy is thus something that touches topics such as the origins of states as political communities and the nature of governance.

The following brief exposition of the defining aspects of legitimacy, as understood in the relevant literature, refers mostly to the excellent online resource that is the *Stanford Encyclopedia of Philosophy*, and the articles around the topic found therein.[75] After an admittedly selective overview, we will examine how trust ties in with the concept of legitimacy.

WEBER

Most textbooks start any discussion of legitimacy with Max Weber, and his account of it. Originating from his 1919 essay Politics as Vocation, the Weberian tripartite breakdown explains that legitimacy arises from either

---

75 Such as plato.stanford.edu/entries/legitimacy

charismatic, traditional or legal-rational authority. The charismatic individual gains authority by their superior personal qualities, leading others to defer authority to them. In the distant past, these qualities may have been those of the greatest warrior of the tribe, or slightly more recently of the most eloquent speaker of the nascent polis or religious movement. Any group relying on heroic individuals for political authority is liable to face constant challenges to that authority by the ambitious and crises at the departure of a leader; and if power is vested by the virtue of some qualities in one context, then those qualities may turn out to be useless as situations change. Weber saw tradition-based legitimacy as the natural next step after the age of heroes, as communities tire of the chaotic nature of the purely charisma-based individual authority, or the powerful individuals seek to consolidate power in some fashion.

A tradition-based system of legitimation bestows authority in accordance with some historically established method. Established nobilities and kingships, found around the world in times past and present, demonstrate the natural continuity between charisma and tradition. Some heroic ancestor gained a position of power, and wanted to perpetuate the advantages achieved for their family. Privileges such as lighter taxation were obtained to this end, while the new noble class in return promised things such as leadership and security through force of arms to the rest of the populace. Strict lines of succession based on heritage and blood relations were established. Legitimacy of rule is thus evaluated by reference to the set system of inheritance. By binding political authority to tradition, a society can order its citizens in relation to the tradition and set expectations about the future by determining how succession works. These features bring advantages of stability over purely charisma-based legitimacy, because succession and transfer of power are governed by the tradition rather than by contest among the most powerful and ambitious. In practice this seems to shift the power struggles from select individuals to the level of select competing noble families and dynasties. In the end, tying authority to bloodline, or some other tradition, has not turned out to provide exceptionally capable leaders, nor corresponded to evolving understandings of equity. The legal-rational basis for legitimacy may have evolved as an attempt to counter these circumstances.

The legal-rational system of legitimation is founded on known legal principles regulating political authority, which resides in impersonal public offices. The modern bureaucracy is a prime example of the legal-rational system of authority. When authority is based on offices and merit rather than individuals or tradition, meritocracy becomes possible (at least in theory). When the rights and responsibilities of authority are founded on legal agreements, they become intelligible, clearly bounded in their extent and modifiable if circumstances call for it. Where in traditional systems compensation for services to authority came in the form of privileges, legal-rational states often provide their servants with salaries that are fairer and even publicly known. Legitimacy in a legal-rational system stems from accordance with the established laws and offices they govern, which themselves are often liable to democratic deliberation and control.

Weber's three sources of legitimacy are archetypes, rarely if ever found in the wild in their pure forms. There is usually some mixture of them. Certainly charismatic leadership is still extant, whether in the form of a political leader with a cult-like following or the superstar start-up founder. Likewise, tradition inevitably arrives to lend its aura of authority to any existing system of governance over time.

NORMATIVE THEORIES OF LEGITIMACY

In the subsequent literature on legitimacy, Weber's exposition of the three sources has often been called descriptive because it provides frank explanations grounded in historical and real-life observations. Another line of thought has focused on examining the question: on what basis can the exercise of power and authority be justified, in other words said to be legitimate? This line of enquiry is called normative, in contrast with Weber's descriptive approach. The literature making up the normative branch of thought is wide and deep, reaching arguably from the earliest writings on how to order a good society to the contemporary profusion of pondering around the topic. Given that the subject has much to do with the origin of states and exercise of political authority, obligations between the state and the citizen – and ultimately about the nature of humans – this is not much of a surprise. In the context of our particular interests, we will focus on some of the major claims.

What is the difference between effective de facto authority, which any tyrant might possess, and legitimate political authority? According to John Locke state authority is born from the voluntary association of people, originally all free and equal in their natural rights, who then agree to submit themselves to state authority in order to prevent mutual abuse in the absence of laws. In this he aligned closely with his predecessor Thomas Hobbes, but he went on to elaborate a very different theory based on freedom and natural rights. What makes the exercise of power by the state legitimate is whether the state enjoys the consent of the people. Consent can be explicit or tacit, and binds the citizens to obey the state's laws. And consent applies not just at the formation of a state ("originating consent"), but also during the ongoing evaluation of the regime by the citizen ("joining consent"). In this concept legitimacy is lost if the state fails to secure the citizens' consent, or does not honour their natural rights (such as to private property, to defend oneself and to pursue personal interests). The state is justified and legitimate in its authority as long as it maintains consent and upholds the natural rights of its citizens. This concept remains at the root of justifying principles for democratic states to this day.

Locke's consent-based articulation of legitimacy did not appear out of a vacuum but was preceded by a long line of works by Grotius, Hobbes and Pufendorf, among others. These thinkers gradually shifted conceptions away from the older divine rights that characterized the medieval world of the church and nobility, representing the Weberian notions of traditional authority.

Since Locke, several variations on the theme of consent have been developed, demonstrating the concept's enduring vitality in western minds. These can be broadly split into two main groups: one focusing on public reason in the footsteps of Kant, and the other on democratic participation in the spirit of Rousseau as the source of consent and thus legitimacy. These two are naturally complemented by a third approach combining elements from both groups. What all have in common is that they discuss their questions and present their answers specifically with a democratic setting in mind.

For Rousseau, the question of legitimacy revolved around three wills or preferences: the citizen's private and general wills, and the abstract general will as revealed by democratic processes. A citizen's general will represents their interpretation of the common good, whereas private will reflects their personal interests. The abstract general will reflects the common good as crystallized by popular consensus. Mere tacit consent to the existence of the state, as with Locke, is not enough. Rather, legitimacy requires active participation by the citizens – a process through which notions of general will are compared and finally revealed conclusively. For Rousseau legitimacy is thus achieved by a state first enabling democratic voting and participation, and second abiding by the general will as revealed by those processes. This may seem to imply that the general will is merely another expression for "simple majority", but it is not quite so. Rousseau seems to have thoroughly deliberated on different majority voting rules and their moral consequences. Despite the seeming contradiction with his concept of general will, he was an advocate for majority rules for deciding the most fundamental and momentous issues, elaborating arguments why such adjustments would lead to more genuine expressions of the general will. In these arguments he, like Locke, drew inspiration from the writings of Grotius and Pufendorf.[76]

In contrast to Rousseau's participatory position on legitimacy, public reason approaches attempt to identify some set of universal values and reasons justifying authority, or the use of coercive power, between citizens and state. An exemplary recent take on public reason theory can be found with John Rawls. In his quest for values and reasons that all might agree on, Rawls limited himself to the architecture of the political system. Regardless of their views and values otherwise, how should everyone wish to construct the political process? With this framing Rawls restricts the domain of public reason to matters concerning constitutional essentials and basic justice, including the procedures for selecting judges, government officials and candidates for political office. While at first this may sound deceptively simple, Rawls included things such as the principles covering the distribution of resources in society. Thus, matters affecting wealth and income distribution, and by that extension nearly everything the state does, fall under the scope of public reason for him. As the minimum shared values that might function as the basis for a legitimate commonwealth, Rawls proposed ideas such as equal basic liberties, equality of opportunity and a just distribution of income and wealth. A state that could secure these "paradigmatic values of justice and public reason" would fulfil the "liberal principle of democracy" where authority is legitimate only when it is exercised in accordance with a constitution all reasonable citizens can endorse in light of their common human reason. So what Rawls was effectively saying was that the reigning western liberal values are those that every human, if they are reasonable, should agree on.

For Rawls and other public reason theorists, legitimacy is thus intimately connected to some set of values, and their realization by the state.

Both the participatory and public reason approaches stress the importance of the practical dimensions of the political process – constitution, voting systems and the principles governing office-holding matter. The so-called instrumentalist and proceduralist approaches make the practical considerations their benchmark, and evaluate legitimacy on the strength of the outcomes the particular decision making process is able to produce.

---

76   Voting the General Will: Rousseau on Decision Rules. Schwartzberg, Melissa. *Political Theory*, 36, 2008.

The proceduralist perspective sees democratic decision making as legitimate insofar as it follows some appropriate set of procedural rules. The result of a vote is legitimate if the aggregative process is fair. In light of the endless gerrymandering present in many democracies, the fairness of the voting process is not a given. Another proceduralist argument is that allowing for democratic deliberation, meaning public discussion and evaluation of policy alternatives or candidates, allows for more epistemically robust decision making. Therefore, in this version of the argument legitimacy depends on the degree and quality of deliberation promoted by democratic institutions.

The essence of pure instrumentalist argument is that there exists some ideal state of affairs, and that any system of governance is legitimate to the degree it is able to meet the hypothetical ideal. In some of these interpretations democracy has no special intrinsic value outside its potential for reaching the imagined ideal state of affairs. What the imagined ideal state would be is of course a pertinent question, and a cause of controversy in the literature. To determine the legitimacy of a given political system and process, one needs to have a clear view of the ideal state – the measuring stick – and of the relevant variables affecting each system's ability to produce outcomes. A tall order and something ultimately dependent on value judgements when it comes to determining the ideal state of affairs.

The proceduralist arguments bear close relation to Rousseau and his emphasis on the importance of voting mechanics in manifesting the general will, because they enquire about the finer details of the political process and how those details translate into legitimate outcomes. The instrumentalist approaches, caring mostly or only about the results the system produces irrespective of everything else, come in turn very close to another school of thought, one that will be the capstone of our rapid review of this topic.

The utilitarian approach considers legitimacy dependent on the beneficial consequences derived from state authority. The leading figure of this line is of course Jeremy Bentham. By his estimation, legitimacy is linked to the consequences of the laws set by the state. If the laws effectively promote the people's happiness and wellbeing, then the state is legitimate. In a more contemporary version, Christopher Wellman argues that since the organized state is the only way to escape the anarchic state of nature, people have a Samaritan duty to help each other to the safety and benefits of the organized community. The ultimate legitimation for the state comes not only from the benefits it provides to an individual directly, but also from those it provides to others. The logic here is that what benefits others and their flourishing tends to help you too, and a system that helps everyone is beneficial if you ever face misfortune. Therefore, the formation of a state is a mutual responsibility for everyone, and provides benefits to each.

And so, this concludes our short review of the major lines of thought about legitimacy. The theories presented here have much depth and many variations, and we have merely summarized the major claims made. This does regrettable injustice to the thinkers in question, but is necessary for our own interests centred on trust.

TRUST AND LEGITIMACY

Having climbed to our new vantage point, we can now survey the landscape of legitimacy through our spyglass of trust. Let's start with the Hobbesian view, shared by Locke and many others, about the state of nature before organized community, the war of all against all and the consequent rationale for people to come together for peaceful living in an organized society. Certainly this is an incomplete perspective, given that humans have always lived with their families and tribes – groups of some sort. The image of individual human beings surviving alone in the wilderness is a fantasy, attested by our fundamentally sociable natures and habits. It seems reasonable to assume that organized societies grew from the first families and tribes. As populations increased, formalizing relations became necessary and so the first rules appeared, later to be inscribed on tablets of law.

Regardless, the Hobbesian view captures some essential ideas that help us reflect on the role of trust in society. The insight about chaos and terror in the absence of enforced order is certainly true. A vacuum in authority will inevitably be filled with abuse and ruthless seizing of advantages. Arts and sciences cannot flourish without stability, any more than human beings can. The direct connection between order and prosperity can be observed in the generally anarchic and miserable conditions afflicting societies where authority has broken down. More fundamentally, historians such as Ian Morris have argued that over time larger and larger political units, and thus areas of stability, have brought about a similar stepwise decrease in rates of violent death. Paradoxically, the peace-bringing consolidation has mostly been realized through wars and violent competition between states.[77] European history leading up to the formation of the EU

---

77 Arguments expressed in his book *War – What is it Good For?* Farrar, Straus & Giroux, 2014.

seems like a perfect example here. The process of interstate competition between European nations on one hand and the pressures from the American, Soviet and Chinese giants on the other pushed the European countries together. Despite the often disastrous and destructive road to peace, the overall pattern is clear: stability and internal peace are of first-order importance for the development of any society.

So, to put it dramatically: across the fence of organized community a lawless wilderness of danger awaits. Should the social order break down, the risk of undesirable outcomes obviously shoots up. What is the role of trust in all this? At minimum the loss of order implies a severe deficit of trust. But is this deficit a cause or a consequence of the loss of order? Possibly both. Before delving into the murk of state failure, let us go back to the beginning.

Should any group come together in a Hobbesian fashion and make a conscious decision to form a state where previously none existed, we may say it would represent a supreme act of trust. The members of this group would have decided to join their individual fates with those of the rest. The quality of this decision becomes apparent if we recall that trust is sensitive to the magnitude of the stakes; on a minor issue we are easier with it, but the graver the concern the higher the bar for trust. Such an immaculate state conception would of course be nearly as sensational as the Catholic one, being all but unheard of in the real world. Nowhere on a fully populated earth do circumstances allow for a fully fresh start. Perhaps the closest we can get to this type of state formation is through secessions that establish a new state out of an older one. The rebellious formations of the US or my native Finland are great examples.

From a trust perspective these acts of establishing new states are not only supreme expressions of trust within the new communities, but often even more so of distrust of the previous overlords. Finnish independence, gained in 1917 in the chaotic circumstances surrounding the Bolshevik revolution, typifies this tendency. Finland had long been the eastern province of Sweden, but thanks to its geographical location formed the battleground for clashing Swedish and Russian interests – a struggle centuries old. The tumultuous Napoleonic years had provided a decisive break in the contest. The combination of rising Russian power and Swedish stumbling resulted in the disastrous Finnish war of 1808–1809. Finland was conquered, and the Russians advanced as far as the shores of modern Sweden. A British intervention to pacify the Baltic was not enough to turn the tide, and Finland was finally ceded in 1809, leading to the creation of the autonomous Grand Duchy of Finland under the wings of the Russian empire.

Although Finnish independence had already been evoked in the preceding century, the new situation soon charged the nascent movement with new vigour. Despite relatively relaxed governance by the Russians, a burgeoning national awakening swept through the country during the 19th century, in line with European trends. Inspired by the desire for independence the people managed to produce a golden age of Finnish arts, perhaps most notably collecting the remnants of oral folklore forming the Kalevala poems of epic mythology. Simultaneously the Finnish language was elevated from the shadow of Swedish and Russian, which had dominated the governmental, commercial and academic discourses. A distinct national narrative and identity was being born.

While the enthusiasm for independence had been growing ever since the beginning of the Grand Duchy, so long as Finnish autonomy was respected no serious seditionary efforts were made. Things began to change as the 19th century turned into the 20th and pressure increased towards the Russification of Finland. It was not merely a cultural programme – the efforts included severe restrictions on autonomy and self-determination, ranging from censorship to military integration and the elevation of the Russian language in official use. These actions by the imperial authorities were not met with much excitement among the population of the autonomous principality. Protests and addresses proved to be in vain, and in 1905 the resistance took a serious turn with the assassination of the Russian general-governor of Finland, Nikolay Bobrikov. Tense relations continued throughout the First World War, but the collapse of the old order in Russia finally opened a new path forward. With the blessing of the newly dominant Bolsheviks, Finland became independent in 1917, after over 100 years of Russian rule and some 600 as a part of Sweden before that.

The idea of independence may have been older, but the period of autonomy served to prepare the ground for the birth and growth of an independent nation. The 19th century saw the crystallization of a unique Finnish identity, shaped by questions of language, the rediscovery of old mythos and the flourishing of arts reflecting the unique Finnish heritage. These in turn meant a distinct sense of Finnishness separate from the neighbouring Russians and Swedes. A verse attributed to Adolf Ivar Arwidsson describes the sentiment succinctly: "Swedes we are no longer; Russians we do not wish to become; let us therefore be Finns."

The rupture with the past caused by separation from Sweden gave room for the blossoming of the unique Finnish heritage and culture; the new Russian pressures moulded them into a political programme. Importantly, the establishment of the Grand Duchy in 1809 eventually turned out to be a blessing from an institutional standpoint. First, to keep the country on its feet, and later to promote its separation from Swedish influence and heritage, new arrangements were needed. In what may initially appear to be acts of considerable enlightenment the victorious Russians granted the Finns the right to maintain their old laws and constitutional arrangements, including their own civil service. The senate combined legislative and executive organs of the nation, and a bank that was to become the Central Bank of Finland was set up in 1811 to manage the monetary separation from Sweden. These developments coincided with expansion of education and the first steps towards an industrial economy. Slowly but surely the institutional foundations for a thriving nation were laid.

The perpetuation of the existing legal and bureaucratic practices may give an impression of benevolence, but in reality stemmed more from the weakness of the Russian position than from any sense of righteousness: being in the middle of the struggle with Napoleon meant Russia had scant time to waste on the Finnish question and the central government's control over the lands was weak. Leaving the conquered nation to tend for itself was just an expedient solution in the middle of much bigger problems. Indeed there are indications that the new emperor reigning from 1825 to 1855, Nicholas I, originally had a more restrictive view about Finland's position. But again more urgent issues elsewhere, this time in the form of the Decembrist revolt in St. Petersburg, led him to opt for the status quo.

Real institutional progress was achieved in the latter part of the century under the reign of the liberal-minded emperor Alexander II, who reigned from 1855 to 1881. A national currency and postage stamps were created, and regular meetings of the estates were resumed. The economy was reformed along liberal lines, aligning with the new ideas coming from western Europe. This meant new initiatives in seafaring and industrial and commercial development, which led to a burst of economic growth in the country.

Things really began to change during the time of his successor Alexander III (1881–1894), and especially after Nicholas II came to power in 1894. In 1890 the post office was merged under the control of the Russian one, but that was a minor issue compared with the changes that were to come in 1899 and after. Among the reforms the small Finnish army was incorporated into the imperial one, censorship was stepped up, the Finnish civil service was opened up for Russians and Russian was made the official language of public life, and planning was stepped up to dissolve the Finnish markka and make the rouble the official currency. Many other efforts to Russify the country were planned and taken, as well, and by 1910 Finland's governance had effectively been taken over by Russian nationals, mostly of a military background.

Russian liberalism especially during the latter part of the 19th century gave the tools for the nation to govern itself; Russian illiberalism in the final years of the Grand Duchy heightened the rationale to do so.

It may be assumed that if the 1808–1809 war had ended in a Swedish success, Finland's continued existence as a part of Sweden would not have brought about the new independent institutions such as its own currency, nor an equally strong search for a national identity. As such the circumstances of an autonomous Grand Duchy prepared the ground for an independent Finland later on.

Various aspects of the story of Finnish independence allow us to analyse how trust may be involved in questions of legitimacy.

The creation of a new unique Finnish national narrative through the resuscitation of old myths and elevation of the vernacular Finnish was essential in establishing a new identity that was separate from the old Swedish and the newly imposed Russian one. This new identity formed the basis from which independent values and interests could be articulated in opposition to Russian dictates. Despite these events, Finland continued to have a significant Swedish-speaking population, and kept looking towards Sweden in particular and the west in general for ideas and example. This translated into very different values from those guiding the Russian empire, manifested for example in differing perspectives on constitutional matters or democratic participation. Values in turn tend to be tightly connected to perceived interests of many sorts.

The different values and interests arising from a new national narrative easily lend themselves to an acrimonious understanding of what is legitimate and what is not. Recall that legitimacy could be based on the consent of the citizens, procedural considerations or perhaps fulfilling some set of values. If there exist marked differences in perceptions about the relationship between the constitution and the head of state, as in Finland under Russian rule, or of the importance of participation, these are clearly grounds for problems with legitimacy. If power is felt to be acquired unjustly, it may be difficult to consent to its exercise. Should you perceive the process of governance as backward and inefficient, or against your values in general, legitimacy seems unlikely to result. In other words, the competing theories can all accommodate and explain the Finnish challenge to the legitimacy of Russian rule (as they should).

From a trust standpoint the nascent national consciousness has similarly clear consequences. Different fundamental values and resulting standards of behaviour between the people of the Grand Duchy on one hand and the imperial Russians on the other, as exemplified by the legal and process-related issues, are sure to affect the integrity dimension of trust. In step with the birth of a national identity came ideas of national interest. When various freedoms and institutions were lost at the end of the 19th century and the start of the 20th, it became clear to Finns that there might exist serious conflicts of interest with the Russian empire. This must have registered negatively on the benevolence aspect of trust antecedents. As the highest echelons of governance became populated by Russian nationals speaking a language mostly unintelligible to the majority of the population, promoting systems of governance broadly viewed as antiquated, inefficient and unjust, the populace cannot have had strong faith in the capability of the system to provide for their needs. Therefore, the new developments must have appeared dubious from the ability dimension of trust as well.

Fundamentally, wishing to break away from a previous order implies that the separatist community believes itself able to conduct its matters better alone than within the confines of the previous arrangement. This wish to cease cooperation, by definition, is therefore a statement of distrust. Likewise, it represents a rejection of the social contract offered by the dominant power.

Lack of legitimacy is likely to find a companion in lack of trust. If there are deep unhappiness and feelings of grievance and unjust rule, these are bound to affect the people's willingness to cooperate with the state and submit to its rule. Trust for its part is about taking the risk to cooperate, and everything that goes into making that choice. Thus, it is apparent that the two, trust and legitimacy as understood normatively, are closely connected.

The connection between the two shines even clearer when we consider the main lines of normative legitimacy theories. As a common starting point legitimacy was thought to flow from the consent of the people. Consent in turn was seen to be dependent on the satisfaction of some set of values, the beneficial outcomes of state action or procedural or efficiency-related reasons. Now compare these with the three antecedents of trust: ability as in capacity to deliver what is promised, benevolence as goodwill towards the trustor, and integrity as in common values and standards of behaviour. The value-based approach by the public reason theorists shares with integrity the importance of values. Beneficial consequences of state action as the benchmark of legitimacy connect clearly to evaluations of benevolent or malicious intent. The proceduralists think legitimacy is connected to the quality of the political process or outcomes it is able to produce, just as the ability dimension of trust sees capacity to deliver as a condition of trust.

The theorists of normative legitimacy have collectively produced explanations of the concept that very closely match our prevailing theory of trust and its constituents. Or perhaps the opposite observation would be more accurate, given that the consensus definition of trust that we use only came to be in the 1990s, far later than most of the relevant theories of legitimacy. Regardless, the neatness of alignment between the broad lines of both sets of theories is remarkable.

Of course, this discussion of legitimacy is somewhat superficial, and claiming trust and legitimacy to be equivalent concepts would not do justice to the depths of theories covering either subject. Yet it is obvious that there is a connection between the two. This connection is not merely a product of the similarities between the theories, but is also corroborated by common sense. Trust in the state is unlikely to exist without the state's existence and actions being felt to be justified, or legitimate, and legitimacy can hardly be sustained for long in the absence of a level of trust. The two are not the same thing, yet they seem to go hand in hand. Legitimacy is about the acceptance and justification of rule, consent to it, all of which must necessarily rely on at least some measure of trust. One might accept the rule of a dictatorial regime as a fact of life, but deny that it has any justification and therefore legitimacy. Consent by definition means giving permission to a third party to do something, and by this virtue comes close to risk-taking on behalf of the trustor towards the trusted party. By voluntarily consenting to something that can affect you, one effectively makes the choice to trust. As such, consent is another concept closely orbiting trust. What separates consent from trust is that it can be thought of specifically as the act of giving permission without reference to the reasons why, or of any reciprocal expectation, in contrast with the multivariable risk-taking process unfolding over time in a relationship context that trust is.

Bearing in mind the tight connections between legitimacy and trust, and to pursue our interest in untangling trust's impacts in society, let us rephrase legitimacy as a specific instance of trust: the trust the populace has in the state and the prevailing political system connected to it. More liberally we might allow some degree of freedom in the use of the concept, so that legitimacy can also be possessed or lacked by some specific part of the state, rather than the whole, such as its highest political leadership or perhaps some particular law or institution. Distrust of a particular sub-organ of the state does not necessarily lead to distrust of the state as a whole, and vice versa. In other words trust in the head of state would mean they can be considered legitimate, and likewise distrust of them would translate into illegitimacy, but not necessarily for the state itself. The same may be said of the state: if it enjoys some necessary level of trust from the citizens, it is legitimate; if not, then it is perceived as illegitimate. And yet some singular organ of the state might still retain the trust of the citizens. Hence, we could see legitimacy as a spectrum, with trust in the state and political system as a whole at one end and trust in no part of it at the other end.

Over time each citizen observes and encounters the state in action. These experiences shape our understanding of its public capabilities in their many forms: the quality of infrastructure and social services provided, the handling of public finances and taxation, general responsiveness to citizens' needs, perceived level of corruption in the civil service and the nature and dysfunctions of the political system and so on. Drawing from these lessons the citizen will start to form opinions about the state and its ability to perform the functions ascribed to it. These evaluations are further coloured by the development of personal values and contrasting examples afforded by international peers. The outcome of these evaluations affects the citizen's level of trust in the state and its organs. Does the state provide adequate services in return for the level of taxation? Can public officials be trusted to promote the common good, or are they merely lining their own pockets? Is the state able to maintain peace and order in my area? Answers to these sorts of questions affect the level of trust the state enjoys from the ability perspective, and ultimately how legitimate it is perceived to be.

Individuals imbibe their values and standards of behaviour from their family and surrounding society, learning to value things that align with the prevailing circumstances in their thoughts and actions. This is the common starting point. Yet time, experience and deliberation may also yield insights and new ideas. Slowly the individual may start to recognize their own perspective as unique and different, sometimes radically so. This dawning of new thoughts tends to be connected to novel interpretations of causes and effects in relation to something desirable or undesirable, leading to the formation of values in clear contrast to the normal way of just internalizing the messages from one's surroundings, often happening without much thought about their validity or deeper consequences. The degree to which one's private values harmonize with those espoused by the state and wider society is bound to impact the individual's evaluation of the legitimacy of the state and society they participate in, and their willingness to underwrite the social contract. Should a decisive difference in values exist, the goals, policies and actions of the state may be an affront to the individual, making it impossible for them to afford any feelings of legitimacy to the state. An obvious and terrifying example is the conflict Nazi Germany had with its Jewish population. In response to the Nazi rise to power and the related conflict in values and interests, many Jews renounced the social contract and emigrated. Values and behavioural standards – the integrity dimension of trust – shape our interpretations of legitimacy.

These examples from the ability and value perspectives are also closely connected to evaluations about the state's benevolence towards its citizens. Clearly, the open antagonism of the Nazi regime cannot have evoked any illusions of benevolence in its Jewish subjects. Contemporary challenges channelling contests to legitimacy from a benevolence angle can be found with climate change and the various forms of income and wealth inequality in many countries. As the name of the climate activist movement Extinction Rebellion implies, many feel that climate change is a matter of life and death – and that rebellion is needed to set things right. Their basic premise, supported by science and common sense alike, is that rising temperatures jeopardize our living environments, with many undesirable second-order consequences. The threats to the environment take many forms from rising sea levels to desertification, as well as extreme temperatures and destructive weather patterns. In the face of these circumstances, it is an understandable position to consider parties causing climate change, or neglecting to address it, as illegitimate. The charge against states is that of omission of the duty to safeguard the future through adequate climate action.

Another contest in many countries, of present importance and an almost eternal nature, concerns the distribution of income and wealth in society. The poor and the rich are equal in their eagerness to promote their own (often short-term) interests, and therefore support factions seeking to raise taxes for the sake of better public services and equality, or to decrease them in the name of freedom and fairness. When one of the factions gains too much power, the environment tends to become hostile and intolerable to the other. The outcomes are usually either a revolt of the frustrated masses or a flight of the moneyed and mobile in search of a more accommodating environment. Often both show up in close connection. Popular revolts tend to follow economic troubles and high perceived income and wealth differences. Given the middle classes in the US have not experienced much if any growth in real incomes in the past 40 or so years, while the top 1% incomes have ballooned, it is no wonder the union seems to grow more fragile by the year, as is marked by increasingly hostile political camps and movements. When a large enough share of people feels the system is working against their interests, rather than for them, the result tends to be revolt.

It is interesting to note that many of the major history-shaping internal conflicts, from the French revolution in the 18th century to the Bolshevik one in the early 20th, as well as the Chinese cultural revolutions, had a common thread: they were mainly purges of the wealthy and educated in the name of the masses, despite their different ideological justifications, whether anti-royalist, democratic or communist. Perhaps even the Nazi events had such a dimension, although mostly ethnically motivated. In the end, all were preceded by economic and other crises, and followed by humanitarian disasters.

If the US provides a current example of excessive control by the rich leading to feelings of illegitimacy among those less well off, a recent counterexample mentioned earlier may be found in the typically more left-leaning France. Under the leadership of the socialist president Francois Hollande, a 75% tax rate was announced for those earning over a million euros in late 2012. The measure, with other wealth taxes, led to an exodus of the well-off, signalling a renunciation of the social contract in the face of what were felt to be illegitimate policies. A few years and tens if not hundreds of thousands of emigrants later, the new income tax policy was reversed.

Not surprisingly, a benevolent or hostile attitude of the state towards the citizens or members of a given group tends to affect the level of legitimacy afforded to it by those subjects. In practice the benevolent or hostile stance manifests as concrete policies, often benefiting some groups over others. This is of course the essence of all political choices, but going too far in one direction (whether too much or too little) tends to make the situation intolerable for some members of society. State policies are usually justified through some set of values, and as such it is clear that the benevolence dimension is closely tied to values and, thus, the integrity dimension. Evaluations of the benevolence of the state can also be a matter of its ability to fulfil the promises made. This is the case with climate change. Nearly every state is making wonderful statements about how important it is to tackle the issue, yet the actions taken have not measured up to the words spoken. This dichotomy is at the heart of the Extinction Rebellion movement. But then again the fascists of 1930s were famed for their organizational abilities, making the trains run on time and the autobahns fast; the problems with those regimes stemmed strictly from the realms of values and hostile attitudes. As such the ability dimension appears slightly more independent of the integrity and benevolence duo. Nonetheless, all of these matter in evaluating the legitimacy of a regime.

Trust develops as a process depending on the feedback loop of past experience guiding future behaviour. Keeping this in mind we can ponder how transparency and responsiveness of governance may affect legitimacy. The incentives of a government in the public eye provide an excellent starting point.

Any regime has an incentive to embellish its competences and hide its failures, as any individual does. This nearly universal tendency is an outcome of the pain and potential consequences of failure, whether large or small, which we would rather avoid than face. There is always the incentive to strive for as positive an image as possible, in the hopes of the potential benefits it may yield. The unfortunate result of these instincts is that they may, however, lead to deceiving and misleading behaviour. The price of this misdirection may be small or insignificant between individuals in a private setting, but when it concerns the highest representatives of a state, the stakes are potentially of existential importance (for the individual and the state alike).

In the context of trust and legitimacy, obstructionism and misrepresentation impact the feedback loop of observation and evaluation essential for trust assessments. When important information is lacking, the trust evaluation is on less firm ground than it might optimally be. When some critical piece of information is hidden, trust may be granted where none is merited. Alternatively, in a total absence of information it may be impossible to make the investment of trust, even if it would be warranted. The importance of information for trust comes up commonly when shopping on the internet. How many times has a lack of prior knowledge about a vendor, perhaps accentuated by a lack of reviews from other customers, resulted in a purchase from another more expensive but already trusted source; and, on the contrary, how many times has taking the plunge and trusting the cheap yet unverified vendor resulted in getting scammed? In the first example lack of information leads to lack of trust and no transaction where it would be warranted; in the second it leads to a purchase where it is not warranted. Imagine a world where customer reviews for these services were not available. Having to trust blindly, how would that affect buying habits with internet vendors? It may be assumed the less information there is, the riskier the investment of trust will be, and so the bar for placing trust will be higher. This is why internet sales platforms have created systems for verification and review, albeit imperfect, which seek to transparently create a feedback loop of trust through public evaluation of vendors.

Periodic elections generate a similar feedback loop in a political context. Politicians and parties whose actions and ideas have not generated approval find their backing diminished, while others find their support increasing in response. Through the process political leadership and state actions come to reflect the changing values and wishes of the people. The functioning of the feedback loop connecting expectations to actual experience and from there finally to re-evaluation is often dramatically compromised by the parties' attempts to present themselves in as vague a manner as possible, to attract voters as broadly as possible and to shield themselves from critique. Other considerations and incentives therefore derail the trust process from an optimal path. The optimal situation from a trust perspective would be one in which parties set maximally truthful expectations by clearly defining their unique political stances and sticking to them; and neither hiding nor obscuring their actions and the outcomes of those actions. In other words, providing fully truthful information based on which the electorate could then adjust their views. Obviously real-life concerns make this ideal unreachable. Although the particular incentives may differ, the overall logic of divergent interests exemplified by political parties applies in many situations and organizations throughout society, not just in politics or in relation to the state.

When information is missing, misleading or misrepresented, the trust evaluation will be different from what it would be if we had all the facts – leading to mistrust, and possibly distrust later on. The greater the misrepresentation, the greater the degree of mistrust and the eventual readjustment when expectations collide with reality. And should it become apparent that false representations were given on purpose, the response tends to be negative.

Organizational and individual logics of self-interest often tend to result in incentives for obscuring or misleading, even when the actor's intent towards those affected is good. If the actor's intent is not wholly benevolent, or perhaps merely not quite within the boundaries of legality, the incentives for obscuration and misleading multiply, because actions and motivations will inevitably need to be hidden lest they generate insurmountable resistance. States and governments genuinely interested in promoting the common good will be keener to open their processes and activities to audit by the eyes of the public. This tendency develops in the first place out of valuing the common good above private interests, thereby directing efforts towards effective solutions over the extraction of benefits. Institutional transparency and openness to improvement will result in a more robustly functioning feedback loop of trust than would exist in a more opaque and closed setting. In practice these feedback loops are built on things such as: a political system able to reflect the wishes of the citizens, as in a representative democracy; an intelligible legal system that is perceived as impartial, fair and reliable; opportunities for citizens to credibly appeal the decisions concerning them and so on. As a result of various institutional forms of two-way communication states enable the trust-building feedback loop where citizens can more accurately assess their relationship with the state and each other, and adjust their actions accordingly, which in turn may effect changes in state function for the better. Transparency alone is not necessarily enough, because the outcome may also be negative for trust and therefore legitimacy, should citizens be utterly dismayed at what they perceive in the state but unable to affect or fix things. It is precisely the benevolent adaptability of the state in response to the evolving needs of citizens that turns the feedback loop into a potential source of trust and legitimacy. States enabling systems of sensitivity to address common concerns are likely to enjoy a higher level of trust, not just between the state and the citizens, but also among citizens by promoting standards of peaceful and responsive solving of problems. From a general political theory point of view we might add these arguments to the merits of freedom of expression and participatory forms of governance, which are typically promoted from the basis of equal rights and freedom instead of trust and its many benefits.

These insights about the trust process and the feedback loop enabled by transparency and responsiveness conform with real-world observations. We generally find countries promoting freedom of expression and participatory forms of governance have high trust scores. They also tend to score highly on transparency.[78] Countries with less participatory governance tend to score low on transparency and trust, which is precisely what we may expect when the incentives for obstruction are stronger. Therefore,

---

78   *Transparency of Government Policymaking*. World Bank: tcdata360.worldbank.org/indicators/
      h7da6e31a For an easier article, see also, for example: www.usnews.com/news/best-
      countries/most-transparent-countries

we might conclude with the common sense understanding that a fair and benevolent state will be eager to promote openness, transparency and responsive governance – and thereby trust – whereas states dominated by private interests will have all the opposite incentives leading to generally lower levels of trust and, by our definition, legitimacy.

As mentioned, the downside of all transparency, openness and responsiveness for any organization is that they expose the particular actor and its representatives to critique. Indeed, one of the strongest explanations for the current crisis of legitimacy in the west and elsewhere stems from the argument that technological changes have increased transparency to the point where the faults and mistakes of various political institutions and actors have come to light like never before, thus driving a widespread disaffection. In addition, self-organizing in the age of the internet is easier than ever before, lowering the bar for all kinds of demonstrations of displeasure. We will explore these arguments more thoroughly when we look into the relationship of trust and technology in the next chapter.

A problem with defining legitimacy as trust in the state is that both are somewhat nebulous concepts to begin with. Measuring them conclusively is difficult, and especially so considering that both are highly multidimensional. Thus, perhaps the most profound problems arise from their very relative nature. One can be very distrustful of the political system and leaders of one's country, yet perceive that the situation could be far worse. Winston Churchill's saying about democracy as the worst form of government, except for all the others that have been tried, captures the sentiment perfectly. It is easily conceivable that someone might respond with very low scores on a trust survey, yet think they are in actuality living in the best system with the best government in the world – and the most legitimate. It can be speculated that forms of government and public institutions both affect the level of trust among citizens and are also a reflection of it.

Ultimately the proof is in the pudding: when there is open revolt, we can definitely say trust has been lost. Typically the road to civil wars and revolutions, reflecting complete breakdowns of trust and legitimacy among the people, is paved with intensifying riots, demonstrations and political polarization. Although these do happen in very healthy and trustful environments, too, they can also signify lack of trust and legitimacy. What is crucial here is the degree to which the demonstrators pose a direct challenge to the state itself and its justification for existence. In the normal course of things, many issues will be demonstrated about in a limited fashion, taking aim at some single point of contest, without calling into question the state's existence. But we may expect such questioning to increase in step with a widening gap in values or views about the benevolence or ability of the state to provide for the people's needs. When the gap becomes unbridgeable civil disorder and worse follow. In benign and trustful circumstances citizens find the state to be their ally in effecting the changes desired.

A legitimate state is one whose institutions and actions the people find justified and acceptable – worth their consent. Normative theories of legitimacy present several answers to the question of consent, and why people should grant it. Whether it is fulfilment of values, beneficial consequences or procedural considerations, there is an apparent connection to be made between the main theories of legitimacy and the antecedents of trust. Following this insight I propose trust in the state as an alternative definition of legitimacy. This new definition has the benefit that through trust's antecedent dimensions it covers and explains the spectrum of legitimacy theories, and grounds them in a broader understanding of human behaviour, cooperation and social capital.

Why is trust in decline in the west?

SO FAR, WE have attempted to argue for the importance of trust in societal development by demonstrating how it may impact everything from individual life to innovation, our concepts of knowledge and the legitimacy of a political order. All of these show why trust really matters. In other words the operating assumption for us is that more trust is good, and that the declines seen over time in the US and Europe alike are a negative indicator of the health of our societies. Having established how essential trust is, the sharp declines in trust seen in statistics become more than a curiosity – they are a flashing warning sign.

From these conclusions we naturally arrive at two questions. First, why is trust eroding? And second, what can we do to reverse the process? Addressing this pair of dilemmas composes the final section of the book.

INCOME INEQUALITY

"The tsunami of wealth didn't trickle down. It surged upward."

WARREN BUFFETT IN *TIME MAGAZINE, 2018*[79]

In the section covering some of the economic aspects of trust, we discussed how pre-tax income inequality has exploded in recent decades, with negative impacts on trust. What has led to such divergence in pre-tax incomes? The answer is obviously complex, but we will attempt to elucidate a few key factors. Let's dig in.

One obvious explanation for the explosion in income inequality, especially in the US, can be found in the very uneven impacts of globalization. By globalization we mean the integration of previously closed and economically less developed nations, such as China, into the international capitalist economic order. The impacts of this integration process have been many. Aided by wise domestic policies and foreign investments deployed in search of high returns, many previously poor countries have enjoyed sky-rocketing standards of living. Indeed, as a consequence of rapid economic development the number of global poor has been steadily decreasing over the past decades, with hundreds of millions lifted out of poverty. China and South Korea are perhaps the most prominent examples. Both were previously poor countries, but are now places where wealth abounds and world-class industries grow and prosper. This has all been extremely positive.

On the flipside of these developments, much industry has been transferred from the west to lower-cost developing countries. In the process, especially industrial jobs have been lost and wages for the remaining ones have stagnated thanks to lower demand and a greater pool of candidates competing for a decreasing number of open positions. To complicate things further, the shareholders of western companies have benefited from various cost reduction and tax evasion opportunities, as is evident from the all-time-high profit margins among US companies for example.[80] In tow, high-level executives and other top professionals have seen their incomes grow rapidly. So in the west, the decades of globalization look very different depending on one's vantage point on the income ladder. Those who were already well off have benefited handsomely; others less so.

The problems of income inequality are especially acute in the US. As we saw from the graphs presented earlier, European income shares have in contrast remained relatively static in recent decades. It seems likely that lack of growth and persistently high unemployment are bigger problems and causes of inequality and distrust for European countries in general, and possibly also explain in part why there has been far less change in European income shares in the first place.

So while globalization has been a mostly unambiguous win for countries such as China, in the west the outcomes have been mixed – in a way that has exacerbated income inequality. The working and middle classes have seen their jobs evaporate and wages stagnate, while the shareholders and high-level professionals running companies have reaped the benefits. The unequal outcomes of globalization have contributed to increasing income inequality, thereby seeding distrust in society. Indeed, scepticism and distrust seem like understandable reactions in the face of policies clearly benefiting a small segment of society at the expense of others.

Globalization of the capitalist economic regime is on the one hand a policy choice (regarding free capital and worker movements, for example), and on the other inevitable and uncontrollable. Less developed countries can always adopt economic practices proven effective elsewhere. In doing so, they increase trading opportunities and competition on a global level,

---

80   See for example: www.gmo.com/europe/research-library/why-we-are-not-worried-about-
      elevated-profit-margins

creating pressure on the incumbents of the system. In this sense, at least some measure of globalization was always inevitable, while a significant part of it has been down to policies explicitly advocating for it.

The rise of information technology, and of companies exploring the opportunities therein, has resulted in a very similar dichotomous dynamic. With the advances of information technology we have acquired not just smartphones and the internet, but also a vast array of automation technologies. And so many jobs have simply been automated away, instead of outsourced. This trend is set to continue, and the World Economic Forum estimates that 85 million jobs will be lost to automation and information technology advances between 2020 and 2025.[81] Luckily, all this new technology also requires people to make use of it, and on the beneficial side the WEF estimates that 97 million new jobs will be created as a result. Although the net effect is positive, it seems likely that the losers and winners will often be different people.

Another feature of information technologies is that they often build on network effects. This is the commonality between MS Office tools, file formats such as the MP3 and social media services like Facebook or Instagram – they all become more valuable as they gain new users. Social media is useless if you're the only one around. But if there are a hundred, a thousand or a million users, it consequently becomes all the more interesting – and valuable – a place to be. The same applies across many tech products and services. One outcome of this network dynamic is effective natural monopolies, such as enjoyed by Google search or YouTube, for example. As a consequence the internet-based economy is often characterized as a "winner takes all" environment. In other words, the one winner reaps gigantic profits, while competition dies out. Given the intangible software nature of the products of these firms, they also often employ very few people compared with older industrial-age businesses. This combination of features easily yields massive income inequalities, as huge profits are concentrated in very few hands. It is no surprise that the founders of Microsoft, Facebook and Amazon are the richest people in the world.

As with globalization, it is easy to see how the technology-driven trends could exacerbate income inequality, and thus further deteriorate societal trust.

On top of these longer-term influences on income inequality, we of course need to consider the actions of the central banks after the financial crisis of 2007–2008. Ever since, the central banks of western economies have been hard at work to reverse the damage originating from the crash of the housing market in the US and the global fall-out that resulted. The tools of their trade, interest rates and money supply, have been liberally used in ways not even imagined before the crisis.

This was at first thought to be a temporary policy to contain an acute situation, but the same tools have been employed every time the stock market or the economy have started to look even a bit pale. So although the 1951–1970 Federal Reserve chairman William Martin described the job of the central banker as to "take away the punch bowl just when the party gets going", the actions of the recent decades have been to the contrary, forcing markets to drink up at every sign of hangover and looming sobriety.

And this has no doubt helped the economy as a whole – including significantly helping those at the lower end of the income distribution, by saving jobs and encouraging investment in general, stimulating the economy and helping companies keep going during difficult times.

But the most visible result of low interest rates and continuous monetary support has been ballooning asset prices across every imaginable class. From bonds and equities to real estate, prices have soared. The most recent and most stupendous example of this was seen with the onset of the corona-crisis. Once the pandemic's impacts became clear, stocks crashed. This was to be expected. After all, growth expectations were slashed and turned negative as countries, companies and industries closed in response to the spreading disease. Central banks, conditioned by a decade of action, responded immediately. Consequently, despite global economic prospects darkening massively, asset prices bounced back and exceeded the previous levels just a few months later. In the markets, Covid never happened.

The combination of low or non-existent real growth and massive monetary intervention has left the majority looking at the taillights of the asset owners, speeding ahead with the rocket fuel generously provided by the central banks. Once again, wealth and income inequality have soared. This is not to say the decisions made by the banks were wrong. On the contrary, it seems likely that everyone is better off thanks to their actions. Yet one of the outcomes has also been a widening gulf between the asset owners and the rest.

So perhaps the overall effect of the central bank action was that the lower- and middle-income groups did not experience as big a backslide into poverty as they otherwise would have, but at the same time the asset owners gained massively. While everyone benefited, income inequality increased nonetheless.[82] And that, as we recall, is poison for trust.

---

82   Assets such as equities provide passive income in the form of dividends etc.

Central banks have created possibly the biggest asset price bubble of all time. At some point the punch bowl will run dry, or perhaps the bacchanal just can't take it any more. What happens at that point is anyone's guess, but it seems the risks are gigantic.

There are undoubtedly many more reasons for recent developments in pre-tax in-come inequality across the west. Yet these causes, globalization with its clear winners and losers in western countries, technological developments and the monetary policy that has disproportionately boosted asset owners, must be absolutely central. The fundamental case here is that the diverging economic fortunes between those at the very top and the rest are one major cause of the trust declines we see in the statistics. This economic explanation seems most pertinent to the US, but points out towards a universal principle regarding trust and income inequality.

For the sake of clarity, it must also be stressed that this is not an argument for zero income differences. Quite the contrary. The economic environment presents us with another view of the dualistic nature of trust, on one hand thriving on similarities, while also requiring freedom for its fullest expressions. It seems apparent that the enforcement of too strict income equalization measures easily leads to massive distrust. If the economically meaningful differences between people are effectively overruled, this restricts the operations of the trust feedback loop that enables people to adjust their behaviour in the face of changing circumstances. In effect, superior performers would not be rewarded, nor slackers punished; failing firms would not go bankrupt and successful innovators would find it hard to grow and capture market share. In an economic setting too much homogenizing equality goes against the reality of human variability and the very real performance differences between companies. Persisting with such policies is thus bound to raise considerable ire and be unsustainable in the long term. The incentive problems that have plagued socialist countries across time bear witness to this reality.

Hence a similar ambivalence seems to apply for trust. Freedom and guidance are both needed, but too much of either will ultimately be dysfunctional, and the golden path requires a balancing act between the two poles, in line with the needs of the specific time and place. In the present case it seems, however, that the US especially has veered towards too much income inequality, and too great differences, with the outcome that trust in the fairness of the economic system has deteriorated sharply.

THE INFORMATION DELUGE

"Societies have always been shaped more by the nature of the media by which men communicate than by the content of the communication."

MARSHALL MCLUHAN, *THE MEDIUM IS THE MASSAGE: AN INVENTORY OF EFFECTS*, 1967

Information technology affects much more than just our jobs and incomes. Indeed, as the name implies, it has everything to do with information and our relationship with it. As mentioned previously, it is widely noted that the advent of mass book printing led to the reformation and the religious wars of 16th century Europe. The ongoing revolutions in information technology seem even more profound than those unleashed by Gutenberg. Of the consequences, we are just starting to get the first taste.

The present international economic structures have come into being in the absence of borders and in the presence of technologies allowing effective command and control over vast distances. New technologies and novel legal opportunities have thus not just shaped economic structures, but also reverberate as second-order effects on income distributions, trust and politics in the west and elsewhere. The far-reaching impacts of technology, or media as he preferred, was the subject matter of choice for Marshall McLuhan, perhaps the most well-known theorist and analyst of media.

A central thesis of McLuhan's farsighted 1964 book *Understanding Media* was that the new electronic media and communications technologies, for him meaning mainly radio and TV, were profoundly altering the societies embracing them. More profoundly, every technology by its nature as an extension of human capabilities is prone to induce a certain mindset and way of being among the people using it, reflecting the essential characteristics of the technologies themselves. As such the age of books, and factories following them, was typified by sequential, serial and fragmented ways of being and perceiving. The structures of a book or a newspaper as the principal forms of communication, or of the assembly line at the centre of economic life, provided the organizing principles for society more broadly. Printed text on a page follows a clear linear structure, presenting thoughts in a logically unfolding sequence. This is a medium of communication wholly different from the sprawling conversations of an oral culture lacking writing, for example. And inevitably, said McLuhan, the form of printed text imprints itself upon the reader's mind, subtly setting a standard for how to think, how to communicate, how to build an argument and so on. In line with these changes, society itself changes to accommodate the new opportunities inherent in the new technology. Before Gutenberg's innovations the products of writing were far fewer in number, and restricted to a much smaller educated elite. Thus, Gutenberg unleashed not just a deluge of books and newspapers, but also a broad revolution in literacy, thinking and behavioural patterns, reaching down to the very foundations of society itself.

With the factory and assembly line life in industrializing societies was again upended. McLuhan noted that "mechanization depends on the breaking up of processes into homogenized but unrelated bits".[83] Mass production of homogenized items, whether McDonalds hamburgers or passenger cars, is the hallmark of an industrial society, and something that separates it from the earlier eras of technology. In line with the reigning technology, the habits of society adjust. To befit the requirements of production, jobs became highly specialized in an image of the consecutive steps forming an assembly line. The changes in the nature of work were mirrored in the whole knowledge-producing infrastructure of science, which became ever more siloed on smaller and smaller niches at the expense of cross-science cooperation and broad systemic thinking.

Against this inherited fragmented, specialized, linear and analytical culture of books and factories, a new electronic age has slowly been dawning. In this new era "Electricity unifies these fragments (created by the earlier industrial culture) once more because its speed of operation requires a high degree of interdependence among all phases of any operation." What was before fragmented and homogenized to fit the industrial modes of operation is now recomposed to take advantage of the speed and flexibility allowed by electricity. Automated, customizable just-in-time production replaced centralized industrial-age factories with their massive inventories of homogeneous products. In tow, societies changed once again to accommodate the new.

In other words while mechanization created fragmentation and separation, electronic technologies enabling automation and instantaneous communications create an "extended nervous system" feeding us with

83   *Understanding Media*, McLuhan, Marshall, Routledge Classics, 2001. Page 385.

real-time information from every connected corner of the earth, meaning from everywhere in the 21st century, in effect bringing closer places that were once obscure and distant to us. One side effect of this new connected "global village" is a constant information overload. Or, as McLuhan said it, "With electric speeds governing industry and social life, explosion in the sense of crash development becomes normal."

McLuhan spoke of electric communications as analogical to the human nervous system. The internet and cell phones redeem McLuhan's predictions in a convincing manner, connecting us to everywhere all the time. Yet a nervous system of the body functions to serve a single being, so that its actions are suitable for the environment it finds itself in, improving harmony and fitness. The electronic nervous system of information technology has perhaps had a similar effect in the realm of the economy, tying together distant countries with supply chains and trade. As side effects of economic integration and information technology, nationalism as an idea has fallen out of favour, while at the same time tribalisms of different sorts have taken root, fulfilling another set of McLuhan's predictions. Despite the many impacts, the growth of the new electronic nervous system has as yet failed to achieve a social homeostasis as upheld by the biological one. On the contrary, it seems many societies embracing information technology are veering towards greater instability, rather than improved self-regulation.

The destabilizing impacts of information technology and the internet are the subject of an extensive account by the former CIA analyst Martin Gurri. In his 2014 book *The Revolt of the Public* he traced the roots of an increasing trend of instability, protests and revolts to the ways new technology has changed our engagement with information and, consequently, with authority. The foundation of his analysis is the observation that information technology, first with proliferating TV channels, then with the world wide web and finally through social media and smartphones, has flooded us with new perspectives, new ideas, new information and new narratives. This situation of information overflow is in sharp contrast to earlier ages, where a few respected newspapers and one or two state-controlled TV channels were largely in control of the official narratives and the interpretation of events as they unfolded. This state-guided control of narratives broke down with the proliferation of new information channels, and as a consequence the legitimacy of existing power structures is being challenged everywhere.

Gurri painted a convincing picture of hierarchical industrial-age institutions being challenged by nimble and fluid networks of the new information era. In short, the modern state and other institutions evolved during the industrial era and, as McLuhan explained, continue to mirror the old industrial modes of operation. Thus we have highly specialized, highly hierarchical and altogether quite inflexible public organizations hopelessly trying to control the interpretation of events and maintain an image of competence in the wild information environment of today.

The effect of the mismatch between existing institutions and the new information sphere is two-fold. First, the official narrative will constantly be contested by massive numbers of alternative interpretations of events. Second, the failures of official institutions become visible in a world of abundant information in a way that was once inconceivable. Both of these will eat away at the legitimacy of existing institutionalized power, whatever form it may take.

The newly tractable incompetence of the experts and authorities was once again in plain sight with the abrupt fall of Afghanistan in a matter of days in the summer of 2021, something that establishment figures could not comprehend. Comments and guarantees from the highest authorities turned out to be false mere days later, as the progress of events proving otherwise was live-streamed on the internet to the eyes of amazed publics across the planet.

Thus the better the public understand the institutions, the less they seem to trust them. In precarious circumstances such as these, challenges and denials of authority are bound to become more frequent. Indeed, the trend of instability and protest perceived by Gurri is corroborated by the data. A report by the Center for Strategic and International Studies states that "Mass protests increased annually by 11.5% from 2009 to 2019 across all regions of the World".[84] Although the data here covers only the period of 2009–2019, the trend has clearly been towards more unrest. It is a mirror image of the trust statistics we reviewed at the beginning of this book. New technology both exposes old centres of power and gives tools to contest them. Naturally, existing institutions have an incentive to preserve and enhance themselves, while those on the outside are keen to pry some off for themselves.

According to Gurri, a large part of the problem lies with the excessive promises of competence made by various institutions. For example, governments promise to make the world better, and people happier, while in reality they can only do so much. Yet excessive promises create excessive expectations, which is a combination inevitably leading to severe disappointments. To counteract this, Gurri calls for greater humility and admission of uncertainty from the institutions. Given the incentives present in democratic politics, this is of course very difficult to achieve in the realm of politics in the west.

84 *The Age of Mass Protests – Understanding an escalating global trend.* Brannen, Samuel; Haig, Christian; Schmidt, Katherine. Center for Strategic and International Studies, March 2020.

Once citizens have had enough of their disappointments, they find it easier than ever before to organize mass action, aided by social media and messaging services.

The development of information technologies has also led to a seemingly unrelenting growth in the volume of data created. This information overflow means that maintaining an official all-encompassing narrative is increasingly difficult for any organization. With the proliferation of information sources and online communities conducting and spreading analysis and opinions, the publics (since there are many of them, focused around different issues) may often have equal or even better understanding of any given issue than the people officially in charge of it. Or, at any rate, a completely different view on the subject. In an age of information and transparency, weak positions become all too clear to the public, again with corrosive results for perceived competence. One consequence of this is, as Gurri says "The more you know, the less you trust."[85]

Another side of this information abundance is that the data available far exceeds our human capacity to make sense of it all. In other words, the more data, the more difficult it becomes to differentiate between real signals and mere noise. This leads to a curious juxtaposition where the information age results simultaneously in far more and better information, and far more confusion. The deluge of data makes it easier to find fault and critique various institutions and more difficult to perceive what is actually relevant information. And so, false accusations and frail defences abound. Thus, it is not just that trust in institutions is shaken by the new information order, but trust in information itself.

This messy state of affairs is exacerbated by conscious efforts to direct public discussion, or simply make a muddle of it, by various actors for their own ends. For example, it has long been common among competing powers to try to inflame the dormant conflicts within opposing societies. The weapons of choice for these attempts are propaganda and disinformation campaigns, commonly employed in the battle between capitalism and communism, US and Soviet Union, as a prime example. But of course, competition among states never ceased, and so we still have operations where Russians for example have been caught trying to sow confusion in the west. We know these "active measures" of information warfare are commonly employed by many actors, but it remains difficult to assess their impacts. Most often, the mode of operation is not to present outright lies, but to offer selective information to sow distrust and division.

85   *Revolt of the Public*. Gurri, Martin. Stripe Press, 2018.,

Whereas the influencing was previously mostly done through unwit-
ting pawns such as journalists and NGOs (the peace and disarmament
movements in the west during the Cold War were famously heavily sponsored and influenced by the Soviet Union, often through seemingly independent intermediaries), the internet has predictably changed the landscape of information operations. With the advent of the web, social media
and smartphones, each and every citizen is potentially directly reachable.
This was indeed the pitch by which Cambridge Analytica, a notorious and
now defunct political consulting firm, with its supposedly highly developed
psychological profiles of voter groups and targeted advertising campaigns,
claimed to be able to "manage" elections to its clients' benefit.

It remains unclear how effective these information operations have
been. Some claim they have won elections, others say they are highly inef-
fective compared with the money, time and effort required. It seems likely
that both claims are true, and that the impact varies with time and situation.

Nonetheless, disinformation has become a hot topic in the west. Fed
by St. Petersburg troll factories, Trump tweets and conspiracy theories in
obscure corners of the web, the material for alarm is readily available. Still,
recalling the breakdown of centralized narratives and information control
as described by Gurri, another reason for worrying about fake news arises.
Attempts to control fake news and disinformation provide a wonderful
framework to subvert not just legitimately false information, but also the
type that might worry or challenge the established centres of power. As
such, clamping down on disinformation provides a potential avenue for
an attempt, on the side of the stated mission, to re-establish information
control by the incumbent powers within a society.

Given the central position certain companies enjoy in the present
information ecosystem, they have become sort of gatekeepers with their
ability to affect what most people can see through selective presentation of
search results, posts and comments. This position dimly mirrors the role
of the major TV channels or newspapers of earlier eras, although is separated from it by the existence of an endless number of smaller alternative
communication channels: blogs, forums and the like, and the interactive
nature of it all. Nonetheless, Facebook, Google, Amazon and Twitter seem
to have become, presumably under the threat of regulation on antitrust
grounds (they are effective monopolies), collaborators with establishment
power in deciding what is acceptable discourse and what is not, what can
be said and posted, what cannot. In short, a handful of for-profit Silicon
Valley firms have become in practice the censors and arbiters of information in charge of a large part of the western information ecosystem.

It must be recalled that these same companies have a business model that relies on capturing and holding our attention to get us to click their links, stories and videos. From this they derive ad revenue and our private data, which they then monetize in various ways. And as it turns out, emotional, outrageous, angry and highly partisan content seems to be the best way to generate engagement, clicks and attention. Thus, the best content for media companies to push in terms of revenue and profit generation is highly similar to typical disinformation material in its divisiveness.

So we find ourselves in a situation where we are supposed to trust the companies making money from outrage and click-bait to simultaneously act as fair and responsible judges of free expression and factual information. Realistically, the only thing these companies can be trusted to care about is their own bottom line. At the end of the day, for any public company, all other considerations are subordinate to profits. This is true for the social media giants, but is particularly acute for the imploding traditional newspapers and media, which have lost print or airtime-based ad revenues and are desperate to stay alive online by any means necessary.

There is an enormous jumble of incentive problems at the heart of the present architecture of media and economy. Having a few giant companies, or indeed a handful of people, who are the controlling shareholders, in charge of vast tracts of what we see and what we can say on the net is problematic in itself. Knowing in addition that in general all media businesses operating on the internet have incentives that are predatory on our attention and divisive in their influence does not help, either. On top of this they then have the mandate to monitor and police speech and action on the net, which is to some degree contradictory to their own interests in generating content that yields the most clicks and holds attention.

This seems an absurd situation – and it is. It is no doubt an indication that we are still in an early leg in our trek through the information age, and that our society and practices are still seeking a more optimal form when it comes to adapting to the internet. What that optimal form may be is not yet clear, and is in any case beyond the scope of this book. But it seems apparent that the incentive problems of our information spaces will continue to influence trust in our societies negatively, until a more robust and reasonable set of incentives and institutions is found.

As McLuhan mentioned, the communications technologies themselves have far greater impacts on our societies than the contents of those communications. Before the internet and electronic communications, our thinking and communications were dominated by the printed text in book or newspaper forms. Contrast a book or an article-long argument with the limited-character tweet or short video story on Instagram or Snapchat. Which of the formats seems more and less likely to produce measured, intelligent, analytical and self-reflective communications, and thereby similar modes of behaviour? Social media and smartphones, in addition to robbing us of our attention and concentration, have also accustomed us to more emotional and instinctive forms of communication, thinking and behaviour. That seems like a step backwards for society, trust and human wellbeing in general.

These impacts are corroborated by research. A Canadian study from 2012 focused on the effects of texting on some 2,300 youths aged 18–22 and found that relative texting frequency correlated negatively with reflectiveness and moral life goals, and positively with materialism and out-group prejudice. In other words, the more the subjects spent time texting, the less they spent time on self-reflection and moral thinking, and conversely the more they focused on materialist goals and expressed negative attitudes towards others.[86]

Another study, from 2017, concentrated on the impacts of social media use on the same personality dimensions, and found results in line with the study on texting frequency.[87] Elsewhere, social media use has been connected with mental health problems such as poor self-esteem, negative body image and depression.[88]

All in all, the number of studies showing similar results seems to be growing. If social media use is reducing sympathy for out-groups, whether ideological, ethnic or any other kind, it seems fair to assume the influence is also negative for trust in general.

All this was noted long ago, and social media use has only intensified since. With this in mind, it is no surprise that internet and social media platforms have effectively turned into battlegrounds of mutual abuse across every imaginable line of demarcation. Likewise, especially in the US, the more traditional news media have taken to naked ideological and partisan advocacy at the expense of seeking common ground or a nuanced understanding of events.

Thankfully, some studies also find contradictory results,[89] which gives us hope but makes for a muddled overall picture. Yet it is abundantly

86 *Texting Frequency and The Moral Shallowing Hypothesis*. Trapnell, Paul; Sinclair, Lisa. The University of Winnipeg, news.uwinnipeg.ca/wp-content/uploads/2013/04/texting-study.pdf

87 Social Media, Texting, and Personality: A Test of the Shallowing Hypothesis. Annisette, Logan; Lafreniere, Kathryn. *Personality and Individual Differences*, Volume 115, September 2017.

88 Social Media Use and Adolescent Mental Health: Findings From the UK Millennium Cohort Study. Kelly, Yvonne; Zilanawala, Afshin; Booker, Cara; Sacker, Amanda. *EClinicalMedicine* 6, *The Lancet*, 2018.

89 Does Time Spent using Social Media Impact Mental Health?: An Eight Year Longitudinal Study. Coyne, Sarah; Rogers, Adam; Zurcher, Jessica; Stockdale, Laura; Booth, McCall. *Computers in Human Behavior*, 104, 2020.

clear from experience and everyday evidence that social media is changing the ways we present and see ourselves as well as others, and how we communicate. These changes cannot help but have consequences.

Still, the picture is not all dark. If social media can help people coordinate and work together, it can also help build trust. As Gurri explained, social media sites have been instrumental in bringing people together for protests and revolts. But far more people have used the services for other constructive ends: to form hobby groups, discuss investments, take care of neighbourhood issues or create and promote art. As such, it is obvious that the potential and present impact of the internet in forming new communities and building trust must also be enormous. Likewise, recent years have seen a proliferation of apps and internet-based platforms providing new channels for tailored mental health support and counselling – starting to counteract the negative influences on this side as well.

Based on the evidence from studies and statistics from the past 15 years, it seems that, for now, the destabilizing effects of social media and the internet are dominating. All this probably reflects a common pattern when adopting new technologies: the commercial opportunities are tapped first, and the negative consequences will be addressed later, as they become more visible and pressing.

TECHNOLOGY, ECONOMY AND TRUST – SUMMARY

As McLuhan noted, when our technologies change, we change and so do our societies. For the past century, we have been taking steps further and further into the electronic information age. And the road taken has led us to a completely new landscape. The economic and technological factors eroding trust perhaps represent policy errors in some respects, but also our difficulties in adjusting to the suddenly peculiar surroundings.

In this section we have focused on the economic and technological causes of declines in trust. The primary cause on the economy side of things was identified in the research literature as pre-tax income inequality, meaning the diverging income development of people on the higher and lower ends of the income spectrum, before wealth transfers. This trend has been especially strong in the US, where the income share of the lower 50% of wage earners of the total national income has steadily declined during the past 40 years, to barely half of what it was in 1980. In short, the fruits of economic growth in the past 40 years have gone directly to those already at the top of the economic ladder. The situation in Europe is somewhat different, with only modest changes in the national income shares towards higher inequality. No doubt this reflects in large part Europe's major problem – the lack of economic growth in the first place. In addition, Europeans have likely been more keen to keep everyone on board in terms of income development, placing relatively more focus on minimum wages, education availability and similar measures.

The causes of this growth in pre-tax income inequality are many. First, we have the many impacts of globalization. The past decades have witnessed an enormous deindustrialization of the west, with production outsourced to lower-cost locations, mostly in Asia. The result has been a loss of industrial and middle-class jobs in a process that has severely hurt prospects and wage development in these sectors of the job market. On the other side of globalization is an influx of new workers from third countries entering western job markets. This obviously adds to the supply of talent in the market, further reducing the bargaining power of every worker, to the benefit of the companies and shareholders.

Another significant development has been the victorious march of information and automation technologies. These technologies have made many older positions redundant, leading to the disappearance or significant decline of many roles. New jobs have been added in software and technology companies, but they often have significant skill and knowledge requirements. Thus technological change has left many without work and lacking the skills needed to take part in the new information economy. Again, divergence in economic fortunes is an obvious outcome.

Finally, we have the policy choices that have created income inequality. As explained earlier, central bank policies since the financial crisis have helped stabilize western economies against any and all disturbances. Certainly, this has helped people maintain their jobs. But it has also been very convenient for the already well-off asset owners, as record low interest rates and monetary easing have boosted prices to previously unknown heights.

As we can see, there have been many factors, all contributing similarly to create increasing income inequality, which in turn has been poisonous for trust within western countries.

In addition to its obvious influence on the economy, technological progress has also changed the way we relate to ourselves and others. The internet, the smartphone, social media and all manner of apps have profoundly altered our information environment. In this new landscape we find new opportunities and new threats, and adjust accordingly with new behaviours. This proliferation of new information channels has broken down the previously much stronger control the establishment had over various narratives. Thus we have alternative information sources, with alternative views, enabling us to question the official stories. This by itself lends a measure of distrust of the establishment narratives. But the situation is made worse by the transparency and speed of the internet, which helps expose the fumbles and incompetence of the authorities like never before.

Once a cause for discontent is found (let's be frank – it's never difficult), the apps and social media make it very easy to organize protests online and offline, in a way that is simply impossible for the authorities to fully monitor or control. And so we have constant petitions, complaints and a tsunami of real-world protests and uprisings.

At the heart of all this are the incredible incentives present in the attention economy of the internet. Media companies make money by the click, and what gets clicks is outrage. Thus many media outlets have transformed to click-baiting, and more or less partisan advocacy at the expense of a finer understanding of the world. Simultaneously, the same companies that make money with outrage are also supposed to act as the guardians of free speech and expression.

In an environment like this, it is no surprise that we find evidence suggesting that social media use seems to make us less self-reflecting and more malicious towards others. Again, trust shrinks and distrust grows.

CHANGES IN CULTURE, VALUES AND SOCIETY

"There is no such thing as society... There are individual men and women, and there are families."

MARGARET THATCHER, IN AN INTERVIEW IN 1987

Having looked at how the way we trust is intimately connected to our own backgrounds, including lessons learned from our parents and the community and society we grow up in, it is surprising to come across this quote from Margaret Thatcher. Not leaving much room for interpretation, the comment announces a complete lack of belief in a commonly shared society. The statement is made even more astounding by the fact that she was herself the head of a state, which presumably exists to serve a community of people, a society. It seems strange to demand compliance from citizens after such an utterance. Regardless, Thatcher probably did not aim to deny the existence of communities and societies – rather, she thought them irrelevant next to the individual and their responsibility for their own life. Yet her comment underscores the triumph of the individual over considerations of community, forming the starting point and backdrop for our analysis of the cultural and societal changes that are leaving trust out in the cold.

Individualism has long roots in the west, most notably with the enlightenment and its focus on human rights, liberty and reason. These new ideas placed the individual at the centre of the social universe, where things like aristocracy, nation, state and religion had previously held greater sway. Many of the concepts were derived from Judeo–Christian religion – for example, equality before God becoming equality before the law and among the people – making the new secular ideology a successor to the earlier religious worldview. In short, the scepticism lit by the scientific and humanist ideas in the renaissance matured with the enlightenment, and in the process started supplanting the values that had guided the west until then.

However, the argument here is not quite that individualism is unequivocally in opposition to trust. A blunt claim to that effect fails to acknowledge the facts that the advance of individualism and retreat of religion coincided with the creation of the modern state with its trust-bearing institutions, and was a major impetus for these changes. These institutions enabling individual expression and empowerment have clearly been good for trust, because they have enabled the dynamic feedback loop of adjustment described previously. Indeed, the most individual – western – countries have long been among those with the highest levels of trust. Some measure of research supports this view of a positive relationship between trust and individualism.[90]

What we are instead proposing is that the ideological positions originating partly from what may be called the individualist line of thought, derived principally from humanist and enlightenment ideas, have advanced to such a degree that they are beginning to erode the foundations on which western, and especially European, countries have historically been built. For example, the ascent of universalist individualism has coincided first with the descent of religion and more recently the nation state – two previously major sources

90   Individualism-Collectivism and Social Capital. Allik, Jüri; Realo, Anu. *Journal of Cross-Cultural Psychology*, January 2004.

of identity and community. Simply put, what has been eroding trust in recent decades is a confusion or separation between older and newer values, and their implications for the basic ideas underlying the concepts of communities. As a result, we are seeing a widening gulf of values between a left promoting new identities and a right maintaining ties to older ideas about a religious and ethnic basis of community, which have previously provided the core legitimizing values for western countries. The following statistics from Pew Research Center show a striking divergence in values in the US:

DEMOCRATS AND REPUBLICANS MORE IDEOLOGICALLY DIVIDED THAN IN THE PAST

Distribution of Democrats and Republicans on a 10-item scale of political values

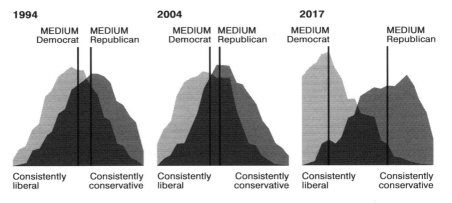

NOTES: Ideological consistency based on a scale of 10 political values questions. The light grey area in this chart represents the ideological distribution of Democrats and Democratic-leaning independents; the medium grey area of Republicans and Republican-leaning independents. The overlap of these two distributions is shaded dark grey. Original graph with democrats in blue, republicans in red, overlap in shaded purple.

SOURCE: Survey conducted June 8–18, 2017.

Whereas in 1994 and as late as 2004 there was a clear overlap in terms of values held by Democrat and Republican voters in the US, by 2017 the supporters of both parties had drifted towards the extreme ends of their ideological positions. Previously the majority of people had occupied the centre ground, where the values between mainline supporters of both parties overlapped significantly. By 2017, the middle ground had nearly vanished to a small minority, and most people occupied ideological positions with little in the way of overlap with the opposing group. Political polarization had exploded and, in tow, trust imploded.

Although the graphic presents the situation in the US, similar divergence is clearly happening in Europe as well. What separates most European countries from the US and the UK is their multiparty political systems. The polarization in Europe has thus come in the form of new nationalist parties on the right, while left-wing parties have adopted identity politics-based positions in place of their earlier redistribution focus. At the same time the traditional parties around the centre seem increasingly confused between the new poles of identitarian left and right. Therefore the changing values have expressed themselves somewhat differently in Europe and the US. In Europe the vectors of change have been the growth of new parties and shifting popularity among the rest, whereas in the US and UK the changing sentiments have forced the existing two parties to drift further apart ideologically.

The individualist Margaret Thatcher was no leftist, though – and we shall shortly explain the connection between individualism on the left and the traditional right where Thatcher held dominion. Besides individualism as a major force dismantling old ideas, we could add economic incentives and psychological trauma originating from the events of the first half of the 20th century as having added further weight to the challenge against the preceding legitimizing values.

If anything, Thatcher was a supporter of business. In this capacity she famously fought trade unions, promoted privatizations and liberalized the British economy, leading to the big bang in London's financial markets that boosted the City's status in the global trading market. But Thatcher did not come up with these policies herself. Rather, she was a high-profile proponent of a liberalizing economic current that had started far earlier. One might consider economics in general and Adam Smith in particular as the origins of the arguments for all types of economic freedom. And not be wrong. But perhaps in this instance it is more fitting to ground the Thatcherite and contemporary economic liberalism in the response to the economically insular interregnum between the world wars, which was embodied in the institutions pioneered during and shortly after the Second World War. The World Bank, International Monetary Fund, World Trade Organization and the like worked to reduce barriers to trade and promote economic integration. The most important European champion in this arena was the European Coal and Steel Community, the forerunner of the present European Union.

These institutions aimed to dismantle hindrances to profit and prosperity. The idea was that all barriers to business effectively reduce overall welfare by diverting economic activity from its potentially most profitable courses. Thus, the logical outcome of this line of thought is to promote free capital and labour movement, and to reduce regulation across the board, which should in theory leave everyone better off in the long run. In Europe, this was not just an economic consideration but, especially early on, a project of peace-making after the disasters of the first half of the 20th century.

To the credit of the economics and economists spreading these ideas, the logic is mostly valid. The problem lies in the real-world frictions between the economically optimal and the humanly desirable. Indeed, as we have seen, the inability of economic models and economists to consider the human, cultural and societal dimensions of the policies they recommend is a very common issue. This is where we can also make a connection between individualist thinking and economics in general. Economics sees the individual as a consumer, as a utility maximizer, and then considers them in a uniform aggregate. But it scarcely acknowledges values, cultures and communities, which are of course meaningful for real-life individuals, influencing their behaviour in many, often diverging and contradictory, ways.

This is an understandable weakness, because such intangibles are challenging to incorporate into a formal and logical analysis of economic behaviour. And economics is still a young science. But it is a weakness nonetheless.

Taking into account the liberalizing institutions of the post-war era, and the economic thinking guiding them, we can ask what kind of second-order attitudes they would generate. An obvious result would be opposition to the norms and values upholding structures that create barriers to economic optimization. Thus to some extent the economic internationalism that relies on minimizing all obstacles to business activity is inherently antithetical to the ideas of fixed communities with their borders, the nation state and the concept of a common society in general. This line of thought is a significant origin of the business-minded individualism, or rather anti-collectivism, of Thatcher and the international economic elite – rooted in opposition to anything that might stand in the way of blunt economic interests.

As part of the liberal economic regime, mass immigration has been accepted and encouraged as a tool of economic invigoration – for example, to counter the seemingly endless shortages of labour that companies complain about at regular intervals. Accordingly, the past 50 years have seen a considerable change in the populations of western countries in a conscious yet unadvertised move away from the concept of nation state in Europe, and ethnic origin or specific cultural heritage have lost their places as legitimizing or constituting elements of state and society more widely. The process has effectively overturned the whole ideology that underpinned state and society during the preceding centuries. The US always stood somewhat apart from nationalist narratives, because it was built on specific ideas and values, rather than on ethnic heritage as in Europe. Yet historically the US always remained closely tied to its European cultural origins. The rise of the generally oppositional nationalist elements in western political systems as a direct result of immigration policies offers an example of how ideas originating in purely economic considerations fail to consider wider societal developments and outcomes.

It is curious, if perhaps a bit cynical, to note that the immigrant flows that were encouraged on the heels of the disintegrating imperial system after the Second World War provided economic advantages to the receiving countries – or at least the companies operating there. Immigration supplies new labour resources and increasing this supply depresses wages in the receiving country. This is a double win for the companies, who now have a greater choice of employees at a lower cost. More people and workers also mean more demand and a bigger market to sell to. Therefore, immigration not only helps companies achieve greater revenues, but can also help keep costs down by suppressing wages. It is no surprise, then, that they are keen to periodically complain about labour shortages and offer immigration as the solution. There is evidence of these sorts of wage effects from the first era of globalization from the 19th century to the First World War, which saw significant immigration within Europe and from Europe to the US.

The economists Alan Taylor and Jeffrey Williamson note in a study that the debate about immigration reducing wages in receiving countries, while increasing them in the sending countries, originates already in the 19th century, when the effect was first observed. They then proceed to tackle this very issue head on, finding that immigration from Europe to the New World between 1870–1913 had very significant wage effects on both ends. They estimate that without emigration away (making labour more scarce), wages in the European countries under investigation, Ireland, Italy and Sweden, would have been 24%, 22% and 8% lower. In the receiving new world destinations the influx of immigrants swelled the labour force and had an opposite effect – without immigration they estimate that wages would have been higher by 27% in Argentina, 17% in Australia, 18% in Canada and 9% in America.[91] Similar impacts are found for other countries as well, and the results are confirmed by numerous studies. Mass migration comes with significant wage effects that can exacerbate income inequality to the detriment of trust.

Thus, open immigration policies achieved for western companies similar advantages to those the imperial system provided – more and cheaper resources (labour in this case) and more consumers to swell the addressable market at home. But this time without the cumbersome direct rule and its economic and moral costs, while fulfilling the ideological needs of post-war western societies. And as long as the immigrants are happy with their new homelands, the framework nobly provides a chance of a better life for the newcomers. On the face of it, these movements might be innocent enough. The problem lies with the increasing income inequality and political tensions the system begets, leading to decreasing trust in the receiving countries.

The sea change in values and attitudes underlying our contemporary divisions originated of course not just in economic optimization. Just as much of an impact, or perhaps even the decisive one, must have originated in the experiences of the Second World War. The Nazi menace can well be described as nationalism gone mad, taken from a healthy appreciation of community and the idiosyncratic features of one's own nation to an outright hatred of other groups. The result was annihilation of the European Jews and other groups, mass exodus of dissenters and intellectuals in a gigantic brain drain, with the US gaining many of Europe's most talented scientists, and the utter material and moral ruination of Europe and much of the world. After such ordeals, it is no wonder that the survivors and generations following the war wanted to get as far as possible from the instigating ideologies. And so, it was not just economic thinking but also this experiential perspective that set the stage for thorough questioning and reversal of the earlier ideas that were perceived to have contributed to the disaster. Thus over the years following the war, intellectual currents started drifting towards more cosmopolitan values, away from the concepts of nations and communities. What started as a drift has turned into a new course that is now visible in the wholesale re-evaluation of the past and the present.

One way this shows up is in our current tendency to view the past 500 years of western history with a highly negative tint, in a nearly one-sided fashion that seems to stress the moral failures as seen from the present and discount the many positive developments and achievements during

---

91   *Convergence in the age of mass migration*. Taylor, Alan; Williamson, Jeffrey. European Review of Economic History, April 1997, Vol. 1, No. 1.

the period. Yet the positive sides far outweigh the bad, and are indeed many, including the abolition of slavery – which had hitherto been a global institution almost from the dawn of time; the development of medicine and science that have saved millions of lives; and the economic and technological progress that has lifted the majority of humanity out of abject poverty. No other age has seen so much progress on such a wide front.

Perhaps the pessimistic take on our collective western history is because of the pain of what was lost (relative power, wealth and status versus the non-western world), because of shame (about how it all ended with mass murder and self-destruction in Europe, slavery and its heritage in the US), as a result of the increasingly diverse populations who do not share a common past, or perhaps just because of technological change and new economic incentives. Most likely all of these things matter, affecting us and our outlooks both consciously and subconsciously.

The fragmentation of the western self-image has been perfectly mirrored in the increasingly bleak displays of contemporary arts. On the streets, the movement has claimed statues, names and works of art as its enemies. In philosophy, a path has been travelled from 19th century early existentialism in the face of a faltering religion to the full experience of absurdity after the Second World War. From there, the road led towards postmodernist relativism and scepticism, questioning all values and knowledge, including all claims of authority. After the postmodern critiques, we seem to have arrived again at a nascent set of new values, at least among some groups, which seem to forgo the earlier relativism and stand squarely against the past. And so, we have since the 19th century, through the dismal first half of the 20th century, arrived in the 21st century having first lost a faith, then losing a sense of everything and now undergoing a wholesale rejection of the past and the present. All of these developments situate themselves in the emotional, moral and to some extent intellectual void left by the harrowing experiences of the wars and the retreat of the Christian faith, which framed the western mind for some 1,500 years.

Regardless of its origin, the present hostility towards the past seems somehow akin to a re-evaluation of an ex-lover after a painful break-up. The good memories are suppressed, while any and all reasons to forget and move on are encouraged. The present for its part is often interpreted as continued oppression, supremacy and imperialism within the now diverse western societies. All in all, the reigning western values and attendant ideological atmosphere would be fertile ground for a thorough psychological analysis.

The ideological environment favouring immigration since the Second World War, whether grounded in economic or morality-based arguments, has dominated to the degree that it is now widely regarded as a universal good in mainstream and official discussion, as exemplified by the dictum "diversity is strength", repeated everywhere from schools to company reports. And with good reason, in many respects – think of the many scientific, economic and cultural contributions made by immigrants. Likewise, it would be unthinkable in today's society to treat people differently depending on their backgrounds. Nonetheless, this admirably positive and in many ways justifiable view ignores the negative consequences of the phenomenon, for example for trust, constituting a blind spot in our collective understanding.

A major negative consequence is the widening ideological gulf between the left and the right that we saw earlier in this chapter, which in large part stems from differing views of immigration. In extreme cases this opposition from nationalist groups may indeed stem from outright hatred and bigotry, which can only be denounced. But it would seem that an increasing portion of the opposition is based on growing worries about cultural dispossession, a legitimate fear of the loss of one's own culture and community. Given the increasingly multi-ethnic societies we live in today, with cities like London and Amsterdam having only some 40% of their populations from the native English and Dutch backgrounds, this is not an empty worry. Even in distant Finland the national statistics office estimates that in a mere 30 years, by 2051, more than 50% of newborn babies will be of immigrant backgrounds.[92] Should these population trends persist, by the end of the century native Europeans will be a small minority in a completely transformed continent. This is of course an issue with two sides, arising from the combination of high immigration and high birth rates among certain immigrant groups, contrasted with low birth rates among European populations.

For many understandable reasons, given the very polarizing nature of the topic, discussion about population developments is effectively shut out of mainstream media. The issue easily fuels negative emotions and uncivil behaviours that should absolutely be guarded against. Yet by failing to engage with the topic we are taking a big risk. With our accumulated understanding of trust and its myriad workings, we are better able to understand both sides of the argument, acknowledge the full gravity of the issues at stake and figure out civilized and respectful ways towards a common future.

The differences between left and right with regards to immigration don't just stem from disparate sensitivities to cultural dispossession, but also reveal differing concepts of relevant society and community. On the mainstream and left we have the primacy of the very agreeable understanding

---

92   Article in Finnish: www.hs.fi/kotimaa/art-2000006330829.html

that every individual needs to be treated equally and fairly regardless of their background, from which they effectively if not always explicitly continue to assert that ethnicity should also not be any sort of basis for community or citizenship – in opposition to the earlier idea of the specific ethnic nation state inherited from the preceding centuries, and in line with the general primacy of the individual in the west. Likewise, on the left we are also liable to find the most stinging critiques and negative views about western history. On the opposing side, on the right, we have those who continue to maintain that a historically established ethnic background (of one or more ethnicities, as is the case with Finland and its traditional Finnish- and Swedish-speaking populations) should remain the foundation of community and the state that serves it, holding on to the more traditional concept of the nation state. This tendency is most obvious in Europe, where polities were founded on distinct tribes that eventually formed larger nations. In the US the picture is obviously a bit more mixed, with the reactionary right most likely attaching to certain values and customs in addition to their European heritage, rather than the concept of specific nationality as understood in Europe.

This all means the opposing camps hold fundamentally different views about the nature and existential justification of their societies. The nationalist elements hold on to an ethnicity-based view that is no longer an accurate reflection of the contemporary reality on the ground. The left-mainstream position on the other hand is unclear about the raison d'être for the specific western political units and states as they exist today, other than pure inertia. Managing common affairs is of course always necessary, but are states that were originally formed around the concept of a specific nation fit for the job in the post-national age they so eagerly promote?

What started as a crisis of faith and turned into a broader existential crisis of all meaning, is now transcending the individual and crossing over into society as a whole. This crisis of meaning is showing up as the divergence in essential values and perceived merits of the societal developments that have happened during the past several decades, contributing to the ongoing erosion of trust we see in the statistics. Both sides of the argument seem to have become incomprehensible to the other, and the right especially views the state with an increasing degree of distrust. No doubt the resistance to Covid-19 vaccinations has stemmed in part from this general state- and authority-related distrust. Recalling the role of values and trust in knowledge, we can understand why there seems to be very little understanding between the left and right, and why seemingly absurd scepticism abounds. A loss of trust is clearly contributing to the confusion.

The interplay between economic interests and post-war morality has also led to an interesting phenomenon, where the traditional roles of the left and the right have switched to some extent. The left has effectively abandoned its traditional working-class voter base, and has taken up the fight to promote sexual and ethnic minority rights, the environment and immigration in general. These causes often rest on the recognition of the individual as an equally valuable human being and worthy of inclusion in a given society regardless of their background. This is of course a noble idea, and in terms of giving voice to the previously unheard it no doubt has the capacity to strengthen trust among these people. The result of this switch of priorities, however, is that in encouraging immigration the left is now effectively economically aligned with the global economic elites, histori-cally represented by the right wing, and promoting policies that effectively suppress the wages of their traditional voter base. In the US the Democrats have overwhelmingly become the party of big business, taking the mantle from the Republicans. In Europe the picture is a bit more mixed thanks to the left-wing parties maintaining generally more sceptical attitudes towards business. An obvious sign of the alignment between the left and business interests is the enthusiastic corporate adoption of various diver-sity agendas, which sometimes read almost as if they come straight off left-wing party pamphlets. The liberal economic policies promoting corporate interests and differential income developments were sold to the left with a language of tolerance and equality.

In this space we find the right trying to suppress immigration, and in the process going against its historical ally, big business, to the wage-level benefit of what used to be the core left-wing voter base. Hence the Brexiteer Boris Johnson and his quip "fuck business".[93] As an outcome, working-class voters across the political spectrum have flocked to the new anti-establishment right-wing parties, whether represented by the Trum-pian Republicans or new nativist parties in Europe.

In the course of these developments the parties' traditional positions during the contest of capitalism and communism have become switched. The previously radical and economically heretical left have become the mainstream, adopting policies supporting big business rewritten in a sweeter language and presumably against the economic interests of their original voter base, while the opposing new right has become the new her-esy and anti-establishment scare.

---

93   www.telegraph.co.uk/politics/2018/06/23/eu-diplomats-shocked-boriss-four-letter-reply-business-concerns/

All this discussion has been to contemplate the ways economic interests, values and ideas have coalesced to produce outcomes that impair trust in our societies. Given the issues affecting minorities and immigration, this is a matter of great delicacy, and must be approached sensitively. Immigration seems to be the focal point in many ways, being related to income inequality as well as the growing gap in values between left and right.

There is another way immigration seems to be contributing to declining trust, which is in a way perhaps the most obvious one. Recall how we construct trust through our evaluations of ability, common values and standards of behaviour, and the perceived benevolence of the other. A diversifying society is comprised of people from all corners of the earth, professing many religions, promoting different cultural traditions, having different histories and even looking unlike each other. In short, a diverse society is one where the spread of identities, values, knowledge, skills and attitudes is inevitably far greater than in a more homogeneous one. In many ways this can be a benefit, potentially making a country richer in its internal life and understanding of the world. Yet it also by definition makes trust that much harder to come by because the differences between people are greater, making it harder to align on the dimensions of trust.

Numerous empirical studies confirm this unfortunate relationship between ethnic diversity and trust. A meta-analysis of 87 empirical studies on the subject finds a consistent negative relationship between trust and ethnic diversity, which seems to be more pronounced in cases where the respondent lives in close proximity to other ethnicities.[94] An OECD Trustlab study on trust between different ethnic groups in Germany and the US finds that ethnic groups show clear ingroup bias, trusting their own group more and others less. Interestingly, relating once again to income inequality, they also find similar disparities in trust between low- and high-income groups within and between ethnicities.[95] All in all the story seems clear – people of similar stock trust together.

Based on our understanding of trust, and in light of its ongoing decline in our societies, it would seem that the present-day phrase "diversity is strength" is more wishful thinking than reality. Of course, differences need to

---

94   Ethnic Diversity and Social Trust: A Narrative and Meta-Analytical Review. Dinesen, Peter
       Thisted; Schaeffer, Merlin; Sønderskov, Kim Mannemar. *Annual Review of Political Science*,
       Volume 23: 441–465, May 2020.
95   *Ethnic Bias, Economic Success and Trust: Findings from Large Sample Experiments in
       Germany and the United States through the Trustlab Platform*. Cetre, Sophie; Algan, Yann;
       Grimalda, Gianluca; Murtin, Fabrice; Putterman, Louis; Schmidt, Ulrich; Siegerink, Vincent.
       SDD Working Paper No. 106, OECD, October 2020.

be respected, and they can indeed be a great source of new ideas and perspectives. But the ancient maxim "divide and conquer", implying the opposite direction of travel, seems closer to the mark than its contemporary inversion.

The theory of trust helps us understand the many causes for the perceptible loss we are currently experiencing. Understanding the issue will in turn help us begin to mend the situation. Trust is formed from our evaluations of ability, benevolence and integrity but, just as importantly, it develops in a learning relationship where the quality of interactions between the trustor and the trustee determine whether cooperation will continue. This means that for trust to really flourish, the feedback loop of trust needs to be free to operate, enabling people to express their views and act according to their own genuine interests – rather than under some external compulsion. In relation to diversity, the meaning of this is two-fold. First, yes, it seems that increasing diversity will have negative consequences for trust. But second, it also helps us appreciate tolerance, freedom and a just society in general as essential enablers of the trust feedback loop. Only in situations where people can freely and safely be who they are and pursue the things they find worthwhile, are treated fairly and equally and have the opportunities to voice their displeasures and promote what they value can the learning process of trust operate unhindered – allowing voluntary cooperation to develop to its fullest extent, and trust to bloom.

At the start of this chapter we referred to the triumph of the individual over considerations of community. On the right the arguments arose from economic interests, from personal liberty and responsibility, and often in opposition to feared statism and communism. On the left, individualism came from the concept of everyone being equal, therefore effectively making any distinctions between people arbitrary and thus to be opposed – also undermining ideas about borders, nations and communities. This sets the background for the present divisions between the left–mainstream and the opposing new right. Their battlegrounds are culture at large and the community itself. The dual nature of trust, stemming on one hand largely from commonalities, while also thriving on tolerance, freedom and justice and the operations of the trust feedback loop, helps us understand where the claims from both sides have merit – and what they are missing.

As we explored in the section on knowledge, the concept of trust also helps us understand why the two sides have severe trouble comprehending and communicating with each other. Our knowledge is dependent on our ability to trust given sources of information. Trust for its part stems in large part from common values and perceived benevolence. As it stands, both sides of the argument prioritize different values, and are likely to perceive the other side as hostile to their own interests. Under these circumstances trust is hard to come by, and consequently we see little mutual understanding and increasing polarization and division within our societies.

The whole situation must be contrasted with our historical background. Specifically, this background involves the collapse of the modes of thought associated with Christianity, including its values and worldview at large. Importantly, the Christian faith provided meaning for the lives of its adherents. The end of faith coupled with the unimaginable terrors of the world wars no doubt contributed to a growing crisis of meaning, coupled with a steady erosion of the values that were founded on Christian principles. This existential crisis led first to questioning all meaning in life, then to the relativism and cynicism of postmodernism, and from there to the present with its dismissive attitude towards the western past in general. These mental developments, further or perhaps even directly animated by the catastrophic consequences of Nazi nationalism, have been mirrored in the real world with the opening of western societies, leading to the present diverse situation befitting the post-modern and post-postmodern philosophies that dominated the times. The reactionary right wing may be seen as a reflection of these changes. With them the existential crisis that originated with the loss of faith and meaning has advanced to take a concrete form in the fear of cultural dispossession, and simultaneously found its solution in the opposition. Assuming the population trends discussed earlier will hold, this concrete form of the existential crisis is bound to spread among European populations.

The fear on the right might also be reworded as a wish for cultural or civilizational sustainability. This is of course a deliberate wording to bring into view the commonalities between the major anxieties across the spectrum of our societies. The left wants environmental sustainability, but doesn't acknowledge any value in maintaining traditional western culture or population. The right wants to maintain this traditional culture and people, but has severe issues with taking climate change seriously. The problem is thus that while both are highlighting legitimate issues, they are simultaneously unable to grasp the opposing side's message. Given the serious and delicate nature of both topics, the resulting acrimony seems guaranteed to make the already difficult situation even worse – and our societies ever more dysfunctional. Yet it seems that to bring peace back, and indeed to have a common future at all, sustainability issues of both kinds need to be addressed.

But enough of this sorry issue. Let us turn to another one – the problem of climate change.

CLIMATE CHANGE

"We deserve a safe future. And we
demand a safe future. Is that really too
much to ask?"

CLIMATE ACTIVIST GRETA THUNBERG AT GLOBAL CLIMATE STRIKE, NEW
YORK, 20 SEPTEMBER 2019

"No challenge poses a greater threat to
our future and future generations than a
change in climate."

PRESIDENT BARACK OBAMA, 2015

I was looking for a fitting quote for this climate section, and happily found
plenty of them. Then it struck me. They all come from influential people.
All profess their worries, underline the gravity of the situation and call for
action. The two above highlight the degree of alignment between the most
prominent activists and powerful leaders. Surely, with everyone who matters weighing in, shouldn't the matter be firmly in hand by now?

The answer is sadly a resounding no, which seems absurd when contrasted with the abundance of attention the subject has garnered. But the
ease of finding relevant quotes and the alarming reality of the issue highlight the essence of the problem: it is easy to talk about it, but action has
been lacking, and clear and comprehensive plans to address it are yet to be
found – reflecting the complexity and difficulty of it all. With each passing
year of inaction, the situation keeps worsening and the distance between
measures taken and required keeps growing. One consequence of this is
increasing anxiety and distrust among the population, who perceive all too
well the problematic nature of the issue.

A recently published article highlighted popular attitudes on climate
change, and showed the extent of anxiety it generates. The study covered
10,000 respondents aged 21 to 25 across 10 countries around the world, asking them about various climate-related topics. Across the board the feelings
are, very understandably, that the matter of climate change is not handled
adequately. Sixty percent of respondents said they were either "very worried"

or "extremely worried" about climate change. What's worse, this state of affairs seems to cause the young considerable distress and anxiety. Forty-five percent said feelings about the subject affect their daily lives negatively. An amazing 75% said they found the future frightening. Given that they correctly perceive the issue as a potential existential threat, it is no wonder.[96]

The following chart displays some of the main results from the survey, showing a widespread worry of the most harrowing sort. The outlook for today's youth (and why not for everyone else, too, who is looking to live more than a few years) seems very dark. Most of the data points repeat the same message. The last two responses related to family security and hesitation about having children reflect a woeful outcome of all this distress — difficulty and unwillingness to go on and maintain society at all. A more despairing outlook can hardly be imagined.

THOUGHTS ABOUT CLIMATE CHANGE

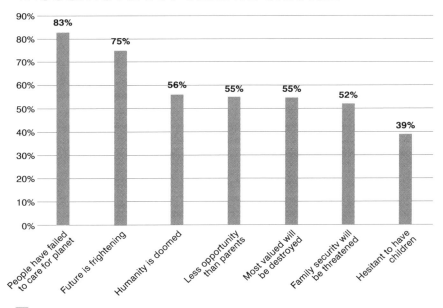

All countries average, % of respondents agreeing with statement

SOURCE: Climate anxiety in children and young people and their beliefs about government responses to climate change: a global survey. *The Lancet*, Volume 5, Issue 12, December 2021

96   Climate anxiety in children and young people and their beliefs about government responses to climate change: a global survey. Hickman, Caroline; Marks, Elizabeth; Pihkala, Panu; Clayton, Susan; Lewandowski, Eric; Mayall, Elouise; Wray, Britt; Mellor, Catriona; van Susteren, Lise. *The Lancet*, Volume 5, Issue 12, December 2021.

The paper also takes a look at the other side, the cause of anxiety – identified in government inaction. The results speak loudly, with only a minority seeing government action as sufficient to alleviate their anxieties.

THOUGHTS ABOUT GOVERNMENT RESPONSE TO CLIMATE CHANGE

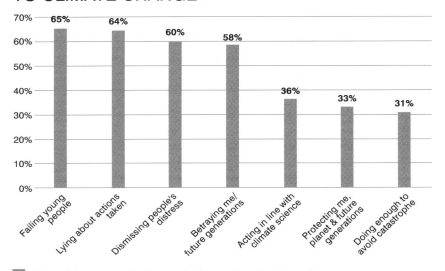

All countries average, % of respondents agreeing with statement

SOURCE: Climate anxiety in children and young people and their beliefs about government responses to climate change: a global survey. *The Lancet*, Volume 5, Issue 12, December 2021

Most pertinently for our interest in trust, the authors of the study also asked about the peoples' trust in governments' responses to the problem at hand. It can hardly come as a surprise that trust was very low. Only in India did 51% of respondents, representing a minimal majority, trust the government to capably handle the issue. In the west in general, and especially in the US, trust in the government was generally weak.

Thinking about this distrust from the perspective of our trust framework, it is easy to see why trust around the issue is low. First, let us assume that the pessimistic outlook with regards to climate change is true. In light of this assumption, how should we see the actions of our governments and other institutions of power? It is increasingly looking like the powers that be are either incapable of the action required or unwilling to do what it takes. In the first instance trust is broken at the realization that govern-

"GOVERMENT RESPONSE CAN BE TRUSTED"

% of respondents agreeing with statement

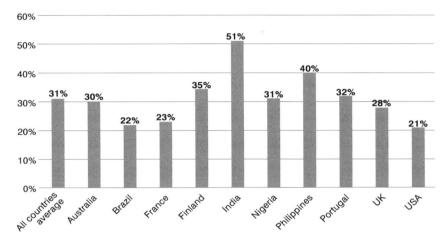

SOURCE: Climate anxiety in children and young people and their beliefs about government responses to climate change: a global survey. *The Lancet*, Volume 5, Issue 12, December 2021

ments are much less able than previously thought, sinking trust on the ability dimension. The situation is worse if we feel the government is capable but unwilling to do what it takes. Unwillingness in this case implies either a completely different understanding of the situation and values, or an attitude of effective hostility to those concerned about the environment. These together would mean a break of trust on the benevolence and integrity dimensions, damaging trust in a much deeper sense than a mere admission of inability would do.

Thinking about the other aspect of trust, the dynamic adjustment process of the trust feedback loop, allows us another perspective. The constant expressions of worry, exemplified by President Obama, and promises of action by governments create expectations among the public. When these communications repeatedly fail to lead to any material action, the continuous disappointments are bound to lead to negative revisions in trust.

So we have an issue causing severe existential angst, with governments perceived to be dishonest at best and antagonistic at worst, and consequently cratering trust in governments, as shown by the survey results. Circumstances such as these hardly seem favourable for internal peace and stable politics.

At the time of writing this in autumn 2021, my hometown Helsinki is constantly harassed by Extinction Rebellion protests. Key traffic points keep getting taken over by masses of protestors, and government meetings are disturbed by chanting outside. The left-green government seems confused by the situation, probably perceiving itself to be on the same side as the rebels. To make it all the more baffling, the green minister of the interior, ostensibly the greatest ally of the protestors themselves, was pressured to condemn the people engaged in the traffic disruptions – people she in all likelihood agrees with. This bewildering situation reflects perfectly the quotes from Greta Thunberg and Barack Obama at the beginning of this chapter – the streets challenging the establishment over an issue they seem to be in complete agreement with.

Despite all the protests, all the concerned words and pretty promises, the reality of the matter is that neither the Extinction Rebellion protestors nor the left-green government itself have presented concrete or credible plans on how to resolve the problem of climate change. In fairness to the protestors, the greater weight of responsibility surely lies with the authorities. Most importantly, however, this situation is not just a local problem in Finland, but a scene being replayed across the globe. Time passes, distress advances and trust keeps evaporating.

The findings on climate anxiety imply that at the heart of the various climate protest movements is a creeping sense of doom and a hopeless future, likely filled with strife and poverty – especially keenly felt by the young population. Based on the present scientific understanding of the issue, and on the probable political and societal outcomes of rising temperatures, it is indeed difficult to avoid such a conclusion. At any rate, the risk of very bad outcomes can hardly be ruled out, even if certainty about the future remains out of reach. As it happens, it might be guessed that similar feelings of anxiety about a lost future are felt among the right-wing rebels against the present population trends and the policies upholding them, as referenced in the previous chapter. To complicate things even more, immigrant minorities in the west likely share in the future-oriented fears thanks to their understandable anxieties about the anti-immigrant parties, in a mirror image of the fears felt on the right. Thus, whatever the cause, movements situated on the left and right ends of our politics share similar fearful attitudes towards the future, often accompanied by a maddening loss of hope. With mental landscapes of despair dominating our societies, it is no wonder trust is suffering.

If we are to restore and build more trust within our western societies, we need to figure out a way towards a more hopeful future – for everyone involved.

What can we do about it all?

"Admitting the facts is the beginning of all wisdom."

J.K. PAASIKIVI, PRESIDENT OF FINLAND, 1946–1956

WE BEGAN OUR journey through the world of trust with a review of the worrying statistics showing trust in decline across the US and Europe. Proceeding through the various theoretical viewpoints, we arrived at a more comprehensive understanding of what trust is all about, and how it manifests in many contexts. We undertook this trek to achieve the main task of this book – to bring to consciousness the absolutely essential contribution of trust in the stability, growth and prospering of societies in general.

Having acquired conceptual tools to understand the phenomenon more broadly, we then followed up with a set of hypotheses for the causes of declining trust across the west. To summarize, these reasons were:

1) pre-tax income inequality driven by factors such as globalization, technological development and central bank policies
2) technological developments disrupting centralized narratives and our information sphere in general
3) the fragmentation of the value basis of our societies, driven mainly by individualism, the death of religion and the traumatic experiences of the 20th century, immigration and attitudes towards it
4) climate change and the present lack of effective actions to mitigate it.

Although this book's major aim is to help us to a new and more nuanced comprehension of the operating of our societies, through the concept of trust, something would be sorely missing if we did not attempt to address the problems identified. This is where we shall now turn. What follows are short high-level sketches of potential solutions, intended as an invitation for more thorough thinking around the issues.

PRE-TAX INCOME INEQUALITY

As we saw earlier, higher pre-tax income inequality is associated with lower trust. Statistics on income developments in turn show that the past decades have seen a significant decoupling of economic fortunes between those at the top of the skills and incomes pyramid, and the rest. This is likely due to many factors, including technological change and automation, globalization that has benefited the capital owners and high-level managers, but exported middle- and working-class jobs to lower-cost locations, and central bank policies since the great financial crisis that have helped everyone, but especially those who own the assets in our countries. This short summary of the situation forms the backdrop against which we may ponder practical ways of reducing income inequality.

Technological change is inevitable in modern scientific and capitalist societies, yielding great benefits such as rising standards of living. As a side effect we undergo creative destruction that leaves old industries obsolete, leading to job losses and often making skills acquired in the past redundant. Recent decades have seen a rapid movement away from the old industrial world to the new information economy. Furthermore, automation is poised to grab ever larger chunks of jobs previously done by humans. Both of these trends imply that there has likely been, and will probably continue to be, an exceptional churn in the types of jobs available and the skills they require. The trends of accelerating technological change place increasing demands on societies in terms of keeping up with relevant skills and competences. This obviously increases the needs for education and re-education as change takes place.

The fast-paced digital evolution means that traditional multi-year university degrees are probably unsuited for the needs that arise, often mid- or late-career. Rather, flexible shorter-term courses and qualifications seem more appropriate for learning things like new programming languages or use of new AI-based tools and the like. It may be that the present education ecosystem needs to be complemented with new forms of educational options – a process that has already started with the birth of various online-based institutions and course offerings. New flexible and evolving forms of practically oriented education and qualifications seem likely to continue to proliferate, gain credibility and prominence. As far as I know, no country has yet made it a conscious strategy to broaden its educational basis towards this sort of flexible approach, with appropriate accreditations and the like. This might be something worth considering.

The point of this skills- and education-based approach is to mitigate income inequality by making it faster and easier for people to upskill themselves, improving their wages and job prospects, and avoid or reduce unemployment in times of change.

Un- and under-employment are forms of inequality affecting economic fortunes in a trust-eroding fashion, keeping people's incomes below what they really should be for a dignified life. Unemployment is especially a European issue, resulting from stagnant economies and poorly designed incentive structures. Excessive risks and costs of hiring combined with costly and difficult firing procedures reduce firms' eagerness to employ, and abuseable social security benefits may make productive work less attractive than it should be. Persistent unemployment issues are especially a problem in the southern European countries. In the north, places like Denmark and Sweden seem to have resolved the issues, having low unemployment and yet maintaining high-quality social security benefits and workers' rights. Thus, many countries with unemployment problems might find solutions and tangible benefits from studying the examples set by these countries in reforming their labour market practices and social security programmes.

Under-employment means suboptimal work circumstances, often meaning one has to hold several jobs to make ends meet. In practice the term can refer to various situations, such as working fewer hours than necessary, working in a job one is considerably overqualified for or just earning too little from a single job to support oneself. On casual analysis under-employment seems more common in the US, but has begun to appear in increasing amounts in Europe as well. This is likely a result of stronger worker rights and minimum wage regulations in Europe. The various app-based food delivery and mobility services seem to rely on avoidance of typical labour regulations, and have resulted in vast numbers of new low-paying jobs, often employing immigrant labour with fewer alternatives on the regular job market. The solutions here must absolutely rest on the same initiatives already suggested: focus on effective education, labour market practices and workers' rights. In addition, minimum wage policies should be reviewed and updated when necessary, to ensure a living wage can be earned from honest work.

All of this ties back to the restructuring of our economies thanks to globalization and exporting of jobs to lower-cost locations. Following the Covid-19 freeze of global supply chains, and in response to the intensifying competition between China and the west, it seems probable that western firms will continue to repatriate production and diversify their suppliers to more secure close locations. If this trend gains strength, it should help reverse the job-destruction that accompanied the preceding outsourcing boom, with positive outcomes for wage growth for the working and middle classes. This nascent trend appears to align with broader geopolitical objectives, as well as helping mitigate income inequality issues.

As mentioned earlier, immigration has also grown the pool of workers and the supply of labour, no doubt suppressing wages, especially at the lower end of the distribution. A rethink of immigration policies might thus be warranted from an income inequality perspective. Taken together, these sorts of policies and directions should help divert income shares back to labour and away from capital – which has taken an increasing slice of the overall pie in recent decades.

LABOUR SHARE OF INCOME IN THE US 1950–2016

Three-fourths of the decrease in labor share in the united states since 1947 has come since 2000. Labor share of nonfarm business sector,[97] total compensation share of gross value added, %

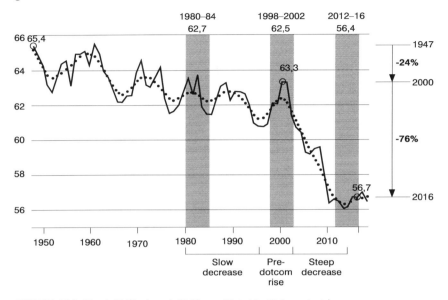

SOURCE: BLS (March 2019 release); McKinsey Global Institute analysis

The idea is not to endorse inward-looking protectionism at all. Free trade enables specialization and prosperity in ways impossible to achieve by a single country going it alone. Rather, the point is to figure out ways to rebalance the excesses of the previous trend that benefited capital at the expense of labour, and created trust-eroding income inequality as a side effect.

This also brings us to our last point about income developments. The best thing for everyone is of course growth in real incomes. This brings about a better quality of life, which is the reason we place value on economic development in the first place. Economic growth bestowing us with increasing incomes rests on rising productivity, which itself comes from organizational, technological and scientific innovations that make it

---

97   Detrended using Hodrick-Prescott filter (restriction parameter=6); adjusted for self-employed income (nonfarm business sector, 75% of total economy), from Labor Productivity and Costs database, Bureau of Labor Statistics.

possible to do things in a better way than before. Thus, to foster income development for all, we should remain mindful of not just how to share the pie, but also baking a bigger one. The best way to accelerate growth is to maintain high investments in education, research and development activities that turn ideas into incomes and wealth. Europe especially has been lagging for a long time in innovation. Devoting more money and focus on research is thus something that should always pay off, resulting in new innovations, new companies, new jobs and new wealth. Then we need to make sure the fruits of growth are shared reasonably, so that there is both fair wage growth for all and fair rewards to the innovators and risk takers, so that the incentives to innovate and generate more growth remain robust.

TECHNOLOGICAL CHANGE

Technological change matters not just from an economic perspective, but also for social reality at large thanks to the way it moulds structures and interactions in societies. Specifically, the change in our technological landscape has had a profound impact on the media. Newspapers and TV channels have lost prominence and migrated online, while new social networks have become central hubs from which information spreads. The internet, computers and smartphones have completely upended the way we engage with information. Just as the underlying technologies of communication have changed, so too have the incentive structures guiding profit-seeking agents in the new information environment. These incentives arise from economic models where engagement and clicks by users generate the most monetary value. The greatest attractor for engagement and clicks is of course outrage, showing up as racy and divisive headlines and points of view. This has resulted in a media landscape that is pushing us towards monetizable actions by making us react on primitive emotions rather than reasoned thought.

As McLuhan put it, the medium is the message (or massage), and the message of the present media is that emotions overrule reason and that outrage pays off, with endless complaints about injustice and screaming against even the minutest piece of discomfort, where ideology trumps all forms of fact and reality. It is an environment where the most extreme positions drown out reasoned debate, an environment that is utterly toxic to objective intellectual analysis and mental health.

That is to say, we are in a complete mess with our information space. In some sense the internet has revealed the very deep differences in worldviews between people, which is a real and legitimate phenomenon that in earlier ages was concealed by the narrower information space. In many ways it seems we are also seeing the limits of human reasoning abilities, not quite at home in an environment of increasingly complex issues and undigestible amounts of information. Yet the problem is in large part connected to the underlying incentive structure that thrives on division and outrage. How to rework the incentives so that they promote calm and collected impartial analysis over brainless partisan shouting is of course the big question. I do not pretend to have answers here, but raise the issue and call for creative thinking around it.

A perhaps deeper set of incentive issues is found in the tension between historical hierarchical organizations of authority such as the state and the spontaneous, non-hierarchical networked world created by communication technologies. In times that require quick reactions, official responses are often hopelessly late, after anonymous experts on the net have already analyzed the situation. When transparency is greater than ever, state incompetence becomes all the more visible. In many ways the inherited structures seem outdated and unable to maintain the authority they claim to possess, leading to eroding trust and legitimacy.

Again, I offer no clear solutions. There seems to be a two-fold development going on. One arises from the reality of the networked age, which would seem to favour nimble, flexible small organizations over larger ones. The other from the fact that the world is now global, and a competition between the largest powers and biggest companies, where size and scale are more important than ever. The eternal forces of competition hence continue in many ways to favour larger units over smaller ones. Taken together, these developments would imply a direction of travel where high-level cooperation, such as on the EU stage, remains absolutely essential, but might be complemented by devolution at the local level. The separatist movements in Catalonia and Scotland, eager for devolution but just as keen to stay in the EU, are perhaps a reflection of these pressures. Issues benefiting from collective weight, such as those concerning trade rules, defence or common foreign policy might optimally be organized at a supranational level – but everything that can be brought as close as possible to the local relevant group of people, should be, implying a two-tier structure. This might enhance the flexibility and speed of operations. More importantly, trust thrives in circumstances of low power distance – where power is exercised locally, by the people one most easily identifies with. Likewise, the closer the relevant group of people are to their representatives and decision makers the better the trust feedback loop can operate between them. Ideas and causes become represented with higher definition, and changes in the electorate's trust in their candidates translate more readily into the composition of the representatives and the policies they conduct.

What this all means in practice is, of course, a difficult question. Whatever else, it is apparent that the sources and structures of authority are in flux in the west, and a world that continues to operate largely with industrial-era frameworks is bound for more stress.

China offers another perspective on the situation as it strives for another solution to the pressures of the information age. The Chinese answer seems to be coalescing around rigid control of the information space, coupled with extensive surveillance and social scoring systems incentivizing desired behaviours. In essence it is attempting to use information technologies for control rather than liberation. How well it can actually restrain free discourse remains to be seen.

It is to be hoped that the west will remain keen to promote individual rights, and maintain limitations on government power and oversight – to secure freedom and foster trust between the state and the people. It should always be remembered that the state and the government exist to serve the people, not the other way around. The ousting of President Trump from social media platforms contrasts curiously with the Chinese situation. On the one hand it shows that even the ostensibly most powerful person in the country is not invulnerable. On the other hand, the prospect of virtual exile and ostracism at the decision of an independent profit-seeking firm is somewhat chilling. If a president cannot avoid this fate, what protections do average private citizens have against arbitrary abuse from the firms in control? Can, and should, private firms be trusted with such powers? These are pertinent questions in need of answers, with consequences that will undoubtedly reflect in citizens' trust in the information ecosystem.

A tacit coalition seems to be forming between the presently Democrat-aligned government and the Silicon Valley firms operating the social media and internet space, perhaps driven by gentle threats of antitrust action. Ostensibly the parties are working together to protect citizens from the wilderness and outrage of the online environment. What will result from this in reality is another question. Incumbent firms will hardly be happy to alter or erode the incentive structures and business models from which their profits flow, despite the unhealthy externalities.

The obvious fear is that the outcome of the alliance is control and censorship in a light-weight imitation of the Chinese policies, rather than a fair and free environment to explore the large and small, the mundane and the challenging issues of the day.

Another interesting development in the intersection of trust and tech is the rise of blockchain technology. It is currently being used mainly for virtual currencies such as Bitcoin, but its potential as a scalable, reliable, trust-free, decentralized and public system of records seems flexible enough for wider use. Indeed, it has been proposed that the technology could be used for a wide variety of applications including trading, financial services, smart contracts and online voting systems. Despite the grand promises, so far success is visible only in the currency space, if even there. Should blockchain prove to be a viable technology more broadly, the prospect of updating and improving core social systems such as finance, contracts and voting is compelling.

Blockchain-based currencies achieve their trust-free status thanks to the system's decentralized, encrypted peer-to-peer nature bolstered by data-replication where copies of the database are maintained at each node, with a node representing an individual computing device forming a part of the blockchain network. These and other features mean the system does not rely on intermediaries for its operation, as the present financial system does with its banks, settlement houses and the like acting on behalf of their clients. On blockchain, trading and transactions can be direct between parties, so presumably not reliant on central points of failure. The information of a trade is automatically appended to the whole blockchain, updating the system at large about the transaction. These features have potentially enormous consequences.

At first glance it is not clear that the monetary system is a particular source of distrust at the present. Yet, the financial crisis is not far behind us and it certainly shook trust in many ways. Taking a historical view shows that the events of 2007–2009 were not an anomaly, but a recurring phenomenon. If a blockchain-based financial system proves to be more stable, mitigating the recurring crises would obviously be a boon. As we have seen, our financial system relies on key central actors – the banks and central banks – for its smooth functioning. Should the banks become jeopardized, and trust in them evaporate, the resulting problems can spread far across the rest of the economy thanks to the way banks are at the centre of handling assets and liabilities, accounts and moving money across firms and people. Therefore, if a blockchain-based system can liberate us from banks as systemic points of failure, without bringing in new and worse vulnerabilities, it might lead us to a more stable and trustful financial future. Central banks have taken note, and all the major ones are experimenting and designing their own digital currencies, though it is unclear whether the reason is financial stability or the ability to exert greater control over the economy.

Another aspect of money is the fact that states (aided by central banks when sufficiently pressured) have always issued more of it to boost their spending power, in effect leading to excessive public debts, rising taxes and decreasing purchasing power for the people through inflation. Independent digital currencies based on blockchain paint the prospect of moving away from this often abusive relationship. Alluring promises aside, independent cybercurrencies seem to be in a constant flux, with repeated price bubbles and subsequent crashes. This has made them poor media for payments and trade in practice. The constant price variance does not help with gaining public trust in them as reliable stores of value either.

Despite the high promise, blockchain-based currencies and financial systems remain viable in speculation only. Whether they manage to develop into a new stable backbone of the financial architecture is still an open question. There can be no doubt that vested interests benefiting from the present setup are enormous, and will mobilize to resist drastic and adverse change. How these tensions are resolved is likely to be a source of high drama in the future, should blockchain-based solutions begin to make good on their promises of superior performance. There can be no doubt that such developments might also have deep ramifications for people's trust in the financial system as a whole.

In the end, the effects of technology on trust are as varied and changeable as the applied sciences themselves. In the ongoing transformation we have to settle in the first instance for trying to understand it all and, should we reach that lofty position, then start to ponder on the implications for trust. We have attempted this here, but it is obvious that much is left in the dark. When it comes to ideas to address the deficit of trust we are experiencing, obvious solutions are sadly in short supply. Regardless, let us summarize some starting points for further discussion that might lead to improvement.

The problem of perverse incentives in the click- and view-based internet economy is a clear issue degrading the quality of our communications. Twitter is the most egregious example of this, being antithetical to reasoned debate and thorough thinking by design. How in practice to turn the incentives around to rewarding the rational rather than the emotional is a very difficult question – but well worth considering. The solution would probably involve the heavy hand of regulation, which is of course to be minimized whenever possible. But in this case the benefits might be worth it, at least to the degree that serious thought should be devoted to the issue.

A related issue is the outsized power of the companies at the core of our information economy: Facebook, Google, Amazon and the like. These companies are simultaneously supposed to be the guardians of our freedom of expression, police against its abuse and maximize their profits. It seems like a tough set of objectives to fulfil, especially when considering the fact that these and other social media companies make their money by maximizing our engagement and the time spent on their services. But, again, what an improved situation would look like is a picture mostly beyond my imagination. Tighter oversight over abuse of often monopolistic market positions seems at the very least necessary, possibly even partitioning the businesses as was done with American oil giants in the early 20th century. The problem of the private internet giants in control of the web infrastructure is closely related to the incentive problems mentioned, and any party wishing to improve the situation should take both into account simultaneously.

Again, it needs to be stressed that unnecessary regulation should be avoided where possible. This applies doubly to censorship, which can only lead to decreases in trust, rather than help it along. Instead we should try to achieve communication structures favouring quality arguments and comprehensive analytical approaches – following McLuhan's insights on the effects technologies have in our social landscapes.

What effects blockchain technologies might eventually have on trust remain a mystery. Given the active private interest in the technology, and ongoing central bank efforts, it seems guaranteed that progress on this frontier will continue.

The development of artificial intelligence technologies is another factor that will come to have deep implications for trust. One aspect is the potential replacement of human effort in many activities, as automation and AI advance. These developments could easily have severe consequences for income inequality, as well as human self-image in general, should we effectively become second-rate in our cognitive abilities next to the machines. Insidious developments could stem from the progress in text, voice, image and video-generation capabilities. It has already become possible to generate these things through AI processes with the results being effectively indistinguishable from those created by real humans. For example, an online video stream could be captured mid-stream and replaced with a fully indistinguishable artificial construction spreading a completely different message. When everything we see online becomes replicable and liable to manipulation, the situation could easily turn precarious for trust. If there are scandals involving, for example, falsified high-level political messages, how would trust keep up? A nightmare scenario would be that people retain trust only in things they can witness in person in the real world, with everything online becoming suspect and distrusted.

In the present, largely thanks to the Covid pandemic, home offices and remote working have become commonplace. Should this trend persist at scale, it could be thought to alienate people from each other, diminishing the face-to-face communal aspects of work that can also generate trust. Similar impacts might also spring from the growth of app-based work coordination, such as with food delivery, which likewise use technological solutions that minimize human contact.

The potential future issues briefly mentioned here seem minor next to the topics covered in greater depth, but might well in time become major ones. All of this is to make obvious that things have changed and will continue to do so. The full impacts of these changes will take time to become intelligible and, in response, actionable. Perhaps the only thing we can say with any certainty is that technology will continue to evolve rapidly, taking our societies along with the process. A quickly changing environment is a bewildering one, and can challenge people's ability to trust as the things previously taken for granted disappear and morph into something new and unfamiliar.

Something we can however say is that we should strive to ensure that technological forces are used for empowerment, improvement and liberation within our societies. Undoubtedly many countries will demonstrate their use as tools of censorship, control and manipulation. Let us choose a different path.

THE SPLIT IN VALUES

Perhaps the most obvious drag on trust in the west is the divergence in values among our populations. The US offers a stark example of this, with people identifying as Democrats and Republicans seeing less and less in common with the opposing side. A recently published survey by University of Virginia Center for Politics highlighted the breakdown with saddening efficiency. According to the study, 80% of Biden voters and

84% of Trump voters saw elected officials from the other side presenting a "clear and present danger to American democracy". When it came to perhaps the driving force of this split, values, 78% of Biden voters and 87% of Trump voters wanted to eliminate the influence of traditional (if Biden voter) or progressive (if Trump voter) values in American life and culture. Results such as these speak of divisions that run very deep. So deep, in fact, that people on both sides are increasingly questioning whether the existing political union makes sense anymore. Forty-one percent of Biden voters and 52% of Trump voters were in favour of blue or red states seceding from the union to form their own country.[98]

Developments in Europe appear to be almost identical. Differences arise mainly out of the multiparty political systems, which in Europe have concentrated the most ardent progressive or traditionalist elements into their own parties on the left and right.

A complete disbelief about views presented by the other side accompanies the breakdown in common values, followed naturally by a lack of understanding. Thus we are in a situation where on both sides the opposition is often described as evil or mad. Understanding trust and its relationship to knowledge informs us about why mutual comprehension has become so elusive. Yet it is precisely mutual comprehension that will prove essential for civilized defusal of the situation.

As long as values remain different, are we doomed to a communications break-down and even worse outcomes? As long as both parties remain unwilling to listen to the other side, rather seeking to censor them out, there can scarcely be hope for constructive outcomes. So, what would mend the situation and get people listening to each other again?

Despite all the differences, the two sides would benefit from realizing that they share a set of common interests, the recognition of which should create space for productive mutual problem solving. The first commonality stems from acknowledging that everyone has an ideal community they wish to live in – and that the shape of this ideal community varies by person and their values. As people promote their own values in pursuit of their own ideal societies, despite their differences they are all effectively looking to create an ideal environment for themselves, however they perceive it. The native voting for an anti-immigration party and the immigrant voting for a pro-immigration party are effectively doing the same: both aiming to mould society to their likeness, to a more advantageous and agreeable

---

98   centerforpolitics.org/crystalball/articles/new-initiative-explores-deep-persistent-divides-between-biden-and-trump-voters

form and hence also into a place they might find more trustful. So, no matter how disagreeable the left and right may find each other, both should at least admit that both are engaged in identical, and quite universal, behaviour – to which they all have full rights.

The second commonality all should agree on is that no matter what the background, everyone should be treated with civility and dignity. Sadly, this base level of courtesy has been declining for a long time, and the disrespectful trend hit a new peak on all sides with Donald Trump's presidency.

So, both sides should equip themselves with the admission that even if the value gap seems unbridgeable, at least the other side is acting in its own interests as they see them – as is legitimate in a democratic system; and deserve to be treated with the same dignity as every human being does. With these admissions the sides might engage in an honest and frank discussion about what might be done to resolve the situation, wherever that may lead. This of course entails taking seriously the grievances and talking points of the other side and mapping where they can be admitted or compromised about and where not.

As it stands, the UK is the only country that has seemingly managed to integrate and defuse the right-wing challenge for the time being, through the painful process of Brexit. Brexit itself was an idiosyncratic mix of Euroscepticism and immigration issues, and scarcely provides a successful or desirable template for others. But it serves as an example of the desire for cultural and national sustainability, provisionally satisfied in the British context. Elsewhere in Europe, such parties have mostly been shut out of power, despite their often considerable popular support. Continued failure to address this challenge is liable to lead to further and more severe problems. For example, given the lack of discernible results through democratic channels, it may be guessed that nativist parties and their members might well lose all trust in a system that continues to exclude them, and mutate into outright separatist groups. In the US, the situation is already extremely volatile.

Any constructive resolution to the situation on both sides of the Atlantic would require both sides of the political spectrum to make painful admissions. Research on trust both helps identify some of the major issues and offers perspective on resolving them. The left-mainstream is unwilling to engage in any critical discussions about fears of cultural dispossession and the downsides of immigration. Yet trust research and theory show quite clearly why immigration can be a negative factor for trust, basically coming down to the fact that the less people have in common, the less they trust each other. The right has problems acceding rights to various sexual and other minority groups, and scepticism about climate change remains a force in many places. Again, trust theory shows why equal rights and freedom of self-expression are important, as they are essential for genuine being and the functioning of the trust feedback loop. Climate change risks outcomes that can scarcely be understood yet. Even if they do not believe the science and prognoses of the climate models, the denialists should accede the limits of their own knowledge and admit that neither can they conclusively deny the potential harms, and that taking action against the most extreme outcomes is the wisest course of action in an uncertain world.

Creating an environment conducive to trust will require everyone to admit painful facts, as well as creative thinking on how to gracefully resolve the existential-level issues we face.

CLIMATE CHANGE

As we have seen, most people agree that climate change is a problem screaming for a solution, yet nobody seems to know how, at least among those in power. Perhaps a handful of severe incentive problems form a wall in the way of breakthroughs. Yet these should not prevent progress if the right perspective is adopted. This is the thesis of Oxford economics professor Dieter Helm, whose brilliant analysis of the issues illuminates a way forward. We will briefly cover the main outlines of his ideas, then add a few notes on how to take matters of trust into account while we forge our way towards a greener, brighter, future.

In his excellent book Net Zero, Helm analyses the problems that have prevented action thus far, and offers a comprehensive plan, which sidesteps the pitfalls that have hampered progress to date. The grand proclamations at international climate summits have proven not much more than hot air. Helm sees several reasons why the good intentions have not translated into effective action in the real world.

A central problem arises from the fact that we tend to measure emissions based on domestic production, rather than on consumption. This has had the effect of further incentivizing the shift of production away from the west to lower-cost locations abroad. By shifting production outside our borders, we have achieved an impression of decreasing emissions – while in practice the products we consume are now produced in more lax jurisdictions, often with greater emissions. Hence, we have dodged the responsibility for cutting emissions at home, and often in reality increased them. A shift to comprehensive consumption-based emission measurements would correct this problematic set of incentives. This leads to the more general problem that the negative externalities from carbon emissions are currently not effectively priced into our economy, which in turn keeps us on an unsustainable economic path. To correct for this problem, we need to count emissions not just from domestic activities but also from imports. Carbon needs a price across the whole economy. Once the carbon content of a product or a service has a price, no matter its origin, the economy will automatically start adjusting to products and modes of operation that are less polluting – in other words, cheaper to produce and thus more profitable.

Typically, unilateral institution of a price on carbon has been thought of as economic suicide, putting firms in the nation doing so at a disadvantage against foreign competition. But Helm contends that setting a carbon price on imports at the border would shield the domestic economy and level the playing field. Furthermore, the carbon taxes would help raise revenues for the state's necessary climate investments – and could be used to cut income or other taxes to compensate for the loss of purchasing power that would otherwise result from the new carbon costs in the economy.

These initiatives need to be further bolstered with extensive investments to transform areas such as communications, energy, transport and agriculture. Another central enabler in the transition to a sustainable economy is research and development, which helps achieve efficiency gains and new sustainable technologies, in the process underpinning economic progress. The state has a key role in these transformative investments, and by increasing funding for relevant research it can bring about similar technological revolutions to those achieved previously with the development of space technology, the internet and mobile communications. Upgrading key infrastructure and investing in research would bring about positive externalities that help create jobs and renew the economy in the difficult transition to a sustainable path.

Helm contends that through measures such as these states can pursue effective unilateral no-regrets action against climate change; action that not only mitigates our pressure on the environment, but also helps upgrade our economies and safeguard prosperity in the future.

What Helm proposes seems eminently reasonable to me, with the caveat that I am an absolute beginner in the art and science of climate change and how to mitigate it. No doubt there exist critiques on Helm's approach, as well as many other ideas about what should and should not be done. The key takeaway here is that there are clear, realistic and achievable ideas out there explaining what to do. The fact of the matter is that we have the necessary plans to get started, the scientific and technological know-how to go a long way and the financial muscle to realize it all. The only thing missing is a firm political commitment to roll up our sleeves and finally get started. The changing and contentious nature of democratic politics has the habit of making this difficult, but a broad cross-party commitment should be reachable in these exceptional circumstances. Regardless of how and in what structure it is achieved, tackling the issue requires a steady long-term commitment that must be above everyday party politics, lest the project falls by the wayside at the first sign of trouble.

To Helm's account I would like to add one thing – something so practical that it is probably almost too obvious to even think for those wrestling with the topic. Yet it might help us restore trust faster than otherwise possible. The issue is of communication and transparency. States are probably already doing many things in response to climate change. Yet often the only thing visible to the public is when a state delegation attends a climate conference to make vague and unbinding promises. Should a country finally muster the courage and start executing a comprehensive plan, such as proposed by Professor Helm, a well thoughtout communication strategy would be an extremely helpful addition to the process. Let us explore why.

The basic idea here is to make visible the actions planned and taken, the impacts achieved and expected in the future and how they measure up to the challenge. By providing a clear roadmap of actions and their estimated impacts, and not shying away from admitting the grey areas requiring research and further study, the state can begin to build trust with citizens and slowly alleviate the fears associated with climate change. So far, states have comprehensively failed to convince the people of their capacity and willingness to master the challenge. No credible plans to address the issue have been presented, probably reflecting the general confusion and lack of ideas. What we have had instead are a series of overly general commitments to address the issue by some distant future date. These statements have proven all too vague, their lack of substance failing to soothe our fears.

Adopting a comprehensive and credible plan to correct the course and communicating it effectively would already by itself constitute a considerable improvement. Should a state adopt such plans, but fail to communicate them to citizens, the climate fears would continue to persist and grow, citizens in all likelihood losing their patience with the state long before the situation is resolved. After all, uncertainty by itself is often a significant source of anxiety, and an efficient communications campaign could do much to mitigate the worries stemming from it. This is why we need to couple effective action with effective communication.

All this information about plans, investments, their timelines and estimated impacts, as well as current and projected emissions, would be very easy to present on a humble website – making it all highly accessible. Functions for citizen engagement and feedback could easily be added. By doing all this a state could make progress in the situation indisputably visible, helping people learn to trust its actions, thus starting to placate the climate worries in the process. Trust is after all gained or lost on account of expectations, the fulfilment of which leads to strengthening trust. By keeping citizens informed, the state can not only adjust expectations, but also showcase the many actions it is taking – signalling its trustworthiness. Of course, such communications would only help if they are honest and realistic, and the actions taken are enough to meet the challenge. The contents of Professor Helm's book show that all this is eminently achievable.

The biggest issue is undoubtedly the lack of effective action, against which Greta Thunberg and Extinction Rebellion keep on raging. Good intentions are certainly there, and commitments about reaching net zero have been made far and wide. But the fact of the matter is, states and other key actors have yet to present credible plans explaining how they intend to deliver on their promises. Helm and others show that the task is not impossible. As often happens in life, presentation matters a lot, not just the content and execution of sustainability plans as they are finally adopted. Clearly explaining climate plans and actions to the people would go a long way to relieve them of their climate angst – assuming the plans are actually realized and the actions measure up to the challenge. This would also create grounds for regaining the trust that has thus far been squandered by confusion and inaction.

Trust as a fundamental force of societal development

THIS BOOK HAS sought to demonstrate the ubiquitous presence of trust as the glue that holds the structures of our societies together. The gifts of trust extend far, thanks to the fact that understanding it provides a robust framework that can be used to analyse and perceive a wide variety of social phenomena from a new, fresh, angle. Yet this book has covered mere surface ripples in a vast ocean of insights for those searching for wisdom and understanding. That is to say, trust with its manifold effects offers an immensely rich field for further study and thinking.

In our exploration of trust we have established how evolutionary pressures bring trust about, and how experiences, especially during childhood, affect its expression. We found that the antecedents of trust can be thought of as a sort of gatekeepers, with trust being a heuristic of risk in cooperation. Yet the same antecedent dimensions could also be turned around and thought of as things motivating us to reach out to others. Knowledge requires trust for its creation and dissemination, and our ability to entertain new ideas seems tied to our trusting facility. Under supportive circumstances trust can accumulate into social capital, an expression of the tangible fruits of trust such as networks, connections and general capacity for collective action. Finally, legitimacy can be seen to rest on people's trust in the state and the political system. We can therefore track the origins of trust from biological and evolutionary factors to its impacts on the individual and society at large, and appreciate how it affects the way we make sense of the world.

In short, through the examination of trust in its many expressions and instances we may attain a comprehensive (though certainly not exhaustive) explanation of a multitude of societal phenomena. Trust has often been intuitively understood as the cornerstone for cooperation, economic activity and functional society, but the various commentators have mostly stopped short of enquiring deeper into the operations that bring about this fundamental role. This book has attempted to examine those mechanisms and thereby underline the essential role of trust in social development in a more tractable manner. This more concrete and comprehensive understanding of the phenomenon may allow for a more intelligent and successful development of societies in the future, and should form a base camp for subsequent forays deeper into the landscape of trust.

One remarkable feature of trust is its dual nature, at once thriving on similarities but also requiring responsiveness, freedom and room for adjustment. It can be claimed that many ideas and practices derive their power from serving one or another aspect of trust, showing up as desire for equality and uniformity of a kind, or the celebration of information and empowerment.

Applying the very simple model of the trust process to a variety of settings allowed us to attain a deeper and more comprehensive understanding of human behaviour and societal development. Trust can for example be seen as an explanation for why like attracts like and why freedom is so valued. As trust can be expected to be higher when power distances are lower and people are aligned in their values and perspectives, we can perhaps deduce why democracies have tended to start small, while large empires tend to be realms of distrust held together only by coercive force, and why hierarchies in general tend to be looked at askance. Of course, this is not to say trust is the only, or even the largest, reason for these things. But it is the thesis of this book that it certainly is a factor that is yet to be fully appreciated.

Trust is a concept that can help us make sense of the bewildering present and the distressing past. The dual nature of trust can serve as a vehicle for understanding nationalism and all kinds of tribalism as political forces, as well as the post-war anti-nationalistic diversity-promoting stance. If nationalism was a thesis based on the value of similarities, and the present its antithesis in celebrating differences and promoting empowerment on that basis, understanding how trust works between its evaluative and processual dimensions provides us with a synthesis that shows why both of these approaches have merit.

We began our journey with a set of statistics showing a stark decline in trust in the west. Here, at the end of the book, we considered hypotheses about what is causing these declines and how we might start to correct our course.

Despite these and other ways trust operates in our lives, trust's very fundamental role in society has mostly remained obscure, probably because it is too obvious and commonplace to garner much thought. By demonstrating trust's presence in various societal contexts, this book has made the case that trust is key to our present predicaments and a subject deserving far greater focus and attention.

Epilogue – values

"Keep your values positive, because your values become your destiny."

GANDHI, SENTIMENT ORIGINATING WITH LAO TZU

ONE OF THE central findings revealed by our investigation is the importance of values in connection to trust. Values pop up time and again, whenever an assessment of another party is being made. Beyond what has already been discussed, it is my firm belief that values are a, perhaps even the, fundamental factor explaining differences in trust between countries. It is not just alignment on values that matters for trust, but also the kinds of values a society holds. Values direct the way we engage with each other, guiding us in subtle ways towards trust or distrust. A society that considers honesty, openness and punctuality as important virtues is bound to see its citizens treat each other in manners far more fruitful for trust than one disregarding such values and behaviours. Positive or negative trust-related externalities therefore offer a perhaps thus far hidden basis for analysis and an explanation for many of our customs and values.

The years since the Second World War have seen values change perhaps faster than at any other time in western history, a development which seems only to have accelerated in the first decades of the 21st century. Religion has effectively exited the stage, especially in Europe, and previous concepts of sexuality, nationhood and the west's history and role in the world have been completely upended. As a consequence, our societies have changed dramatically. The rapid progress of technology has further accentuated the changes, completely disrupting the ways we communicate and connect, consume and create information.

Against this mutating mental and social landscape, we must contrast the stark declines in trust reflecting increasing insecurity across our countries. Given the present outlook with persisting income inequalities, dissonant values, demographic anxieties and the creeping doom of climate change, a lot needs to happen to restore trust in a better future. The scale of the challenges was correctly framed by UK prime minister Boris Johnson at a G20 meeting in Rome, ahead of the 2021 Glasgow Climate Change Conference, when he compared them to those that felled the ancient Roman empire and drove Europe into the dark ages.[99]

Indeed, the present circumstances bear an uncanny resemblance to those faced by the Roman empire in its waning years, from the long retreat from imperial heights to the loss of old faith, to adverse population trends and climate changes coupled with economic collapse. As far as policies and practices uphold these trends, they are also tightly tied to the values professed by a society. This makes it only a slight exaggeration to say that,

---

99   www.theguardian.com/environment/2021/oct/30/cop26-failure-could-mean-mass-migration-and-food-shortages-says-boris-johnson

for all their other merits, many of the ideas and values presently held in the west spell out its own demise. The distressing direction of travel is of course not an explicit aim, but rather takes its course from the implicit second-order effects.

Yet our situation is far more hopeful than the Romans' ever was. Despite the gravity of the challenges, our capacity to overcome them is incomparably better. We have the lessons of history to draw wisdom from, should we choose to do so. We have a base of knowledge and instruments of science infinitely greater, allowing us to devise solutions to even the most perplexing problems. The wealth of technology affords us economic resources to bear even the heaviest investments needed to turn the course.

Finding an orderly and peaceful path to a sustainable, hopeful future hinges on our capacity to take in the situation in all of its multifaceted complexity, and show the necessary responsibility and thoughtfulness in resolving it. The task is great, but eminently achievable.

As values often develop in response to societal challenges and historical experience, we can also expect continued revaluation of values in the west. Environmental considerations will undoubtedly come to permeate nearly all our ways of being and doing. Despite the recent and present trends in the opposite direction, it seems likely that family values will return to prominence in one way or another, at least among those yearning to flourish, rather than wither away.

Through the upcoming transformations, trust is a concept that can help us understand, reconcile and surmount the dilemmas we face.

What we face is nothing less than the real maturity test of the western civilization after the painful 20th century: to accept and heal from our past, not just reject and repeal it; to create new hope and positive expectation for the future, respecting the dignity of everyone; to learn to trust ourselves and each other again.

About the author

MARTIN MIKAEL LILIUS (b. 1983) works as a management consultant, in a profession resting on trust between the client and the advisor. Prior to consulting, he focused on private equity investing. He holds a Master's degree in Applied Economics and Finance from Copenhagen Business School, including studies at Columbia University in the City of New York. Martin Mikael Lilius lives in Helsinki, Finland.

WWW.TRUSTKNOWLEDGESOCIETY.COM

References

Printed references

A Contribution to the Theory of Economic Growth. Solow, Robert M. *The Quarterly Journal of Economics*, Vol. 70, No. 1. 1956.

A new understanding of the history of limited liability: an invitation for theoretical reframing. Harris, Ron. *Journal of Institutional Economics*, 2020, 16.

A prospective longitudinal study of attachment disorganization/disorientation. Carlson, E. A. *Child Develevelopment*, August 1998.

Adolescent Future Orientation: An Integrated Cultural and Ecological Perspective. Seginer, Rachel. *Online Readings in Psychology and Culture*, 6(1), 2003.

Agency Problems in Public Firms: Evidence from Corporate Jets in Leveraged Buyouts. Edgerton, Jesse. *The Journal of Finance* Vol. 67, No. 6, December 2012.

An empirical investigation of mobile banking adoption: The effect of innovation attributes and knowledge-based trust. Lin, Hsiu-Fen. *International Journal of Information Management*. Volume 31, Issue 3, June 2011.

An Integrative Model of Organizational Trust. Mayer, Roger; Davis, James; Schoorman, David. *The Academy of Management Review*, Vol. 20, July 1995.

Are close relationships in adolescence linked with partner relationships in midlife? A longitudinal, prospective study. Möller, Kristiina; Stattin, Håkan. *International Journal of Behavioral Development* 2001, 25.

As Economic Concerns Recede, Environmental Protection Rises on the Public's Policy Agenda. Pew Research Center, February 2020.

Attachment security: A meta-analysis of maternal mental health correlates. Atkinson, Leslie; Paglia, Angela; Coolbear, Jennifer; Niccols, Allison; Parker, Kevin; Guger, Sharon. *Clinical Psychology Review*, November 2000, Volume 20, issue 8.

Attachment theory and its place in contemporary personality theory and research. Fraley, R. Chris; Shaver, Phillip, R; *Handbook of Personality: Theory and Research*, 2008.

Attachment Theory: Basic Concepts and Contemporary Questions. W. S.

Rholes & J.A. Simpson. *Adult attachment: Theory, research, and clinical implications* (pp. 3–14). Guilford Publications, 2004.

Beyond Good and Evil. Fourth Chapter: Apophthegms and Interludes, 68. Nietzsche, Friedrich. Wordsworth Editions, 2008.

Can We Be Happier? Layard, Richard. Pelican books, 2020.

Climate anxiety in children and young people and their beliefs about government responses to climate change: a global survey. Hickman, Caroline; Marks, Elizabeth; Pihkala, Panu; Clayton, Susan; Lewandowski, Eric; Mayall, Elouise; Wray, Britt; Mellor, Catriona; van Susteren, Lise. *The Lancet*, Volume 5, Issue 12, December 2021

Convergence in the age of mass migration. Taylor, Alan; Williamson, Jeffrey. *European Review of Economic History*, April 1997, Vol. 1, No. 1.

Depressive realism: A meta-analytic review. Moore, Michael T; Fresco, David M. *Clinical Psychology Review*, Volume 32, Issue 6, August 2012.

Differences in Parenting Stress, Parenting Attitudes, and Parents' Mental Health According to Parental Adult Attachment Style. Kim, Do Hoon; Kang, Na Ri; Kwack, Young Sook. *Journal of the Korean Academy of Child and Adolescent Psychiatry*, 2019, 30.

Does time spent using social media impact mental health?: An eight year longitudinal study. Coyne, Sarah; Rogers, Adam; Zurcher, Jessica; Stockdale, Laura; Booth, McCall. *Computers in Human Behavior*, 104, 2020.

Emotions, learning, and the brain. Immordino-Yang, Mary. Norton Professional Books, 2016.

Ethnic bias, economic success and trust: Findings from large sample experiments in Germany and the United States through the Trustlab platform. Cetre, Sophie; Algan, Yann; Grimalda, Gianluca; Murtin, Fabrice; Putterman, Louis; Schmidt, Ulrich; Siegerink, Vincent. *SDD Working Paper* No. 106, OECD. October, 2020

Ethnic Diversity and Social Trust: A Narrative and Meta-Analytical Review. Dinesen, Peter Thisted; Schaeffer, Merlin; Sønderskov Kim Mannemar. *Annual Review of Political Science* Vol. 23: 441–465, May 2020.

Exploring the Genetic Etiology of Trust in Adolescents: Combined Twin and DNA Analyses, Robyn E. Wootton et. al. Twin Res Hum Genet. 2016 December

Generalized Trust: Four Lessons From Genetics and Culture. Paul A M Van Lange. *Current Directions in Psychological Science*, February 2015.

Individual-Level Evidence for the Causes and Consequences of Social Capital. Brehm, John; Rahm, Wendy, *American Journal of Political Science* Vol. 41, No. 3, July 1997.

Individualism-Collectivism and Social Capital. Allik, Jüri; Realo, Anu. *Journal of Cross-Cultural Psychology*. January 2004.

Industry concentration in Europe and North America. Bajgar, Matej; Berlingieriu, Giuseppe; Calligaris, Sara; Criscuolo, Chiara; Timmis, Jonathan. *OECD Productivity Working Papers*, January, 2019, No. 18.

It Isn't Always Mutual: A Critical Review of Dyadic Trust. M. Audrey Korsgaard, Holly H. Brower, Scott W. Lester. September 3, 2014

Judgment of Contingency in Depressed and Nondepressed Students: Sadder but Wiser? Alloy, Lauren B. ; Abramson, Lyn Y. *Journal of Experimental Psychology: General* 1979, Vol. 108.

Making Democracy Work. Civic traditions in modern Italy. Putnam, Robert. Princeton University Press, 1994.

Mediation effects of trust and contracts on knowledge-sharing and product innovation: Evidence from the European machine tool industry. Charterina, Jon; Landeta, Jon; Basterretxea, Imanol. *European Journal of Innovation Management*, 2018.

Mediation effects of trust and contracts on knowledge-sharing and product innovation: Evidence from the European machine tool industry. Charterina, Jon; Landeta, Jon; Basterrextea, Imanol. *European Journal of Innovation Management* Vol. 21 No. 2, 2018.

Net Zero. Helm, Dieter. HarperCollins, 2000.

Oxytocin as Treatment for Social Cognition, Not There Yet. Erdozain, Amaia M; Peñagarikano, Olga. *Frontiers in Psychiatry*, January 2020.

Oxytocin's Effect on Resting-State Functional Connectivity Varies by Age and Sex. Ebner, Natalie; Chen, Huaihou; Porges, Eric; Lin, Tian; Fischer, Håkan; Feifel, David; Cohen, Ronald. *Psychoneuroendocrinology*, July 2016.

Politics and Economics. Butler, Nicholas Murray. 1911, 143rd Annual Banquet of the Chamber of Commerce of the State of New York, New York: Press of the Chamber of Commerce, pp. 43–56.

Quality of Life: social cohesion and well-being in Europe. Delhey, Jan; Dragolov, Georgi; Boehnke, Klaus. Eurofound, November, 2018

Radical Distrust: Are Economic Policy Attitudes Tempered by Social Trust? Pitlik, Hans; Rode, Martin. *WIFO Working Papers*, No. 594 December 2019.

Revolt of the Public. Gurri, Martin. Stripe Press, 2018. Page 2013.

Self-Confidence and Personal Motivation. Benabou, Roland; Tirole, Jean. *Quarterly Journal of Economics*, February, 2002.

Self-Deception: A Concept in Search of a Phenomenon. Gur, Ruben C; Sackeim, Harold A. *Journal of Personality and Social Psychology*, February 1979

Social capital, civil society and development. Fukuyama, Francis. February, 2001. *Third World Quarterly* 22.

Social capital, innovation and growth: Evidence from Europe. Akçomak, I.Semih; Ter Weel, Bas. *European Economic Review*, 53, 2009.

Social Capital, Intellectual Capital and the Organizational Advantage. Nahapiet, Janine; Ghoshal, Sumantra. *Academy of Management Review*, 1998, Vol. 23

Social Media Use and Adolescent Mental Health: Findings From the UK Millennium Cohort Study. Kelly, Yvonne; Zilanawala, Afshin; Booker, Cara; Sacker, Amanda. *EClinicalMedicine* 6, The Lancet, 2018.

Social media, texting, and personality: A test of the shallowing hypothesis. Annisette, Logan; Lafreniere, Kathryn. *Personality and Individual Differences*, Volume 115, September 2017.

Social Trust and Economic Growth. Bjørnskov, Christian. *Oxford Handbook of Social and Political Trust* 2017

Social Trust and the Growth of Schooling. Bjørnskov, Christian. *Economics of Education Review*, 28, 2009

The Age of Mass protests – Understanding an escalating global trend. Brannen, Samuel; Haig, Christian; Schmidt, Katherine. Center for International and Strategic studies. March, 2020.

The Art of Rhetoric. Aristotle. Collins Classics, 2012.

The Dark Side of Trust: The Benefits, Costs and Optimal Levels of Trust for Innovation Performance. Molina-Morales, Xavier; Martínez-Fernández, TeresaM; Torlòa, Vanina Jasmine. *Long Range Planning*. Volume 44, Issue 2, April 2011.

The Death and Life of Great American Cities. Jacobs, Jane. Random House, 1961.

The Economic Theory of Agency: The Principal's Problem. Ross, Stephen. *American Economic Review* 63(2), February, 1973.

The External Benefits of Education. McMahon, Walter. *International Encyclopedia of Education*, 2010.

The Importance of Trust for Investment: Evidence from Venture Capital. Bottazzi, Laura; Da Rin, Marco; Hellmann, Thomas. *The Review of Financial Studies*, Volume 29, Issue 9, September 2016

The Importance of Trust for Investment: Evidence from Venture Capital. Bottazzi, Laura; Da Rin, Marco; Hellmann, Thomas. *The Review of Financial Studies*, Volume 29, Issue 9, September 2016.

The influence of political ideology on trust in science. McCright, Aaron; Dentzman, Katherine; Charters, Meghan; Dietz, Thomas. *Environmental Research Letters* 8, 2013.

The Market for "Lemons": Quality uncertainty and the Market Mechanism. Akerlof, George. *The Quarterly Journal of Economics*, Vol. 84, No. 3, August, 1970.

The Market-Promoting and Market-Preserving Role of Social Trust in Reforms of Policies and Institutions. Berggren, Niclas; Bjørnskov, Christian. *Southern Economic Journal*, Volume 84, Issue 1, 2017

The Politics of Climate. Pew Research Center, October, 2016,

The Role of Trust in Knowledge. Hardwig, John. *The Journal of Philosophy*, December, 1991

The Role of Trust in Organisational Innovativeness. Blomqvist, Kirsimarja; Ellonen, Riikka; Puumalainen, Kaisu. *European Journal of Innovation Management*, April 2008.

The Role of Trustworthiness in Reducing Transaction Costs and Improving Performance: Empirical Evidence from the United States, Japan, and Korea. Dyer, Jeffrey; Chu, Wujin. *Organization Science* Vol. 14, No. 1, 2003.

The Rural School Community Center. Hanifan, L. J. The Annals of the American Academy of Political and Social Science, September, 1916, Vol. 67, *New Possibilities in Education.*

'Til Death Do Us Part(isanship): Voting and Polarization in Opposite-Party Marriages. Insights from the democracy fund voter study group. Fisk, Colin A; Fraga, Bernard L. August, 2020.

Trust – The social virtues and the creation of prosperity. Fukuyama, Francis. Simon & Schuster, 1995.

Trust and innovation: Evidence from CEOs' early-life experience. Kong, Dongmin; Zhao, Ying; Liu, Shasha. *Journal of Corporate Finance*, vol. 69, August, 2021.

Trust-Based Work Time and Innovation: Evidence from Firm-Level Data. Godart, Olivier; Görg, Holger; Hanley, Aoife. *ILR Review*, 2017.

Trust, Growth and Well-being: New Evidence and Policy Implications. Algan, Yann; Cahuc, Pierre. *IZA DP* No. 7464, June, 2013.

Trust, happiness and mortality: Findings from a prospective US population-based survey? Miething, Alexander; Mewes, Jan; Giordano, Giuseppe. *Social Science & Medicine*, 252, January 2020

Trust, welfare states and income equality: Sorting out the causality. Bergh, Andreas; Bjørnskov, Christian. *European Journal of Political Economy*, Volume 35, September 2014.

Understanding Media. McLuhan, Marshall. Routledge Classics, 2001.

Volitional Trust, Autonomy Satisfaction, and Engagement at Work. Heyns, Marita; Sebastiaan, Rothmann. *Psychological Reports* 2018, Vol. 121(1).

Voting the General Will: Rousseau on Decision Rules. Schwartzberg, Melissa. *Political Theory* 2008, 36

War – What is it good for? Morris, Ian. Farrar, Straus & Giroux, 2014.

We feel, therefore we learn: the relevance of affective and social neuroscience to education. Immordino-Yang, Mary; Damasio, Antonio. *Emotions, learning, and the brain.* Norton Professional Books, 2016

What have we learned from generalized trust, if anything? Nannestad, Peter. *Annual review of political science*, 2008.

When Marriage breaks up – Does attachment style contribute to coping and mental health? Birnbaum, Gurit; Orr, Idit; Mikulincer, Mario; Florian, Victor. *Journal of Social and Personal Relationships*, 1997, volume 14.

When overconfidence is revealed to others: Testing the status-enhancement theory of overconfidence. Kennedy, Jessica A.; Anderson, Cameron; Moore, Don A. 2013, *Organizational Behavior and Human Decision Processes* 122.

Why Too Much Trust Is Death to Innovation. Bidault, Francis; Castello, Alessio. *MIT Sloan Management Review*, June 2010.

Graphs and tables

ABI

Americans trust in mass media lowest since 2016 news.gallup.com/poll/355526/americans-trust-media-dips-second-lowest-record.aspx

Bond yields – source ECB – replace with the new graph you have!

Concepts underlying ABI

Democrats & republicans more ideologically divided than in the past. Pew research survey June 8–18, 2017.

EU Net trust index EBU Market Insights: Trust in Media, 2021

Income shares UAS wid.world/document/world-inequality-report-2018-english/

Income shares Western Europe

Secular stagnation www.un.org/development/desa/dpad/publication/development-issues-no-9-low-growth-with-limited-policy-options-secular-stagnation-causes-consequences-and-cures/

Sources of social capital www.socialcapitalresearch.com/sources-of-social-capital

Three-fourths of the decrease in labor share in the US since 1947 has come since 2000. Source BLS March 2019 release, McKinsey Institute Analysis

Trust in EU institutions: www.debatingeurope.eu/2019/09/06/what-should-eu-institutions-do-to-boost-your-trust-in-them/#.YooSWKhByUk

Trust in government in the US, pew research www.pewresearch.org/

politics/2019/04/11/public-trust-in-government-1958-2019/

Trust in others around the world ourworldindata.org

Trust in others in USA, general social survey gssdataexplorer.norc.org/
variables/441/vshow

Trust vs. GDP per capita – ourworldindata.org

www.socialcapitalresearch.com/structural-cognitive-relational-social-
capital / Tristan Claridge

Web references

centerforpolitics.org/crystalball/articles/new-initiative-explores-deep-
persistent-divides-between-biden-and-trump-voters/

dictionary.apa.org/self-confidence

dictionary.apa.org/self-efficacy

dictionary.apa.org/self-esteem

news.gallup.com/poll/321116/americans-remain-distrustful-mass-media.
aspx

plato.stanford.edu/entries/legitimacy/

tcdata360.worldbank.org/indicators/h7da6e31a

Texting Frequency and The Moral Shallowing Hypothesis. Trapnell, Paul;
Sinclair, Lisa. The University of Winnipeg news.uwinnipeg.ca/wp-
content/uploads/2013/04/texting-study.pdf

www.epi.org/publication/ceo-compensation-2018/ – CEO compensation

www.gmo.com/europe/research-library/why-we-are-not-worried-about-
elevated-profit-margins/

www.hs.fi/kotimaa/art-2000006330829.html

www.imf.org/external/pubs/ft/fandd/2020/03/larry-summers-on-secular-
stagnation.htm

www.telegraph.co.uk/politics/2018/06/23/eu-diplomats-shocked-boriss-
four-letter-reply-business-concerns/

www.theguardian.com/environment/2021/oct/30/cop26-failure-could-
mean-mass-migration-and-food-shortages-says-boris-johnson

www.usnews.com/news/best-countries/most-transparent-countries

www.weforum.org/reports/the-future-of-jobs-report-2020

Trust, Knowledge & Society: Trust as the Foundation of Societal Development by Mikael Lilius, 978-9529-461417. Acknowledgements prepared on 11th July 2022.

We are grateful to the following for permission to reproduce copyright material:

The figure "Public Trust in Government: 1958–2021", Pew Research Center, Washington, D.C., May 2021, www.pewresearch.org/politics/2019/04/11/public-trust-in-government-1958-2019/

The figure "What should EU institutions do to boost your trust in them?" 06/09/2019, data source: Eurobarometer www.debatingeurope.eu/2019/09/06/what-should-eu-institutions-do-to-boost-your-trust-in-them/#.YooSWKhByUk. Reproduced with permission of Debating Europe

The figure "Americans' Trust in Media Dips to Second Lowest on Record" by Megan Brenan, Gallup, news.gallup.com/poll/355526/americans-trust-media-dips-second-lowest-record.aspx. Permission conveyed through Copyright Clearance Center

The figure "Evolution of EU Net Trust Index (2015–2021)" from *Marketing Insights: Trust in Media* 2021, EBU Media Intelligence Service, September 2021, hwww.ebu.ch/, p.12. Reproduced with permission of EBU

The figure 'Proposed Model of Trust' from "An Integrative Model of Organizational Trust" by Roger C. Mayer, James H. Davis & F. David Schoorman, The Academy of Management Review, Vol. 20 (3), pp.709–734, July 1995, Figure 1, doi.org/10.2307/258792. Permission conveyed through Copyright Clearance Center

An extract and figure from "We Feel, Therefore We Learn: The Relevance of Affective and Social Neuroscience to Education" by Mary Helen Immordino-Yang & Antonio Damasio in *Mind, Brain, and Education*, Vol.1 (1), pp.3–10, 12/03/2007, copyright © 2007. Reproduced with permission of John Wiley & Sons

Statistics from "As Economic Concerns Recede, Environmental Protection Rises on the Public's Policy Agenda" Pew Research Center, Washington, D.C., February 2020. www.pewresearch.org/politics/2020/02/13/as-economic-concerns-recede-environmental-protection-rises-on-the-publics-policy-agenda/

A figure from "As Economic Concerns Recede, Environmental Protection Rises on the Public's Policy Agenda", Pew Research Center, Washington, D.C., February 2020, Data source: Survey of US adults conducted Jan 8-13 2020, www.pewresearch.org/politics/2020/02/13/

as-economic-concerns-recede-environmental-protection-rises-on-the-publics-policy-agenda/

Statistics and the Figure "Trust in climate scientists by political affiliation in the USA", from "The Politics of Climate" Pew Research Center, Washington, D.C., October 2016, www.pewresearch.org/science/2016/10/04/the-politics-of-climate/

Extracts from "The influence of political ideology on trust in science" by Aaron M. McCright, Katherine Dentzman, Meghan Charters & Thomas Dietz in *Environmental Research Letters*, Volume 8, (4), Nov 2013, Creative Commons Attribution 3.0 licence

The table 'Dimensions of social capital' from "Structural, cognitive, relational social capital" by Tristan Claridge, 20/01/2018: www.socialcapitalresearch.com/structural-cognitive-relational-social-capital

An extract and the table 'Examples of social capital' from "Sources of Social Capital" by Tristan Claridge, 27/09/2019 www.socialcapitalresearch.com/sources-of-social-capital. Reproduced with kind permission of Tristan Claridge

The figure "The lower the better: European interest rates during the Greek crisis" from *Interest rate statistics*, 2004 EU Member States & ACCB, sdw.ecb.europa.eu/, copyright © European Central Bank, Frankfurt am Main, Germany

The figure "Annual GDP growth in the developed economies 1971–2016" from *Development Issues No. 9: Low growth with limited policy options? Secular Stagnation – Causes, Consequences and Cures*, UNDept of Economics and Social Affairs, 02/03/2017, copyright © United Nations, 2017, www.un.org/development/desa/dpad/publication/development-issues-no-9-low-growth-with-limited-policy-options-secular-stagnation-causes-consequences-and-cures, downloaded March 2022. Reproduced with permission of the United Nations

Statistics and the figure "CEO compensation has grown 940% since 1978" by Lawrence Mishel & Julia Wolfe, *Economic Policy Institute*, 14/08/2019, www.epi.org/publication/ceo-compensation-2018/, Figure C. Reproduced with permission of Economic Policy Institute

The Figures "Top 1% v.s Bottom 50% national income shares in the US" and "Top 1% v.s Bottom 50% national income shares in Western Europe" 1980-2016" from *World Inequality Report 2018* by Alvaredo et al., wid.world/document/world-inequality-report-2018-english, figure E3. Data source: wir2018.wid.world for data series and WID.world for the most recent updates

Printed in Poland
by Amazon Fulfillment
Poland Sp. z o.o., Wrocław
03 November 2022

f8ef16a4-34de-4828-abff-3157b2a58404R01